4TH EDITION

COMPLETE GUIDE TO THE
TOEIC® TEST

BRUCE ROGERS

NATIONAL
GEOGRAPHIC
LEARNING

Australia · Brazil · Mexico · Singapore · United Kingdom · United States

NATIONAL GEOGRAPHIC
L E A R N I N G

Complete Guide to the TOEIC® Test,
4th Edition
Bruce Rogers

Publisher: Andrew Robinson

Executive Editor: Sean Bermingham

Associate Development Editor: Yvonne Tan

Contributing Writer: Mark Stafford

Director of Global Marketing: Ian Martin

Senior Product Manager: Paul Grainger

IP Analyst: Kyle Cooper

IP Project Manager: Carissa Poweleit

Media Researcher: Leila Hishmeh

Senior Director of Production:
   Michael Burggren

Senior Production Controller: Tan Jin Hock

Manufacturing Planner: Mary Beth Hennebury

Compositor: MPS North America LLC

Cover Design: Brenda Carmichael, Lisa Trager

Cover Photo: An illuminated trail is left
   by traffic passing through Hong Kong's busy
   financial district: © EugeneLimPhotography
   .com/Getty Images

© 2018 National Geographic Learning, a Cengage Learning Company

ALL RIGHTS RESERVED. No part of this work covered by the copyright herein may be reproduced or distributed in any form or by any means, except as permitted by U.S. copyright law, without the prior written permission of the copyright owner.

"National Geographic", "National Geographic Society" and the Yellow Border Design are registered trademarks of the National Geographic Society ® Marcas Registradas

For product information and technology assistance, contact us at
Cengage Learning Customer & Sales Support, cengage.com/contact

For permission to use material from this text or product,
submit all requests online at **cengage.com/permissions**
Further permissions questions can be emailed to
permissionrequest@cengage.com

ISBN-13: 978-1-337-39653-0

National Geographic Learning
20 Channel Center Street
Boston, MA 02210
USA

National Geographic Learning, a Cengage Learning Company, has a mission to bring the world to the classroom and the classroom to life. With our English language programs, students learn about their world by experiencing it. Through our partnerships with National Geographic and TED Talks, they develop the language and skills they need to be successful global citizens and leaders.

Locate your local office at **international.cengage.com/region**

Visit National Geographic Learning online at **NGL.Cengage.com/ELT**
Visit our corporate website at **www.cengage.com**

Printed in the United States of America
Print Number: 01 Print Year: 2017

Contents

Scope and Sequence

About the Author

Bruce Rogers is a materials writer, editor, and teacher from Boulder, Colorado, USA. He taught at the Economics Institute, University of Colorado Boulder for over 20 years. He has also taught in Indonesia, Vietnam, Korea, and the Czech Republic. He is the author of *The Complete Guide to TOEFL®* and the co-author of *The Complete Guide to IELTS* and *Reading Explorer 5* (all published by National Geographic Learning). He has also written several other ESL textbooks and provided materials for online courses.

Photo Credits

13, 14 (t), 14 (b), 15 (t), 15 (b), 17, 18, 19 (t), 19 (b), 22, 24 (t), 24 (b), 25, 26 (b), 27 (b), 28 (t), 30 (t), 30 (b), 32 (t), 34 (t), 35 (t), 223, 260, 276, 287, 289 (t), 318, 335, 336 (t), 336 (b), 337 (t), 337 (b), 338 (t), 338 (b), 369: PhotoDisc, Inc. Digital Imagery © 2006 PhotoDisc, Inc.

16 (t), 16 (b), 20 (t), 20 (b), 23 (t), 23 (b), 26 (t), 27 (t), 31 (t), 31 (b), 34 (b), 35 (b), 36 (t), 36 (b), 288 (t), 288 (b), 289 (b), 290 (b): Jonathan Stark/Cengage Learning

28 (b), 32 (b), 290 (t): Bruce Rogers

Getting Started

A Guide to the Guide: *How to Use This Book*

About This Book

The TOEIC® Test is an increasingly important test. Over five million people around the world take this test annually. In an era of globalization, a knowledge of English, the global language, is a key to success. One measure of English proficiency is a high score on the TOEIC® Test. And a high score on the TOEIC® Test can be an important factor in being hired, promoted, or selected to travel and work internationally.

However, preparing for this test is not easy. Some of the books written to help you are badly organized, incomplete, or poorly written. Some of the "practice tests" have little resemblance to actual exams.

You need a guide you can depend on. That is why this book was written.

Complete Guide to the TOEIC® Test is a complete, accurate, and up-to-date preparation book. It is based on extensive research and on years of classroom experience in test preparation. It offers a step-by-step program that provides test-taking strategies and the development of language skills. It is based on the following simple philosophy:

- The same points are tested over and over on every TOEIC® Test.
- Each of these testing points is based on a clearly defined language skill.
- These skills can be mastered by guided practice.

The fourth edition of this *Guide* has been revised to reflect the changes in test format made by ETS in 2016. The scoring system, the total number of items, the time limits, and the level of difficulty of the test did NOT change.

Organization of the Guide

1. Getting Started
This is an introduction to the exam.
- **Questions and Answers about the TOEIC® Test**
  This provides basic background about the format and scoring of the test.
- **Important Changes to the TOEIC® Test**
  This provides a summary of the new question types that were introduced to the test in 2016.
- **Eight Keys to High Scores**
  This helps you become a smarter test-taker by suggesting ways to arrange your preparation time, use the process of elimination, mark your answer sheet, control test anxiety, and learn other important test-taking techniques.

2. Listening Comprehension (Lessons 1–4)
This section of the book is designed to prepare you for the Listening Comprehension section of the TOEIC® Test (Parts 1–4). In order to complete the exercises for this part of the book, you must have the accompanying audio program. (See "Guide to Listening Comprehension," page 11, for more information about using the audio program.)

3. Reading (Lessons 5–7)
This section is designed to prepare you for the Reading section of the TOEIC® Test (Parts 5–7).

Each of the seven lessons consists of these components:
- **Lesson Outline**
  This provides a brief overview of the lesson.
- **Format**
  This describes in detail the format of the problems in this part of the test.
- **Tactics**
  This component discusses the best techniques for maximizing your score in this test part.
- **Preview Test**
  This is a shortened version of the test part that familiarizes you with the directions and the most common types of items. Items for this section are used as examples in the next component.

- **Testing Points and Skill-Building Exercises**
  This is the main component of each lesson. It breaks down the testing points into understandable individual units and offers numerous exercises designed to increase your skills.
- **Review Test**
  This component offers a full-length test part so that you can practice testing points, not in isolation but in combination. Together, the seven review tests provide you with the equivalent of another full-length practice test.

4. Two Complete Practice Tests
These resemble actual tests in terms of format, content, and level of difficulty. To get the most of these exams, follow the suggestions in the section titled "How to Take the Practice Tests."

The Audio Script and Answer Key for *Complete Guide to the TOEIC® Test* provides a written version of all the recorded material in the audio program, answers for all the exercises and tests, and explanations when appropriate.

Suggestions for Using the *Guide*

The *Complete Guide to the TOEIC® Test* is designed to be used either as a textbook for a TOEIC® preparation course or as a tool for individual learners who are preparing for the test on their own. If you are working alone, you will need to obtain the audio program that accompanies the book.

Whether working in a class or alone, you should begin preparing for the TOEIC® Test by reading the introductory lessons ("Getting Started"). Then you can work through the lessons one by one, or begin with the parts in which you feel you need improvement. You can usually make the fastest progress by working in the areas in which you are weakest.

When using the book in the classroom, the exercises work well as small-group or pair activities. Students may either work on the exercises together or complete them individually and then check and discuss them afterward.

Following are the amounts of time required to cover each part of the *Guide*. Keep in mind that these times are very approximate and do not include review sessions.

Getting Started	1–3 hours
Lesson 1	2–3 hours
Lesson 2	5–7 hours
Lesson 3	4–6 hours
Lesson 4	5–7 hours
Lesson 5	8–10 hours
Lesson 6	4–6 hours
Lesson 7	7–10 hours
Practice Test 1	3–4 hours
Practice Test 2	3–4 hours

If you have any questions, comments, or suggestions regarding this book or the TOEIC® Test itself, I would very much appreciate hearing from you. Please contact me care of the publisher:

National Geographic Learning
20 Channel Center Street
Boston, MA 02210
USA
ngl.cengage.com

And good luck on the test!

Bruce Rogers
Boulder, Colorado, U.S.A.

Questions and Answers about the TOEIC® Test

Q: *What is the TOEIC® Test?*

A: The TOEIC® (Test of English for International Communication) Test is a standardized test designed to measure a person's ability to understand English as it is used in international business situations.

The TOEIC® Test is designed, produced, and administered by Educational Testing Service (ETS) of Princeton, New Jersey. ETS produces many other standardized tests, such as TOEFL® (Test of English as a Foreign Language) and GRE® (Graduate Records Exam).

The TOEIC® Test was first administered in Japan in 1979 and in Korea in 1982. It is now given in over 90 countries all over the globe. In a recent year, more than 5 million candidates took the test. Every year, four new forms of the test are administered.

Q: *How is the TOEIC® Test administered?*

A: Most TOEIC® testing is arranged by a sponsoring organization (a multinational corporation, for example) and by a local agent that represents ETS. The dates, times, and locations of the testing are generally set by the sponsoring organization. In many places, there are also "open administrations." Anyone may register to take the test at an open administration. These are given at special centers, often at language schools or universities. For more information, contact the TOEIC® representative for your country or visit **www.ets.org**.

Q: *What format does the TOEIC® Test follow?*

A: All the questions on the current TOEIC® examination are multiple choice questions. Items in most parts have four answer choices; in Part 2, there are three answer choices. The test is divided into two main sections: Listening Comprehension and Reading. Each section contains 100 items. Listening Comprehension is divided into four parts, Reading into three. Each part has its own directions. The entire test takes about two hours to complete.

See page 4 for a summary of the new TOEIC® Test format.

Q: *Who takes the TOEIC® Test?*

A: Anyone who travels abroad on business or who has contact with international visitors is a likely candidate for the TOEIC® Test. All types of employees of international organizations may be asked to take the test: managers, marketing experts, sales representatives, customer service agents, flight attendants, hotel employees, customs officials, and others. Many organizations also require job applicants to take the TOEIC® Test. Many individuals take it on their own and include their test scores as part of their résumés.

Q: *Who uses the TOEIC® Test?*

A: TOEIC® clients include trading and manufacturing companies, government agencies, international banks, hotel chains, and airlines. Within these organizations, personnel directors, training managers, human resource managers, and English language program administrators use the scores.

Q: *What contexts are used for TOEIC® questions?*

A: Common contexts for TOEIC® questions are business situations (marketing, sales, contract negotiations, meetings), travel (airlines, taxis, hotels), entertainment (restaurants, movies, plays, museums), and health and fitness (doctors, dentists, exercise programs).

The New TOEIC® Test: Format

Test	Part	Content		Questions (previous)	Questions (new TOEIC)	Time (min)	Points
Listening	1	Photographs		10	6	45	495
	2	Question–Response		30	25		
	3	Short Conversations		30	39		
	4	Short Talks		30	30		
Reading	5	Incomplete Sentences (grammar/vocabulary)		40	30	75	495
	6	Text Completion		12	16		
	7	Reading Comprehension	Single reading passages	28	29		
			Multiple readings	20	10 (paired readings)		
					15 (3-part readings)		
Total				**200**	**200**	**120**	**990**

Q: How is the TOEIC® Test scored?

A: Three scores are reported: a score for Listening Comprehension, a score for Reading, and a comprehensive score. To calculate these scores, the number of correct answers in each of the two main sections is first counted. These scores are called raw scores. Then the raw scores are changed to scaled scores by means of a conversion chart similar to the one on page 281. The scaled scores for the two sections are added together to obtain a comprehensive score. Scores on each of the two sections range from 5 to 495. Comprehensive scores range from 10 to 990.

The chart below provides an approximate guide to interpreting TOEIC® scores:

TOEIC Score	Level	CEFR*
910+	High advanced	C2
701–910	Advanced	C1
541–700	High intermediate	B2
381–540	Intermediate	B1
246–380	Beginner 2	A2
0–245	Beginner 1	A1

*Common European Framework of Reference for Languages

Q: How does the TOEIC® Test differ from the TOEFL® iBT Test?

A: The names of the two tests sound quite similar. Both measure a person's ability to understand English, and both are standardized tests. However, there are a number of differences between the two exams, as shown in the following charts:

Purpose

The TOEFL® iBT Test
To measure the English-language proficiency of applicants for North American universities

The TOEIC® Test
To measure the English-language proficiency of employees, trainees, or prospective employees of international organizations

Format

The TOEFL® iBT Test
- 4 sections:
    - **Reading**
    36–70 multiple choice questions
    - **Listening**
    34–51 multiple choice questions
    - **Speaking**
    6 speaking tasks
    - **Writing**
    2 essays

The TOEIC® Test
- 2 sections:
    - **Listening Comprehension**
    100 multiple choice questions
    - **Reading**
    100 multiple choice questions

Delivery

The TOEFL® iBT Test
Internet computer

The TOEIC® Test
Paper-and-pencil based

Time Limits

The TOEFL® iBT Test
3½–4 hours

The TOEIC® Test
2 hours

Range of Scores

The TOEFL® iBT Test
0–120

The TOEIC® Test
10–990

Language

The TOEFL® iBT Test
Academic English as used in campus settings and university textbooks

The TOEIC® Test
International English as used in business settings

Important Changes to the TOEIC® Test

The 2016 changes introduced to the TOEIC® Test include new question types in Parts 3, 4, 6, and 7.

Listening Comprehension

Part 3: Short Conversations

- **NEW:** Visual aid analysis—Test-takers will read something (e.g., a coupon, a receipt, a map) as they listen, and answer a question that relates to both.
  - ➤ *Look at the graphic. What discount will the woman most likely receive?*
- **NEW:** 3-way conversation—One conversation (out of 13) will involve 3 speakers. Speakers take more turns talking, with exchanges of different sentence lengths. These feature a range of accents: American, Australian, Canadian, and British.
- **NEW:** Inference questions based on spoken phrases that test the speaker's intention.
  - ➤ *What does the woman mean when she says, "We could use some help in the kitchen"?*
- **NEW**: The conversations feature more colloquial language and elisions such as "gonna" instead of "going to" or "wanna" instead of "want to."

Part 4: Short Talks

- **NEW:** Visual aid analysis—Test-takers will read something (e.g., a map, a chart, an order form) as they listen, and answer a question that relates to both.
  - ➤ *Look at the graphic. Where will the listeners be unable to go today?*
- **NEW:** Inference questions based on spoken phrases that test the speaker's intention.
  - ➤ *What does the woman mean when she says, "And why wouldn't we"?*

Reading

Part 6: Text Completion

- **NEW:** One question in each passage will require test-takers to choose the correct *complete sentence* to fill in the blank.

Part 7: Reading Comprehension

- **NEW:** 3 related texts (e.g., product information, online review, and response)—15 questions total.
- **NEW:** More tech-type readings, e.g., text message chains, online chat discussions, webpages, emails, etc.
- **NEW:** Inference questions based on written phrases that test the author's intention.
  - ➤ *At 9:38 a.m., what does Ms. Lo mean when she writes, "I'd like your input"?*
- **NEW:** Sentence Addition questions where test-takers identify the most appropriate place for a sentence.
  - ➤ *In which of the positions marked [1], [2], [3], and [4] does the following sentence best belong?*

Eight Keys to Higher Scores on the TOEIC® Test

Key 1:
Increase Your General Knowledge of English

There are two types of knowledge that will help you improve your TOEIC® scores:
- A knowledge of the format of the test and the tactics used by good test-takers.
- A general command of English (which must be built up over a long period of time).

A step-by-step TOEIC® preparation program such as the one in this book can supply the first type of knowledge. The best way to increase your background knowledge of English is simply to use English whenever you can. If possible, take English language classes. Outside of class, look for opportunities to speak English, especially with native speakers. Read newspapers and magazines in English. Listen to English language news programs and TED Talks on the Internet. Attend lectures and movies in English.

Key 2:
Learn Your Strengths and Weaknesses and Work on Areas Needing Improvement

You probably already have a fairly clear idea of the areas of English in which you need improvement. You may want to use the preview tests that are part of each lesson in this book as diagnostic tools. Take each of these preview sections before you begin your studies. Did you find one or more of the previews particularly difficult? If so, focus more of your time and attention on the corresponding lesson or lessons of this book.

Key 3:
Make the Most of Your Preparation Time

Taking an important test such as the TOEIC® Test is like facing any other challenge in your life. You need to train for it, and your training should be systematic.

Before you begin studying for the test, prepare a time-management chart. Begin by drawing up an hour-by-hour schedule of your current weekly activities. Then pencil in times for TOEIC® preparation. You'll remember more of what you study if you schedule an hour or so daily or three or four times weekly than if you schedule all your study time in large blocks on weekends. After following this schedule for a week, make whatever adjustments are needed. Then keep to your schedule as much as possible until a few days before the test. At that point, studying won't have much effect on your score. It's better for you to relax.

If possible, reserve a special study space where you do nothing but study for the TOEIC® Test, separate from the place where you do your regular homework or other paperwork. This space should be as free of distractions as possible.

Use the "30–5–5" method of studying:
- First, study for thirty minutes.
- Take a five-minute break. Leave your desk and do something completely different.
- When you return, take five minutes to review what you studied during the last thirty minutes and preview what you are going to study next.

It's also a good idea to meet regularly with a small group of people who are also preparing for the TOEIC® Test. Research has shown that this "study group" approach is highly effective.

Key 4:
Be Familiar with the TOEIC® Format and the Directions for Each Section

If you have a clear "map" of the TOEIC® Test in your mind, you won't have any surprises on test day. You'll always know exactly where you are in the test and what will come next. You can become familiar with the format by studying the chart on page 4 and by taking the practice tests in this book.

The directions for each part of the test are always the same; even the same examples are used. If you have familiarized yourself with these directions, you won't need to waste precious testing time by reading them. For copyright reasons, the directions that appear in this book are not the same, word for word, as those used on official versions, but they are similar, and if you understand these directions, you will understand those on actual tests.

Key 5:
Know How to Mark Your Answer Sheet

One of the worst surprises you can get during a test is to suddenly discover that the number of the item you are working on does not correspond to the number on the answer sheet. You have to go back to find where you first got off track, then change all the answers after that number. You can avoid this problem by using the test book itself as a marker. Cover the unanswered items in each column on the answer sheet with the book and then, as you mark each item, move the test book down one number.

Bring several number 2 black-lead pencils, a good eraser, and a pencil sharpener. Don't use a pen or a liquid-lead pencil to mark your answers. Mark the answers by filling in the space completely. Don't mark answers in any other way.

Correct

1. Ⓐ   Ⓑ   Ⓒ   ●

Incorrect

1. Ⓐ   Ⓑ   Ⓒ   ⊗

1. Ⓐ   Ⓑ   Ⓒ   Ⓓ̸

1. Ⓐ   Ⓑ   Ⓒ   ⊛

Always be sure that you have filled in the circle completely and have filled in only one circle per item. If you have to erase an answer, be sure to erase completely.

🔑 Key 6:
No Matter What, Always Guess!

On the TOEIC® Test, unlike on certain standardized tests, there is no penalty for guessing. In other words, no points or fractions of points are subtracted for incorrect answers. What this means to you is that you should always guess at the answer if you are not sure and never leave any items unanswered at the end of the test. Remember, even if you are guessing blindly, you have a one-in-four chance (25%) of guessing the answer correctly in most sections. (In Part 2, your odds go up to one in three, or 33.3%.) If you have no idea which answer is correct, it's probably better to use a standard guess answer such as (C) than to guess at random.

🔑 Key 7:
Use the Process of Elimination to Make the Most of Your Guess

In Key 6, you learned that you should always guess. However, until the last few minutes of the test, it's not a good idea to guess blindly. Instead, you want to make the best guess that you possibly can, and to do so, you need to use the process of elimination. In other words, if you are unable to find the correct answer, you should eliminate unattractive or unlikely choices and then, if more than one cannot be eliminated, guess from the remaining choices. This is not as difficult as it may seem because of the way test writers design many of the items on standardized tests.

Let's look at a diagram of a typical multiple choice item:

Stem..............................

Ⓐ Answer choice

Ⓑ Answer choice

Ⓒ Answer choice

Ⓓ Answer choice

Only one of the four answer choices, of course, can be the best one. This choice is called the **key**. The three incorrect choices are called **distractors** because their function is to distract (take away) your attention from the key.

Stem.............................

Ⓐ Distractor

Ⓑ Distractor

Ⓒ Key

Ⓓ Distractor

However, many items are written so that the distractors are not equally attractive. One or two choices are often clearly incorrect and are easy to eliminate. Another one of the distractors is usually less easy to eliminate because it is somehow closer to the key. This is the choice that most people choose if they answer an item incorrectly. It is called the **main distractor**.

Stem..........................

Ⓐ Main distractor

Ⓑ Distractor

Ⓒ Key

Ⓓ Distractor

Even if you can eliminate only one distractor from a four-choice item, you have improved your chance of guessing the key from one in four (25%) to one in three (33.3%), and if you can eliminate two distractors your chances become pretty good — one in two, or 50%.

What should you do if you can eliminate one or two choices but can't decide which of the remaining choices is correct? If you have a "hunch" (an intuitive feeling) that one answer is better, choose that one. If not, just mark your standard guess answer or, if you've eliminated that choice, choose any remaining letter and go on.

Let's see how this process works in practice by looking at an example from Part 5:

I am eager _____ the new member of the product development team.

    (A) meeting

    (B) will meet

    (C) to meet

    (D) met

You'll probably be able to eliminate choices (B) and (D), because these are both main verbs and the sentence already has a main verb (*am*). Also, choice (D) incorrectly refers to the past. It may be more difficult to choose between (A), a gerund (*meeting*), and (C), an infinitive (*to meet*), but even so, you've improved your chances of getting this answer correct by making an educated guess. And one of the remaining answer choices may sound better than the other. If you guessed (C), you're right! Not all items on the TOEIC® Test follow this pattern exactly, and it is not always easy to eliminate two distractors or even one. Still, the process of elimination is a powerful tool for good test-takers.

O—π Key 8:
Learn to Control Test Anxiety

There is nothing unusual about being nervous before a test. Standardized tests such as the TOEIC® Test can have a definite impact on your future plans. If you were participating in a big athletic event or giving an important business presentation, you would feel the same. There is an expression in English that describes this feeling of anxiety very well: "butterflies in your stomach." These "butterflies" will mostly disappear once the test begins. And a little nervousness can actually work to your advantage by making you more alert and focused. However, too much nervousness can slow you down and cause you to make simple mistakes.

One way to avoid stress on the day of the test is to give yourself plenty of time to get to the testing site. If you have to rush or if you're late, you'll be even more nervous during the testing period.

If you find yourself nervous during the second section of the test (Reading), give yourself a short break — take a "fifteen-second vacation." Sit back, close your eyes, take a few deep breaths, relax as completely as possible — then get back to work. (Don't try this technique during the Listening Comprehension part of the test — you will miss items on the audio program!)

In general, the best way to overcome test anxiety is through a positive, confident attitude toward the test. You can develop this attitude if you become familiar with all aspects of the exam, polish the skills that are required to do well, and take realistic practice tests. The *Complete Guide to the TOEIC® Test* was developed to help you fulfill these goals.

Listening Comprehension

Guide to Listening Comprehension

The first section of the test consists of four separate parts. Each has its own directions and format:

Part 1: Photographs	6 items
Part 2: Question–Response	25 items
Part 3: Short Conversations (13 conversations with 3 questions each)	39 items
Part 4: Short Talks (10 talks with 3 questions each)	30 items
Total:	100 items

This section tests your ability to understand informal spoken English, but only Part 2 is a "pure" test of listening. Part 1 also tests your ability to quickly interpret photographs, and Parts 3 and 4 test your reading skills, since you must read the questions and answer choices before you can answer.

You can make quite a few errors in this section and still get a good score. Errors count less against your total score than errors in the Reading section do. (See the Score Conversion Chart on page 281.)

Concentration is very important to success in this section. You need to focus your attention on the audio program, on the test booklet (except in Part 2), and on your answer sheet. In Parts 1 and 2, particularly, you need a very close, almost word-for-word understanding of the items on the audio program, and you will have to be able to distinguish between words with similar sounds.

The Listening section of the *Guide* is divided into four lessons, each corresponding to one of the parts of the test. Each lesson provides familiarity and practice for that part of the test.

Using the Audio Program

The audio symbol shown above indicates that you should turn on the audio program whenever it appears throughout the *Guide*. Almost all the exercises in this section are also on the audio program. However, directions for the exercises are not recorded. You should read the directions before you begin to work on an exercise. The audio portion of the Practice TOEIC® Tests is also recorded on the audio program.

The Audio Script and Answer Key for *Complete Guide to the TOEIC® Test* provides a written version of the material on the audio program, as well as answers for the exercises and tests. If you have trouble with an exercise, listen to it again before you look at the script and the answer. Don't stop the audio program in the middle of an exercise; always complete each exercise before listening again or looking at the audio script.

Lesson 1 Photographs

Lesson Outline

Format   Part 1

The first part of the test consists of six numbered photographs that are in your test book. For each photograph, you will hear on the audio program four sentences that refer to it. You must decide which of the sentences best describes something you can see in each photograph.

The photographs are pictures of ordinary situations. Some of the photographs involve a person or people; others involve an object or a scene without people.

The sentences are short and grammatically simple. They generally deal with the most important aspects of the photographs.

Each item is introduced by a statement that tells you to look at the next numbered photograph. The pacing for this part is fast: There is only a five-second pause between items, and there is no pause between sentences (A), (B), (C), and (D).

Tactics   Part 1

1. Always complete each item as quickly as possible so that you can preview the photograph for the next item. Don't wait for the statement that says, "Now look at photograph number _____."

2. If you are previewing a photograph that involves a person or people, look for aspects of the photograph that are often mentioned in the sentences:
   - What are the people doing?
   - Where are they?
   - Who are they? (Is there a uniform or piece of equipment or anything else that indicates their profession or role?)
   - What distinguishes them? (Is there a hat, a mustache, a purse, a pair of glasses, a tie, or anything else that differentiates the people?)
   - What do the people's expressions tell you? (Do they look happy? Unhappy? Excited? Bored? Upset?)

3. If you are previewing a photograph of an object, focus on these aspects:
   - What is it?
   - What is it made of?
   - What — if anything — is it doing?
   - Where is it?

4. If you are previewing a photograph of a scene, focus on these aspects:
   - Where is it?

- What is in the foreground (the "front" of the picture)?
- What — if anything — is happening?
- What is in the background (the "distant" part of the picture)?

5. Don't mark an answer until you have heard all four choices. When you hear a choice that you think is correct, rest your pencil on that oval on your answer sheet. If you change your mind and hear a sentence that you think is better, move your pencil to that choice. Once you have heard all four sentences, mark the oval that your pencil is resting on. (This technique helps you remember which choice you think is best.)

6. Try to eliminate choices with problems in *meaning*, *sound*, and *sound + meaning*. (There is more information about recognizing these problems in the main part of this lesson.)

7. Most correct answers involve verbs in the simple present ("The furniture looks new.") or present progressive tense ("The woman is riding a bicycle."). Be suspicious of answer choices involving any other tenses.

8. Never leave any blanks. Always guess before going on to the next item.

9. As soon as you have finished marking the answer, stop looking at and thinking about that photograph and move on to the next item.

Preview Test Part 1

Start the audio program and read along as the directions are read.

Directions: For each item, there is a photograph in the book and four short sentences about it on the audio program. The sentences are not written out, so you must listen carefully.

You must choose the one sentence — (A), (B), (C), or (D) — that best describes what can be seen in the photograph, then mark the correct answer.

Look at the example

You see this photograph:

Listen to the four sentences:

(A) (B) (C) ●

Choice (D) — "The mechanic is repairing the engine." — is the best description of what can be seen in the photograph.

1.

    (A)   (B)   (C)   (D)

2.

    (A)   (B)   (C)   (D)

3.

4.  Ⓐ Ⓑ Ⓒ Ⓓ

5.

A   B   C   D

6.

A   B   C   D

Testing Points and Skill-Building Exercises

The correct answer for a Part 1 item is one that correctly describes what can be seen in the photograph. The distractors — incorrect answers — are incorrect for one of the following reasons:

A. Meaning — The sentence does not correctly describe what is shown in the photograph.

B. Sound — The sentence contains a word that sounds like — but is not the same as — something visible in the photograph.

C. Meaning + Sound — The sentence not only is an incorrect description of what is shown in the photograph but also contains a sound-alike word.

Let's look at the first item from the Preview Test to see examples of each type of distractor.

Sample Item

(A)   She's holding the fruit.

(B)   She's playing a game.

(C)   She's preparing some food.

●   She's playing music on the flute.

Choice (A) involves a **sound** problem — the girl is holding a flute, not a fruit. Choice (B) is a problem of **meaning**. She's not playing a game, she's playing a musical instrument. Choice (C) involves a **meaning** + **sound** problem: The girl is not preparing some food; she is playing a flute. (Flute and food sound somewhat alike.) Choice (D) best describes what is pictured in the photograph.

Focus: Identifying types of distractors for Part 1 items.

Directions: There are five photographs taken from the Preview Test section. The sentences spoken about them are printed next to the photographs. Identify each sentence according to the following system:

M	=	**Meaning** problem
S	=	**Sound** problem
M + S	=	**Meaning + sound** problem
C	=	Correct answer

You may want to stop the audio program between items to give yourself time to decide which answer is correct and what kind of distractors are heard.

 Now start the audio program.

1.

_____ Ⓐ The couple is painting the wall.

_____ Ⓑ The woman is pushing a stroller.

_____ Ⓒ They're hanging a painting on the wall.

_____ Ⓓ They're planting a garden.

2.

_____ (A) There is a lock on the door.

_____ (B) There are some cards on a rock.

_____ (C) There is a card in the time clock.

_____ (D) There are several cars lined up.

3.

_____ (A) The trains are passing through a tunnel.

_____ (B) An empty train is passing a loaded one.

_____ (C) One train is far ahead of the other one.

_____ (D) Both trains are loaded with coal.

4.

___ (A) He's pushing a steel barrel.

___ (B) He's going the wrong way.

___ (C) He has just stepped out of the shadow.

___ (D) He's waiting at a stop sign.

5.

___ (A) The man is holding the book open.

___ (B) They're standing by themselves.

___ (C) The books are all of different sizes.

___ (D) The woman is pointing at the page.

A. Sentences with Meaning Problems

This is the most common type of distractor. Sentences of this type in some way contradict what is seen in the photograph. Some common types of meaning problems are listed below, but many other types are heard during the test.

Meaning Problem	Example
1. The sentence misrepresents the location.	The photograph shows a man eating in a hospital bed. The sentence says, "He's eating out at a restaurant."
2. The sentence misrepresents the photograph's "environment."	The photograph shows people in light clothing sitting in the sun. The sentence says, "It's cold and rainy today."
3. The sentence misrepresents the spatial arrangement.	The photograph shows a car parked behind a fence. The sentence says, "The car is in front of the fence."
4. The sentence misrepresents a person's activity.	The photograph shows a person writing a note. The sentence says, "She's reading from her notebook."
5. The sentence misrepresents a person's facial expression or "body language."	The photograph shows people in an audience with interested and attentive expressions. The sentence says, "They seem to be bored by what they're seeing."
6. The sentence assigns characteristics of one person or thing to another person or thing.	The photograph shows a tall man wearing a hat and a shorter man with glasses. The sentence says, "The tall man is wearing glasses."
7. The sentence misidentifies an object.	The photograph shows a scientist looking through a microscope. The sentence says, "He's using a telescope."
8. The sentence identifies people in a scene with no people.	The photograph shows an empty swimming pool. The sentence says, "The pool is crowded with swimmers today."
9. The sentence misidentifies the material something is made of.	The photograph shows a woman sitting on a stone wall. The sentence says, "The wall is made of wood."
10. The sentence misidentifies a background detail as a central feature of the photograph.	The photograph shows a man walking through an airport. There is a telephone in the background. The sentence says, "The man is talking on the telephone."

Focus: Identifying distractors involving errors in meaning and recognizing sentences with correct meanings.

Directions: Look at each of the photographs below. You will hear a number of sentences describing each one. Decide if the sentence is true (T) or false (F) according to what you see in the picture. There may be more than one true sentence about each photograph, or there may be no true sentences.

 Now start the audio program.

1.

A.　Ⓣ　　Ⓕ

B.　Ⓣ　　Ⓕ

C.　Ⓣ　　Ⓕ

D.　Ⓣ　　Ⓕ

E.　Ⓣ　　Ⓕ

F.　Ⓣ　　Ⓕ

2.

A. (T) (F)

B. (T) (F)

C. (T) (F)

D. (T) (F)

E. (T) (F)

3.

A. (T) (F)

B. (T) (F)

C. (T) (F)

D. (T) (F)

E. (T) (F)

F. (T) (F)

4.

A. (T) (F)

B. (T) (F)

C. (T) (F)

D. (T) (F)

E. (T) (F)

5.

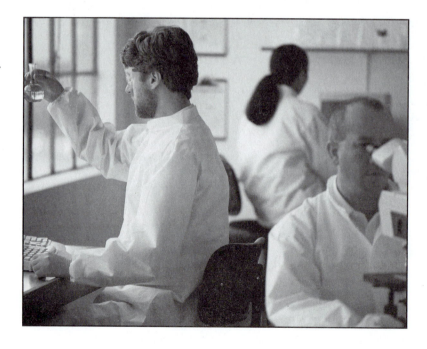

A. (T) (F)

B. (T) (F)

C. (T) (F)

D. (T) (F)

E. (T) (F)

F. (T) (F)

6.

A.	T	F
B.	T	F
C.	T	F
D.	T	F
E.	T	F

B. Sentences with Sound Problems

These sentences test your ability to distinguish similar-sounding words. These words may rhyme (*pile* and *file*, for example) or they may sound alike in other ways (*car* and *card*, for example, or *lock* and *lake*.) Here's an example: The photograph shows a man taking a letter out of a file. The spoken sentence says, "He's taking the letter from the pile." To avoid choosing the incorrect answer, you must be able to hear the difference between *pile* and *file*.

Remember: If you hear a sentence with a sound-alike word, that sentence is not the right answer.

Also remember that if you hear a sentence that seems strange or unrelated to what you see in the photograph, it probably involves a sound problem, even if that problem is not clear to you. These sentences will not be correct answers.

Exercise 1.3

Focus: Identifying distractors involving sound problems and recognizing correct answers.

Directions: There are two parts to this exercise. For Part A, look at the photographs and listen to the sentences — (A) and (B) — about them. Mark the letter of the sentence that best describes what can be seen in the photograph.

Now start the audio program.

1.    Ⓐ   Ⓑ

2.    Ⓐ   Ⓑ

3. 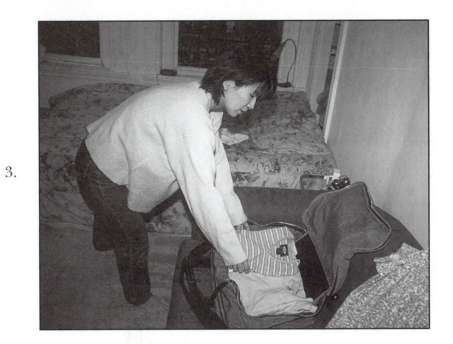 Ⓐ   Ⓑ

4.  Ⓐ   Ⓑ

5. 　　　Ⓐ　　　　Ⓑ

6. 　　　Ⓐ　　　　Ⓑ

Listen to Exercise 1.3 again. Write down the sound-alike word from the incorrect answer and the correct word from the correct answer. You may want to stop the audio program between items to give yourself time to write.

Sound-Alike Words	Correct Words
1. _____	_____
2. _____	_____
3. _____	_____
4. _____	_____
5. _____	_____
6. _____	_____

C. Sentences with Sound and Meaning Problems

This type of item is more common than those involving sound problems. A sentence of this type contains a sound-alike word, but the sentence is also an inaccurate description of what can be seen in the photograph. For example, a photograph shows a man putting a lock on his bicycle. One sentence says, "He's blocking the path." Another sentence says, "He's swimming in the lake." In the first sentence, *blocking* sounds like *locking*, and in the second sentence, *lake* sounds like *lock*. Neither sentence describes what is happening in the picture.

Sentences of this type can be eliminated by either the sound-alike word or the incorrect meaning.

Exercise 1.4

Focus: Identifying distractors involving sound + meaning problems and recognizing correct answers.

Directions: There are two parts to this exercise. For Part A, look at the photographs and listen to the sentences — (A) and (B) — about them. Mark the letter of the sentence that best describes what can be seen in the photograph.

Now start the audio program.

1.  Ⓐ Ⓑ

2.  Ⓐ Ⓑ

3.  Ⓐ Ⓑ

4.  Ⓐ Ⓑ

5.

(A)   (B)

6.

(A)   (B)

Listen to Exercise 1.4 again. Write down the sound-alike word from the incorrect answer and the correct word from the correct answer. You may want to stop the audio program between items to give yourself time to write.

Sound-Alike Words	Correct Words
1. _____	_____
2. _____	_____
3. _____	_____
4. _____	_____
5. _____	_____
6. _____	_____

Directions: For each item, there is a photograph in the book and four short sentences about it on the audio program. Choose the one sentence — (A), (B), (C), or (D) — that is the best description of what can be seen in the photograph. Then mark the correct answer.

 Now start the audio program.

1.

    (A)   (B)   (C)   (D)

2.

    (A)   (B)   (C)   (D)

3.    Ⓐ   Ⓑ   Ⓒ   Ⓓ

4.    Ⓐ   Ⓑ   Ⓒ   Ⓓ

5.

    (A)   (B)   (C)   (D)

6.

    (A)   (B)   (C)   (D)

Lesson 2 Question–Response

Lesson Outline

Format   Part 2

This part of the test consists of twenty-five items. Each item consists of a stimulus on the audio program followed by three possible responses, also on the audio program. Most of the stimuli are questions, but a few may be statements. Your job is to decide which is the best response. Between each item is a five-second pause. Part 2 problems do not involve any reading skills; therefore, this part is considered a "pure" test of listening skills. Your test book simply tells you to mark an answer for each problem.

Tactics   Part 2

1. There are no answer choices to consider before or while the item is being read. You should just concentrate on the question or statement and the three responses on the audio program, and pay no attention to the test book.

2. Try to identify the type of question (information question, yes/no question, alternative question, and so on). The correct response, of course, often depends on the type of question being asked.

3. Try to eliminate distractors. Parts D and E of the Testing Points and Skill-Building Exercises section of this lesson, pages 56-58, will help you recognize distractors.

4. Don't mark an answer until you have heard all three responses. When you hear a response that you think is correct, rest your pencil on that oval on the answer sheet. If you change your mind and hear a response that you think is better, move your pencil to that choice. Once you have heard all three responses, mark the oval that your pencil is resting on. (This technique helps you remember which choice you think is best.)

5. If you hear all three responses and none of the three seems correct, take a guess and get ready for the next item.

6. There is very little time (only five seconds) between items in Part 2. You need to decide on an answer and fill in the circle quickly to be ready for the next item.

Start the audio program and read along as the directions are read.

Directions: In this part of the test, you will hear a question or statement on the audio program. After that, you will hear three possible responses to the question or statement. Each question or statement and each response is given only once and is not written out in your book, so listen carefully. Mark the answer that corresponds to the best response to the question or statement.

Listen to a sample

You hear:

You then hear:

> Choice (A), "At the gymnasium," is the best response to the question "Where have you been, Steve?" You should mark (A).

● Ⓑ Ⓒ

---

1. Mark your answer.　Ⓐ　Ⓑ　Ⓒ
2. Mark your answer.　Ⓐ　Ⓑ　Ⓒ
3. Mark your answer.　Ⓐ　Ⓑ　Ⓒ
4. Mark your answer.　Ⓐ　Ⓑ　Ⓒ
5. Mark your answer.　Ⓐ　Ⓑ　Ⓒ
6. Mark your answer.　Ⓐ　Ⓑ　Ⓒ

7. Mark your answer.　Ⓐ　Ⓑ　Ⓒ
8. Mark your answer.　Ⓐ　Ⓑ　Ⓒ
9. Mark your answer.　Ⓐ　Ⓑ　Ⓒ
10. Mark your answer.　Ⓐ　Ⓑ　Ⓒ
11. Mark your answer.　Ⓐ　Ⓑ　Ⓒ
12. Mark your answer.　Ⓐ　Ⓑ　Ⓒ

Testing Points and Skill-Building Exercises

The questions/statements you hear on this part of the TOEIC® test can be broken down roughly as follows:
Information questions (wh- questions)
Yes/No questions
Other types of questions/statements

Information questions begin with a wh- question word or the word *how*:
When can we begin?
Where's the post office?
How are you today?

Yes/No questions begin with an auxiliary verb or a form of the main verb *to be*.
Did Hiroshi attend the lecture?
Would you like to come with us?
Were you in Nairobi last year?

Other types of questions include embedded questions, alternative questions, tag questions, and negative questions. You may also hear statements.

Do you know who wrote this report? (embedded question)

Do you want to play chess or checkers? (alternative question)

You've been to Seoul before, haven't you? (tag question)

Isn't this interesting? (negative question)

A new manager has finally been hired. (statement)

Exercise 2.1

Focus: Distinguishing between information questions, yes/no questions, and other types of questions.

Directions: Decide whether you hear an information question, a yes/no question, or some other type (embedded question, alternative question, tag question, negative question, or statement), and then mark the appropriate blank. The first one has been done as an example.

 Now start the audio program.

Information Question	Yes/No Question	Other Type of Question or Statement
1. ✓	_____	_____
2. _____	_____	_____
3. _____	_____	_____
4. _____	_____	_____
5. _____	_____	_____
6. _____	_____	_____
7. _____	_____	_____
8. _____	_____	_____
9. _____	_____	_____
10. _____	_____	_____
11. _____	_____	_____
12. _____	_____	_____

A. Information Questions

Nearly half the questions in Part 2 are information questions. These questions ask for specific pieces of information. Questions with *What . . . ?* and *How . . . ?* are the most common.

1. What . . . ?
2. How . . . ?
3. When . . . ?
4. Where . . . ?
5. Why . . . ?
6. Who . . . ?
7. Whose . . . ?
8. Which . . . ?

Responses to information questions may be either short answers (a word or phrase) or complete sentences.

Sample Items: Information Questions

What color is your new car?

(A) I bought a sports car.

(B) New cars are expensive.

● It's bright blue.

This question asks about color. Only (C) provides this information.

How was the party Friday night?

● Very enjoyable.

(B) By car.

(C) Until around midnight.

This question asks a person for his or her general impression of the party. Choice (A) provides this.

What do you think of the plan to open an office in Yokohama?

● I think it's a great idea.

(B) I'll leave the office open.

(C) I'm going next month.

The question asks for an opinion of the plan, such as the one expressed in (A).

How many suitcases are you bringing?

(A) Quite expensive.

(B) They're very full.

● Two or three.

A *how many . . . ?* question asks about quantity (number). The only response containing a quantity is (C).

Questions with *What . . . ?*

The question word *what* is used to ask about things, names, actions, ideas, and definitions, among others.

Sample Questions	Possible Responses
What are you thinking about?	I'm thinking about my family.
What did Cathy say to you?	She just said, "Good morning."
What is George going to do tomorrow?	He's going to a job interview.
What's her name?	It's Joyce Wong.
What happened here?	There was an accident.

What type of . . . ? and *What kind of . . . ?* are used to ask about classification.

Sample Questions	Possible Responses
What kind of music does he listen to?	He usually listens to jazz.
What type of people read this magazine?	Well-educated people, generally.

What time . . . ? is used to ask about the time of day.

Sample Questions	Possible Responses
What time does your flight leave?	At 7:30.
What time is the news on television?	It's on at 11.

What do/did you think of . . . ? asks for an opinion.

Sample Questions	Possible Responses
What do you think of Scott Graham's latest novel?	It's a real thriller.
What do you think of your new supervisor?	I don't know her well enough to say.

What . . . like? is used to ask for a general description or impression. It is also used to ask about the weather.

Sample Questions	Possible Responses
What are your new co-workers like?	They seem very pleasant.
What does your house look like?	It's a small, red-brick bungalow.
What's the weather like here in the winter?	It's cool and often rainy.

What does . . . do for a living? is used to ask about a person's occupation.

Sample Question	Possible Response
What does your brother do for a living?	He's an accountant.

What's the matter with . . . ? and *What's wrong with . . . ?* are used to ask about problems.

Sample Questions	Possible Responses
What's the matter with Joe?	He ate too much and doesn't feel well.
What's wrong with this microphone?	I don't know; it just doesn't seem to work.

What . . . ? is also used before many nouns to ask questions.

Sample Questions	Possible Responses
What size sweater do you wear?	Medium, usually.
What sports do you enjoy?	Tennis and volleyball.
What color is your new suit?	It's dark blue.
What flavor ice cream do you want?	Strawberry, please.

Exercise 2.2

Focus: Answering information questions beginning with *what*.

Directions: You will hear a number of questions, each followed by three possible responses. For each item, choose the letter of the response that best answers the question.

 Now start the audio program.

1. Mark your answer.   Ⓐ   Ⓑ   Ⓒ
2. Mark your answer.   Ⓐ   Ⓑ   Ⓒ
3. Mark your answer.   Ⓐ   Ⓑ   Ⓒ
4. Mark your answer.   Ⓐ   Ⓑ   Ⓒ
5. Mark your answer.   Ⓐ   Ⓑ   Ⓒ

6. Mark your answer.   Ⓐ   Ⓑ   Ⓒ
7. Mark your answer.   Ⓐ   Ⓑ   Ⓒ
8. Mark your answer.   Ⓐ   Ⓑ   Ⓒ
9. Mark your answer.   Ⓐ   Ⓑ   Ⓒ
10. Mark your answer.   Ⓐ   Ⓑ   Ⓒ

Questions with *How . . . ?*

The question word *how* is used to ask about manner and methods.

Sample Questions	Possible Responses
How did she get to Melbourne?	By plane.
How did you get in touch with Mr. Suyoto?	By texting him.
How does he drive?	Slowly and carefully.
How did you make these holes?	With a drill.
How did they get a loan for their business?	By providing collateral.
How do you know Christina?	She works in my office.

How . . . ? can be used to ask about the general condition of someone or something.

Sample Questions	Possible Responses
How's your father doing?	He's doing well, thanks.
How has Ellen been?	As far as I know, just fine.
How was dinner?	Great — we went to a good Mexican restaurant.

How much . . . ? is used to ask about cost or amount. *How many . . . ?* is used to ask about quantity (number).

Sample Questions	Possible Responses
How much is a motorcycle like that one?	Around $5,000.
How much water should we bring?	A couple of liters each.
How many guests were at the party?	There were twenty or thirty.

How do/did you like . . . ? is used to ask for an opinion of someone or something.

Sample Question	Possible Response
How did you like that new movie?	I enjoyed it, but my husband didn't.

How . . . get to . . . ? is used to ask for directions.

Sample Question	Possible Response
How do I get to the post office from here?	Walk down Liberty Avenue until you come to Third Street.

How about . . . ? is used to offer something to someone or to invite someone to do something.

Sample Questions	Possible Responses
How about some French pastries?	I'd love to have some, but I'm on a diet.
How about coming to a barbecue at our house on Saturday?	Sure, that sounds great.

How . . . ? is used with adverbs and adjectives to ask about age, duration, frequency, size, distance, and other characteristics.

Sample Questions	Possible Responses
How old is Fritz?	He's twenty-seven.
How long will this session last?	For another hour, perhaps.
How often does Michelle go skiing?	Once or twice a month.
How far is it from Boston to Washington, D.C.?	It's around 400 miles.
How late is this store open tonight?	Until nine o'clock, I believe.
How soon can you be here?	In about fifteen minutes.

Exercise 2.3

Focus: Answering information questions beginning with *how*.

Directions: You will hear a number of questions, each followed by three possible responses to the question. For each item, choose the letter of the response that best answers the question.

 Now start the audio program.

1. Mark your answer.   (A)   (B)   (C)
2. Mark your answer.   (A)   (B)   (C)
3. Mark your answer.   (A)   (B)   (C)
4. Mark your answer.   (A)   (B)   (C)
5. Mark your answer.   (A)   (B)   (C)
6. Mark your answer.   (A)   (B)   (C)
7. Mark your answer.   (A)   (B)   (C)

8. Mark your answer.   (A)   (B)   (C)
9. Mark your answer.   (A)   (B)   (C)
10. Mark your answer.   (A)   (B)   (C)
11. Mark your answer.   (A)   (B)   (C)
12. Mark your answer.   (A)   (B)   (C)
13. Mark your answer.   (A)   (B)   (C)
14. Mark your answer.   (A)   (B)   (C)

Questions with *When . . . ?* and *Where . . . ?*

The question word *when* is used to ask about time: times of day, days, dates, years, decades.

Sample Questions	Possible Responses
When did Antonio arrive?	Last Wednesday.
When will the planning session take place?	Tomorrow at eleven.
When is Maria's birthday?	On March 3.

The question word *where* is used to ask about locations: rooms, buildings, streets, cities, countries, and so on.

Sample Questions	Possible Responses
Where is the television studio?	It's downtown on Wells Street.
Where is your passport?	In my briefcase.
Where are you going?	To the drugstore.
Where are my glasses?	Over there, on your desk.

Where . . . from? is used to ask about place of origin.

Sample Question	Possible Response
Where is Jaewoo from?	He's from Busan, South Korea.

Exercise 2.4

Focus: Answering information questions beginning with *when* and *where*.

Directions: You will hear a number of questions, each followed by three possible responses to the question. For each item, choose the letter of the response that best answers the question.

 Now start the audio program.

1. Mark your answer. (A) (B) (C)
2. Mark your answer. (A) (B) (C)
3. Mark your answer. (A) (B) (C)
4. Mark your answer. (A) (B) (C)

5. Mark your answer. (A) (B) (C)
6. Mark your answer. (A) (B) (C)
7. Mark your answer. (A) (B) (C)
8. Mark your answer. (A) (B) (C)

Note: An incorrect choice may be an appropriate response for a *where . . . ?* question, but it does not answer the question asked.

    Where is the French Embassy?   *In the filing cabinet.*

Questions with *Why . . . ?*, *Who . . . ?*, *Whose . . . ?*, and *Which . . . ?*

The question word *why* is used to ask about reasons and purposes.

Sample Questions		Possible Responses	
Why did she go to Brussels?		To attend a conference.	
Why did you leave your last job?		Because of the low wages.	

Why don't you . . . ? is used to make suggestions.

Sample Question		Possible Response	
Why don't you order the soup?		Good idea — soup sounds great.	

The question word *who* is used to ask questions about people.

Sample Questions		Possible Responses	
Who were you talking to on the phone?		To my wife.	
Who is that woman in the blue raincoat?		That's Patricia Wedgewood.	

The question word *whose* is used to ask about possession.

Sample Question		Possible Response	
Whose scarf is this?		It's Fran's.	

The question word *which* is used to ask about choices from a limited number of selections.

Sample Questions		Possible Responses	
Which salesperson won the award?		Mr. Ishimura did.	
Which floor is your office on?		It's on the fourth floor.	

Which way . . . ? is used to ask about directions.

Sample Question		Possible Response	
Which way is it to Concourse E?		Walk straight ahead, and you'll see a sign.	

Exercise 2.5

Focus: Answering information questions beginning with *why, who, whose,* and *which*.

Directions: You will hear a number of questions, each followed by three possible responses to the question. For each item, choose the letter of the response that best answers the question.

 Now start the audio program.

1. Mark your answer.	(A)	(B)	(C)
2. Mark your answer.	(A)	(B)	(C)
3. Mark your answer.	(A)	(B)	(C)
4. Mark your answer.	(A)	(B)	(C)

5. Mark your answer.	(A)	(B)	(C)
6. Mark your answer.	(A)	(B)	(C)
7. Mark your answer.	(A)	(B)	(C)
8. Mark your answer.	(A)	(B)	(C)

Exercise 2.6

Focus: Reviewing and practicing all types of information questions.

Directions: You will hear a number of questions, each followed by three possible responses to the question. For each item, choose the letter of the response that best answers the question.

 Now start the audio program.

1. Mark your answer.	(A)	(B)	(C)
2. Mark your answer.	(A)	(B)	(C)
3. Mark your answer.	(A)	(B)	(C)
4. Mark your answer.	(A)	(B)	(C)
5. Mark your answer.	(A)	(B)	(C)
6. Mark your answer.	(A)	(B)	(C)
7. Mark your answer.	(A)	(B)	(C)
8. Mark your answer.	(A)	(B)	(C)

9. Mark your answer.	(A)	(B)	(C)
10. Mark your answer.	(A)	(B)	(C)
11. Mark your answer.	(A)	(B)	(C)
12. Mark your answer.	(A)	(B)	(C)
13. Mark your answer.	(A)	(B)	(C)
14. Mark your answer.	(A)	(B)	(C)
15. Mark your answer.	(A)	(B)	(C)
16. Mark your answer.	(A)	(B)	(C)

B. Yes/No Questions

Sample Items: Yes/No Questions

Did you finish that project yet?

Ⓐ   It was a difficult one.

●   Yes, finally, a week ago.

Ⓒ   No, there's only one.

> The question asks whether, as of now, the project has been finished. Choice (B) supplies this information.

Are you taking the 3 p.m. flight to Paris?

Ⓐ   From New York.

Ⓑ   It leaves in an hour.

●   No, the 7 p.m. flight.

> Choice (A) answers a *where . . .?* question; choice (B) answers a *when . . .?* question. Only (C) properly responds to a yes/no question.

May I talk to you for a few minutes?

●   Sure. What about?

Ⓑ   Yes, thanks to you.

Ⓒ   If you're not too busy.

> The questioner requests permission to talk to the respondent, and in Choice (A) the respondent agrees.

Basic Yes/No Questions

Yes/no questions begin with auxiliary verbs (*do, are, has, should, can,* for example) or with a form of the main verb *be* (*is, are, was,* and *were*). Responses may be short answers or full sentences.

Sample Questions	Possible Responses
Did you watch television last night?	No, I was out last night.
Is Herbert out of town?	I believe he is.
Will Mr. Cho attend the meeting?	Probably not.

Some yes/no questions contain **the** word *yet* or *still*. *Yet* is used in questions and negative sentences to mean that an activity is continuing. *Still* has a similar meaning in some questions and in affirmative sentences.

Sample Questions	Possible Responses
Is the game over yet?	No, it's still going on. / No, it's not over yet. / Yes, it's already over.
Are you still working at TRC Electronics?	No, I don't work there anymore. / Yes, I still work there.

Some yes/no questions contain the word *ever*. *Ever* means "at any time in the past."

Sample Question	Possible Responses
Have you ever been to Kuala Lumpur?	Yes, several times. / No, I've never been there.

Some yes/no questions begin, "Have you had a chance to . . ." This means "Have you had the opportunity to do something yet?"

Sample Question	Possible Responses
Have you had a chance to read that email?	No, not yet. / Yes, I just read it.

In Part 2, the correct responses for yes/no questions are often not simple short answers such as "Yes, I do" or "No, I'm not." There is a range of affirmative, negative, or neutral responses, as shown:

Question: Has Martin finished writing the report?		
Possible Affirmative Responses	Possible Negative Responses	Possible Neutral Responses
I think so. Of course he has. Yes, he finished this morning. I believe he has. Definitely. He's a fast worker. Probably. As a matter of fact, he has.	No, I don't think he has. Not yet, but he's hard at work on it. No, but he should finish soon. No, he gave up on it. No, he's doing something else now.	I have no idea. Why don't you ask him? Maybe — I don't know for sure. Perhaps he has. I'm not sure.

Exercise 2.7

Focus: Answering yes/no questions.

Directions: You will hear a number of questions, each followed by three possible responses to the question. For each item, choose the letter of the response that best answers the question.

 Now start the audio program.

1. Mark your answer.	Ⓐ	Ⓑ	Ⓒ		**6.** Mark your answer.	Ⓐ	Ⓑ	Ⓒ		
2. Mark your answer.	Ⓐ	Ⓑ	Ⓒ		**7.** Mark your answer.	Ⓐ	Ⓑ	Ⓒ		
3. Mark your answer.	Ⓐ	Ⓑ	Ⓒ		**8.** Mark your answer.	Ⓐ	Ⓑ	Ⓒ		
4. Mark your answer.	Ⓐ	Ⓑ	Ⓒ		**9.** Mark your answer.	Ⓐ	Ⓑ	Ⓒ		
5. Mark your answer.	Ⓐ	Ⓑ	Ⓒ		**10.** Mark your answer.	Ⓐ	Ⓑ	Ⓒ		

Requests, Invitations, and Offers

Some yes/no questions have special functions. These functions include making requests, giving invitations, and making offers. A **request** involves asking someone to do something or asking someone to help.

Sample Questions	Possible Responses
Will you come here a minute?	Of course — what do you need?
Would you hand me that pair of scissors?	Sure, here you are.
Can you take a look at this new schedule?	I'd be glad to.
Could you help me move this box?	I can't, I'm afraid — I have a sore back.
Can I have some more ice water?	Yes, here's some.
Could I get a copy of that?	This is the only copy I have, I'm afraid.
May I borrow twenty dollars?	Yes, if you promise to pay me back tomorrow.
Would you mind if we didn't go out tonight?	No, I don't mind — I don't want to go out either.*
Do you mind if I turn on the radio?	No, go ahead.*

*A positive response to questions beginning Do you mind if . . .? or Would you mind if . . .? may begin with the word No. For example, the response "No, go ahead" means "Yes, you may turn on the radio."

An **invitation** is a suggestion that someone go somewhere or do something with the person asking the question.

Sample Questions	Possible Responses
Would you like to join us for a game of tennis?	We'd love to — thanks!
Will you be able to come to the garden show this afternoon?	I'm afraid not, but perhaps tomorrow.
Should we get something to eat now?	Sure — I'm getting hungry.
Do you want to come skiing with us this weekend?	That would be great.
Should we get something to eat now?	All right, let's go.

An **offer** is a proposal to help someone or to allow someone to do something.

Sample Questions	Possible Responses
Could I get you a glass of water?	Thanks, I could use one.
Can I help you?	Yes, I'm looking for some printer paper.
May I show you our new line of fall clothes?	I just want to look around, thank you.
Should I get you a taxi?	No, I believe I'll walk.
Would you like to use my laptop?	Yes, if you don't mind.
Is there anything I can do for you?	You could make a phone call for me.
Would you like me to take you to the airport?	Thanks — it's kind of you to offer.

Exercise 2.8

Focus: Answering yes/no questions involving requests, invitations, and offers.

Directions: You will hear a number of questions, each followed by three possible responses to the question. For each item, choose the letter of the response that best answers the question.

Now start the audio program.

1. Mark your answer. (A) (B) (C)
2. Mark your answer. (A) (B) (C)
3. Mark your answer. (A) (B) (C)
4. Mark your answer. (A) (B) (C)
5. Mark your answer. (A) (B) (C)
6. Mark your answer. (A) (B) (C)

7. Mark your answer. (A) (B) (C)
8. Mark your answer. (A) (B) (C)
9. Mark your answer. (A) (B) (C)
10. Mark your answer. (A) (B) (C)
11. Mark your answer. (A) (B) (C)
12. Mark your answer. (A) (B) (C)

C. Other Types of Questions and Statements

Sample Items: Other Types of Questions

Can you tell me when the next planning meeting will be?

(A) Every month.

● This Monday at ten.

(C) Yes, that's the plan.

> This is an embedded question. It really asks, "When will the next planning meeting be?" The main question ("When will the next planning meeting be?") is part of another question "Can you tell me . . . "

Do you prefer playing tennis or golf?

(A) All right, let's play.

● I like both.

(C) I didn't play tennis.

> This is an alternative question. The correct answer indicates which of the two choices the respondent prefers.

That presentation wasn't very long, was it?

(A) No, it wasn't very difficult.

● You're right — it was quite short.

(C) Thanks, I enjoyed it.

> This is a tag question. Choice (B) responds to the question of whether or not the presentation was long.

Wasn't that a fascinating article?

(A) Yes, he was fascinating.

(B) It will be finished soon.

● Yes, it was very interesting.

> This is a negative question. The questioner believes the article was fascinating, and in (C), the respondent agrees.

There will be a retirement party for Mr. Jones tonight.

● Great — I'd love to go.

(B) Yes, he did look tired last night.

(C) The food at the party was very good.

> This is a statement. The person making the statement says there will be a retirement party tonight. Choice (A) indicates that the person responding wants to go to the party.

Embedded Questions

This type of question usually begins with one of the following phrases:

Do you know . . . ?   *Do you think . . . ?*   *Did you decide . . . ?*   *Did you hear . . . ?*   *Are you sure . . . ?*
Did anyone tell you . . . ?   *Have you heard . . . ?*   *Can you tell me . . . ?*   *Will you let me know . . . ?*

The embedded question may be an information question:

Sample Questions	Possible Responses
Did you decide where you're going for your honeymoon?	We're going to Tahiti.
Can you tell me how to get to the Continental Express office?	Sorry, I'm not sure where it is.

Responses to this type of question are not simply yes/no answers; they must answer the embedded information question. The embedded portion may be a yes/no question.

These questions are introduced by the words *if* or *whether*.

Sample Questions	Possible Responses
Do you know if Mr. Kwon is in his office?	I believe he is — let me check.
Have you heard whether interest rates will go up again?	I haven't heard anything, but they probably will.

Statements may also be embedded in questions. These statements can be introduced by the word *that*, but it is often omitted.

Sample Questions	Possible Responses
Did you hear that Bill was laid off?	Oh, no — poor Bill!
Are you sure this is a bargain?	Yes, it's the best price I think you'll get.

Alternative Questions

Alternative questions ask listeners to choose between one of two (sometimes three) possibilities. They contain the word *or*.

Sample Questions	Possible Responses
Will you arrive in the morning or the evening?	In the morning, I think.
Do you want coffee or tea?	Coffee for me.

Responses to these questions usually name one of the alternatives. Answers may also include the word *either*, *neither*, or *both*. Remember: A yes or no response is not appropriate for an alternative question.

Sample Question	Possible Responses
Do you want milk or sugar in your coffee?	Neither one. / Both, please.

Exercise 2.9

Focus: Answering questions with embedded sentences and alternative questions.

Directions: You will hear a number of questions, each followed by three possible responses to the question. For each item, choose the letter of the response that best answers the question.

 Now start the audio program.

1. Mark your answer.	Ⓐ	Ⓑ	Ⓒ
2. Mark your answer.	Ⓐ	Ⓑ	Ⓒ
3. Mark your answer.	Ⓐ	Ⓑ	Ⓒ
4. Mark your answer.	Ⓐ	Ⓑ	Ⓒ
5. Mark your answer.	Ⓐ	Ⓑ	Ⓒ
6. Mark your answer.	Ⓐ	Ⓑ	Ⓒ
7. Mark your answer.	Ⓐ	Ⓑ	Ⓒ
8. Mark your answer.	Ⓐ	Ⓑ	Ⓒ

9. Mark your answer.	Ⓐ	Ⓑ	Ⓒ
10. Mark your answer.	Ⓐ	Ⓑ	Ⓒ
11. Mark your answer.	Ⓐ	Ⓑ	Ⓒ
12. Mark your answer.	Ⓐ	Ⓑ	Ⓒ
13. Mark your answer.	Ⓐ	Ⓑ	Ⓒ
14. Mark your answer.	Ⓐ	Ⓑ	Ⓒ
15. Mark your answer.	Ⓐ	Ⓑ	Ⓒ
16. Mark your answer.	Ⓐ	Ⓑ	Ⓒ

Tag Questions

Tag questions consist of an affirmative statement with a negative tag (. . . *doesn't he?* / . . . *isn't it?* / . . . *haven't you?*) or a negative statement with an affirmative tag (. . . *will you?* / . . . *did she?* / . . . *are there?*).

Sample Questions	Possible Responses
This is a beautiful beach, isn't it?	It's lovely.
You enjoyed the play, didn't you?	As a matter of fact, I found it boring.
This won't take long, will it?	Just a few minutes.
He didn't miss his plane, did he?	I don't think so.

Expressions such as . . . *wouldn't you say?*, . . . *don't you think?*, . . . *OK?*, and . . . *right?* are sometimes used in place of negative tags.

Sample Questions	Possible Responses
You remember Rachel, right?	Oh, sure, I remember her well.
This is a good place to camp, don't you think?	Yes, it's a nice spot.

Negative Questions

Negative questions begin with negative contractions: *Doesn't . . . ? I Hasn't . . . ? / Aren't. . . . ?* The expected answer is affirmative, but the actual answer may be either affirmative or negative.

Sample Questions	Possible Responses
Isn't this beautiful weather?	It certainly is.
Weren't you tired after the race?	No, not too tired.

Some negative questions are used in special functions: *Won't you . . . ?* is used in invitations.

Sample Question	Possible Response
Won't you come to the party with us?	Sure, I'd love to.

Shouldn't you/we . . . ? is used to make suggestions.

Sample Question	Possible Response
Shouldn't you take your umbrella?	No, I think the weather is going to clear up.

Wouldn't you like . . . ? is used to make offers.

Sample Question	Possible Response
Wouldn't you like some tea?	Thanks, I'd love some.

Statements (Non-question)

There are many kinds of statements used for announcements, requests, suggestions, or exclamations. These are not questions, but can be responded to in a number of ways: with yes or no responses, or with other statements.

Announcements are statements that are used to give information.

Sample Statement	Possible Response
There's a meeting in 10 minutes in the conference room.	Thanks for letting me know.

Please. . ., *Let me know if. . .*, and *I'd appreciate it if. . .* are used in statements that make requests.

Sample Statements	Possible Responses
Please tell David about the changes.	OK, I'll email him now.
Let me know if the package arrives by the end of the day.	I'll call you as soon as I see it.
I'd appreciate it if you could send this package to Singapore.	No problem. I'll mail it right away.

Let's . . . is used in statements that make suggestions.

Sample Statement	Possible Response
Let's take Mr. Robbins to the new Italian restaurant.	That's a good idea.

A special kind of statement, an exclamation, is used to express surprise, delight, or anger. These types of statements frequently begin with *What (a)* + noun, *What (a)* + adjective + noun, and *How* + adjective.

Sample Statements	Possible Responses
What a mess!	I know. I need to clean today.
What a great day!	Yes, the weather is beautiful.
How hot it is in here!	It is pretty warm.

Exercise 2.10

Focus: Answering tag questions, negative questions, and statements.

Directions: You will hear a number of questions or statements, each followed by three possible responses. For each item, select the best response to the question or statement.

 Now start the audio program.

1. Mark your answer. (A) (B) (C)
2. Mark your answer. (A) (B) (C)
3. Mark your answer. (A) (B) (C)
4. Mark your answer. (A) (B) (C)
5. Mark your answer. (A) (B) (C)
6. Mark your answer. (A) (B) (C)

7. Mark your answer. (A) (B) (C)
8. Mark your answer. (A) (B) (C)
9. Mark your answer. (A) (B) (C)
10. Mark your answer. (A) (B) (C)
11. Mark your answer. (A) (B) (C)
12. Mark your answer. (A) (B) (C)

D. Recognizing Sound/Meaning Distractors

Some responses are incorrect because of problems involving sound and meaning.

Sample Items: Sound/Meaning Problems

Did you catch the plane?

- (A) No, I didn't change my plan.
- ● Yes, but I almost missed it.
- (C) No, I didn't catch a cold.

> The question contains the word *plane*. Choice (A) contains the sound-alike word *plan* and is incorrect. The question also includes the word *catch*. Choice (C) contains the word *catch* too, but it has another meaning (to contract an illness).

How did you hear about this event?

- ● My brother told me.
- (B) The event is not held here.
- (C) It starts at nine.

> Choice (B) contains the word *here*, which sounds exactly like the word *hear* in the question. However, choice (B) does not answer the question. Choice (C) answers the question "When does the event start?"

There are three types of sound/meaning problems:

1. **Sound-alike words:** The question and one of the responses have words with similar sounds but different meanings (such as *plane* and *plan* in the first sample item).
2. **Words with multiple meanings:** The question contains a word that has more than one meaning. The word is used one way in the question and another way in one of the responses (*catch* and *catch* in the first sample item).
3. **Homophones:** The question and one of the responses contain a homophone — a word that has the same pronunciation but a different meaning (*hear* and *here* in the second sample item).

Exercise 2.11

Focus: Identifying distractors based on sound/meaning problems, and choosing correct answers.

Directions: You will hear a number of questions, each followed by three possible responses to the question. For each item, choose the letter of the response that best answers the question.

 Now start the audio program.

1. Mark your answer. (A) (B) (C)
2. Mark your answer. (A) (B) (C)
3. Mark your answer. (A) (B) (C)
4. Mark your answer. (A) (B) (C)
5. Mark your answer. (A) (B) (C)

6. Mark your answer. (A) (B) (C)
7. Mark your answer. (A) (B) (C)
8. Mark your answer. (A) (B) (C)
9. Mark your answer. (A) (B) (C)
10. Mark your answer. (A) (B) (C)

E. Recognizing Other Types of Distractors

Some responses are incorrect for the following reasons:

1. Incorrect verb tense

Where did Jacques go?

(A)   He'll go to the bookstore tomorrow.

The question asks about the past (*did . . . go*), but the response involves the future. (*He'll go to the bookstore tomorrow.*)

2. Incorrect person

Do you plan to go with her?

(A)   Yes, she plans to.

The question asks about *you*, so the response should use the word *I* or *we*. Instead, it incorrectly involves the word *she*.

3. Response to the incorrect type of question

When did Maria leave?

(A)   I think she went to the bank.

The question asks about time (*When . . . ?*), but the response provides a destination (*the bank*). This response is incorrect because it answers a *where* question, not a *when* question.

Were you here at noon?

(A)   At a restaurant.

The question asks for a yes/no reply, but the response answers an information question. ("Where were you at noon?")

Do you want one scoop of ice cream or two?

(A)   Yes, please.

The question asks the listener to choose between one scoop or two, but the response is a simple affirmative. This is a proper answer for a yes/no question, not for an alternative question.

Focus: Identifying common types of distractors for Part 2 items.

Directions: You will hear a question followed by a response. In each case, the response is an inappropriate one. Choose the category that most correctly explains why the response is not an appropriate one, and mark the blank accordingly.

 Now start the audio program.

	Wrong Tense	Wrong Person	Wrong Type of Question
1.	_____	_____	_____
2.	_____	_____	_____
3.	_____	_____	_____
4.	_____	_____	_____
5.	_____	_____	_____
6.	_____	_____	_____

Directions: You will hear a number of questions or statements, each followed by three possible responses. For each item, select the best response to the question or statement.

   Now start the audio program.

1. Mark your answer.   (A)   (B)   (C)
2. Mark your answer.   (A)   (B)   (C)
3. Mark your answer.   (A)   (B)   (C)
4. Mark your answer.   (A)   (B)   (C)
5. Mark your answer.   (A)   (B)   (C)
6. Mark your answer.   (A)   (B)   (C)
7. Mark your answer.   (A)   (B)   (C)
8. Mark your answer.   (A)   (B)   (C)
9. Mark your answer.   (A)   (B)   (C)
10. Mark your answer.   (A)   (B)   (C)
11. Mark your answer.   (A)   (B)   (C)
12. Mark your answer.   (A)   (B)   (C)
13. Mark your answer.   (A)   (B)   (C)

14. Mark your answer.   (A)   (B)   (C)
15. Mark your answer.   (A)   (B)   (C)
16. Mark your answer.   (A)   (B)   (C)
17. Mark your answer.   (A)   (B)   (C)
18. Mark your answer.   (A)   (B)   (C)
19. Mark your answer.   (A)   (B)   (C)
20. Mark your answer.   (A)   (B)   (C)
21. Mark your answer.   (A)   (B)   (C)
22. Mark your answer.   (A)   (B)   (C)
23. Mark your answer.   (A)   (B)   (C)
24. Mark your answer.   (A)   (B)   (C)
25. Mark your answer.   (A)   (B)   (C)

Lesson 3 Short Conversations

Lesson Outline

Format   Part 3

This part of the test consists of thirteen short conversations. Each of the thirteen conversations is followed by three questions. The conversations are generally between a man and a woman, although sometimes they are between two women or between two men. Three-way conversations involve two women and a man or two men and a woman. The conversations usually consist of three to five exchanges, but some conversations — especially three-way conversations — may be longer. A few typical patterns are given below:

Speaker 1: Asks a question.
Speaker 2: Responds to the
      question.
Speaker 1: Comments on the
      response.
Speaker 1: Asks a question.
Speaker 2: Responds to the
      question.

Speaker 1: Makes a statement.
Speaker 2: Questions the
      statement.
Speaker 1: Responds to
      the question.
Speaker 1: Asks Speaker 3 for
      his/her opinion.
Speaker 3: Responds with his/her
      opinion.

Speaker 1: Asks a question.
Speaker 2: Responds to the
      question and asks a question.
Speaker 1: Responds to the question.
Speaker 2: Comments on the response.

In your test book, the three questions for each conversation are written out. Four possible answer choices are provided for each question. Your job is to decide which one of these best answers the question. Then you need to mark the corresponding answer on your answer sheet.

Tactics   Part 3

1. Between each question, and between the third question and the next conversation, there is an eight-second pause. During these pauses, you can accomplish quite a bit. You need to mark your answer and then preview the next question and answer choices. They tell you what to listen for.

2. While listening to each conversation, keep your eyes on the corresponding set of three questions and answer choices. Don't close your eyes or look away. Try to evaluate the four choices as you are listening.

3. Remember that distractors are sometimes mentioned in the conversations but are not answers to the question. Don't choose an answer just because you hear a word or two from the answer in the conversation.

4. If the correct answer is not obvious, try to eliminate answer choices that seem to be incorrect. If more than one answer choice is left, take a guess.

5. Mark your answers as quickly as possible so that you can preview the next item.

6. Never leave any answers blank. If you are not sure, always guess.

Preview Test Part 3

 Start the audio program and read along as the directions are read.

Directions: In this part of the test, you hear short conversations involving two or three speakers. Each conversation is spoken only once and is not written out in the book, so listen carefully.

In your book, you will read three questions about each conversation. Following each question are four answer choices. Choose the best one — (A), (B), (C), or (D) — and mark the answer.

SEATING PLAN

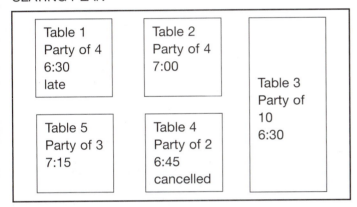

| Table 1 Party of 4 6:30 late | Table 2 Party of 4 7:00 | Table 3 Party of 10 6:30 |
| Table 5 Party of 3 7:15 | Table 4 Party of 2 6:45 cancelled | |

1. Look at the graphic. Where will the man most likely be seated?
   - (A) Table 1
   - (B) Table 2
   - (C) Table 3
   - (D) Table 4

2. How long will they have to wait for seats?
   - (A) A couple of minutes
   - (B) Less than twenty minutes
   - (C) A half hour
   - (D) Two hours

3. Why was the man worried?
   - (A) He didn't have any reservations.
   - (B) He reserved the seats too late.
   - (C) He didn't know if this was a good restaurant.
   - (D) He thought he might be late for a party.

4. What is the problem?
   - (A) The new shipment has not arrived.
   - (B) The wrong order was delivered.
   - (C) The company sent too many packages.
   - (D) The invoice number was incorrect.

5. What can be inferred from this conversation?
   - (A) The problem has already been taken care of.
   - (B) There is no blue paper in stock at present.
   - (C) Ms. Tupton's manager wasn't upset last time.
   - (D) Janice Nelson is a new employee.

6. What is Ms. Nelson planning to do?
   - (A) Make a copy of the invoice
   - (B) Speak to her manager
   - (C) Call Ms. Tupton later today
   - (D) Send a new order

7. What are the speakers mainly discussing?
   - (A) Shopping for clothes
   - (B) An important meeting
   - (C) Dry cleaning some clothing
   - (D) Scheduling a dinner meeting

8. What does Ruby say about the extra fee?

   (A) It's too expensive.

   (B) It isn't necessary.

   (C) She doesn't mind paying it.

   (D) She will pay it with a credit card.

9. Where most likely does the man work?

   (A) A restaurant

   (B) A hotel

   (C) A newspaper

   (D) A dry cleaning shop

10. What does the man mean when he says, "Not as much as I thought I would"?

   (A) He paid less money than he expected.

   (B) He enjoys his job less than he predicted.

   (C) He spent less time at work than he anticipated.

   (D) He gets less salary than he thought.

11. What does the man think about his job?

   (A) It isn't challenging enough for him.

   (B) He doesn't like the long hours.

   (C) He wants to quit immediately.

   (D) It doesn't provide any options.

12. What advice does the woman give?

   (A) To stay on the job

   (B) To take a risk

   (C) To apply for another position

   (D) To give someone a present

Testing Points and Skill-Building Exercises

Many kinds of questions may be asked about the conversations, but they can be divided into these general categories:
A. Overview questions
B. Detail questions
C. Inference questions
D. Three-way conversations
E. Intention questions
F. Graphic-based questions

A. Overview Questions

These questions require you to have a "global" or overall understanding of the dialogs that you hear. There are four kinds of overview questions:

Types of Overview Questions	Typical Question Words
1. Questions about locations	1. Where . . . ?
2. Questions about occupations	2. Who . . . ?
3. Questions about activities	3. What . . . doing?
4. Questions about topics	4. What . . . talking about?

These ask where the conversation occurs. There are a number of ways these questions can be asked:

- *Where are they?*
- *Where is the man/woman?*
- *Where are the speakers?*
- *Where is the conversation taking place?*

The answer choices for these questions are the names of four locations of various types — for example, a restaurant, a bank, an advertising agency, a tailor shop. To answer these questions, you can't simply listen for the name of the location, which is seldom provided in the conversation. You need to listen for vocabulary that is tied to a certain location. For example, if you hear the words *reservations*, *first class*, and *tickets*, the answer will probably be "In a travel agency." However, don't choose an answer on the basis of just one of these words or phrases. The word *reservations* could also be heard in a restaurant or hotel; the phrase *first class* could also be heard at a post office; the word *tickets* could also be heard at a concert, movie, or sporting event.

Sample Item: Location Question

Man: We don't have any reservations. Is it still possible for us to get a table for two?
Woman: You're in luck — a party of two just cancelled their reservations. We can seat you in about fifteen or twenty minutes.
Man: Great! I was worried, but I guess this is our lucky night!

Q. Where are they?

(A) At a theater
(B) At a party
(C) At an airport
● At a restaurant

> The mention of *reservations*, *table*, and *party of two* indicates that they are at a restaurant.

Exercise 3.1

Focus: Linking vocabulary to locations.

Directions: Match the locations below with the appropriate group of vocabulary words by writing the appropriate letter in the blank. The first one has been done as an example.

There is no audio program for this exercise.

a. airport	**g.** construction site	**m.** hair salon	**r.** post office
b. apartment complex	**h.** courtroom	**n.** hardware store	**s.** restaurant
c. bakery	**i.** farm	**o.** hotel	**t.** stationery store
d. bank	**j.** football stadium	**p.** jewelry store	**u.** theater
e. beach	**k.** freeway	**q.** laundromat	**v.** travel agency
f. computer store	**l.** grocery store		

1. __C__
rolls
cake
bread

2. _____
stage
cast
box office

3. _____
bulldozer
hard hat
crane

4. _____
chain
ring
bracelet

5. _____
menu
terminal
keyboard

6. _____
dryer
hangers
detergent

7. _____
terminal
concourse
gate

8. _____
surf
towel
umbrella

9. _____
pens
envelopes
letterhead

10. _____
lanes
drivers
exit

11. _____
suite
front desk
reservations

12. _____
field
barn
fertilizer

Occupation Questions

These questions are very similar to the ones asked about locations, but they ask about the job or profession of one or both of the speakers. There are various ways these questions can be asked:

- *Who is the man/woman?*
- *Who are they?*
- *What is he/she?*
- *What are they?*

- *What is the man's/woman's profession?*
- *What is the man's/woman's occupation?*
- *What is the man's/woman's job?*

The answer choices for these questions are the names of four occupations: banker, bus driver, doctor, police officer, and so on. The occupations are seldom given directly in the conversations. As with location questions, you must listen for key vocabulary that ties the speaker or speakers to one of the answers. For example, if you hear the terms *fare, transfer,* and *next stop,* the correct answer will be "bus driver." Again, don't choose an answer based on just one term; the word *fare* could also be used by people in other occupations — for example, by a travel agent.

Sample Item: Occupation Question

1st Man: Front desk.

2nd Man: Yes, I'd like to have my suit cleaned and pressed. I have an important dinner meeting, so I'll need it by 5:00.

1st Man: Certainly, sir. I'll have someone come by your room in just a few minutes to pick it up.

2nd Man: Please put the charges on my bill. Oh, and I didn't receive the morning paper I asked for. Can you have someone bring that to me as well?

Q. Who is the first speaker?

- (A) A waiter
- ● A hotel clerk
- (C) A journalist
- (D) A dry cleaner

The words *front desk* and *room* indicate that the first speaker is the clerk at the front desk of a hotel.

Exercise 3.2

Focus: Linking vocabulary to occupations.

Directions: Match the occupations below with the appropriate group of vocabulary words by writing the letter of the occupation in the blank.

There is no audio program for this exercise.

a. carpenter	**e.** immigration officer	**i.** painter	**m.** surgeon
b. dentist	**f.** manicurist	**j.** postal clerk	**n.** tailor
c. florist	**g.** mechanic	**k.** secretary	**o.** taxi driver
d. hair stylist	**h.** musician	**l.** student	**p.** travel agent

1. _____
   anesthesia
   scalpel
   operation

2. _____
   transmission
   spark plug
   tune-up

3. _____
   nails
   file
   hammer

4. _____
   stamp
   visa
   passport

5. _____
   drill
   polish
   cavity

6. _____
   brushes
   rollers
   coat

7. _____
   alterations
   tape measure
   suit

8. _____
   first class
   stamps
   parcel post

9. _____
   notes
   arrangement
   orchestration

10. _____
    arrangement
    delivery
    bouquet

Exercise 3.3

Focus: Answering overview questions about locations and occupations.

Directions: Listen to the conversation. Read the question about the conversation and then choose the one option — (A), (B), (C), or (D) — that best answers the question.

 Now start the audio program.

1. Who is the second speaker?

   (A) An electrician

   (B) A banker

   (C) An engineer

   (D) A jeweler

2. Where are they?

   (A) In a grocery store

   (B) On a farm

   (C) At an outdoor market

   (D) In a vegetable garden

3. Where is this conversation taking place?

   (A) At a men's clothing store

   (B) In a courtroom

   (C) At an art gallery

   (D) In a paint store

4. Who are they?

   (A) Printers

   (B) Architects

   (C) Fashion designers

   (D) House painters

5. Who is Thomas?

   (A) A sailor

   (B) A mechanic

   (C) A plumber

   (D) A carpenter

6. Where are they?

   (A) At a coffee shop

   (B) On an airplane

   (C) In an automobile

   (D) In a clothing store

7. Who is the man?

   (A) A police officer

   (B) A gardener

   (C) A security guard

   (D) A pilot

8. Where is this conversation taking place?

   (A) On a bus

   (B) In a taxi

   (C) At the library

   (D) On Clifton Avenue

9. Where are the speakers?

   (A) At a cinema

   (B) At a television studio

   (C) At a bookstore

   (D) At a video rental store

10. Who is Lisa?

    (A) An interior designer

    (B) The director

    (C) A painter

    (D) A newspaper reporter

11. Where are they?

    (A) In a hardware store

    (B) In a dentist's office

    (C) In an artist's studio

    (D) In an electronics store

12. Who is the first speaker?

    (A) A teacher

    (B) A mechanic

    (C) A doctor

    (D) A pharmacist

Activity Questions

These questions ask what one or both speakers are doing or are going to do. These questions can be asked in several ways:
- *What are they doing?*
- *What is happening now?*
- *What is the situation?*
- *What is the man/woman doing?*
- *What is going to happen?*

Answer choices for these questions are the names of different activities: buying a car, painting a room, eating breakfast, getting a haircut, and so on. There are two or three key vocabulary terms that can be connected with a certain activity. For example, if you hear the words *tent* and *sleeping bag,* the answer will be "going camping."

Woman: It must be a big change to go from being a marketing manager to a product designer. So, are you enjoying the job?

Man: Not as much as I thought I would. I didn't think I'd have to work so late to meet the deadlines.

Woman: Well, give it a chance — you've only been in this position for a month. It took me a year of on-the-job training to adjust to the pace around here.

Man: Oh, I intend to. I'm not a quitter. I actually enjoy challenges.

Q. What is the man doing now?

- (A) Working as a manager
- (B) Marketing products
- (C) Training new employees
- ● Designing products

> The woman says that the man has gone from being a marketing manager to a product designer. This means he has changed jobs, and is now designing products.

Topic Questions

These questions ask about the general subject of the conversation. The subject of the conversation can be a person, a thing, or an activity. Topic questions can be phrased in a variety of ways:

- What/Who are they discussing?
- What are they referring to?
- What is the topic of the conversation?

- What are they talking about?
- What is the conversation about?
- What is the subject of the conversation?

The answer choices will be four plausible topics. Incorrect answers may include details that are mentioned in the conversation but that are not the main subject of the conversation.

Sample Item: Topic Question

1st Man: Front desk.

2nd Man: Yes, I'd like to have my suit cleaned and pressed. I have an important dinner meeting, so I'll need it by 5:00.

1st Man: Certainly, sir. I'll have someone come by your room in just a few minutes to pick it up.

2nd Man: Please put the charges on my bill. Oh, and I didn't receive the morning paper I asked for. Can you have someone bring that to me as well?

Q. What are they mainly discussing?

- (A) Shopping for clothes
- (B) An important meeting
- ● Dry cleaning a suit
- (D) Scheduling a dinner meeting

> The main focus of the dialog is on arranging to have the second man's suit dry cleaned. Dry cleaning includes both cleaning and pressing a garment.

Focus: Answering overview questions dealing with activities and topics.

Directions: Listen to the conversation. Read the question about the conversation and then choose the one option — (A), (B), (C), or (D) — that best answers the question.

 Now start the audio program.

1. What are they discussing?

   (A) A boat trip

   (B) Fishing

   (C) A ball game

   (D) Medical care

2. What are they doing?

   (A) Buying clothing

   (B) Going through customs

   (C) Going grocery shopping

   (D) Getting their luggage

3. Who are they talking about?

   (A) A sculptor

   (B) A novelist

   (C) A painter

   (D) A gardener

4. What is the second speaker doing?

   (A) Renting a car

   (B) Looking for retail space

   (C) Trying to find an apartment

   (D) Going shopping

5. What is the conversation about?

   (A) A computer

   (B) A photographer's model

   (C) A sports car

   (D) An old photograph

6. What is Mr. Krueger going to do?

   (A) Have his carpet cleaned

   (B) Get his car repaired

   (C) Have his lawn mowed

   (D) Get his hair cut

7. What is the subject of the conversation?

   (A) A dangerous intersection

   (B) A new store

   (C) An airline accident

   (D) Outdoor lighting

8. What are they going to do?

   (A) Go horseback riding

   (B) Go skiing

   (C) Go on a plane trip

   (D) Go shopping

9. What is the situation?

   (A) The woman is being interviewed for a job.

   (B) The man is trying to sell the woman a computer.

   (C) The woman is applying to a college.

   (D) The man is asking the woman if he can use her computer.

10. What are the speakers going to do?

    (A) Go deep-sea fishing

    (B) Examine some documents

    (C) Watch television

    (D) Go out to a movie

B. Detail Questions

Detail questions ask about specific points in the conversation. However, the answers to these questions are generally not found in a single line of the conversation. It's usually necessary to understand the entire conversation. Some of the most common detail questions are given below, but there are other types.

Types of Detail Questions	Typical Question Words
1. Questions about time	1. When . . . ?
2. Questions about reasons	2. Why . . . ?
3. Questions about plans	3. What . . . do?
4. Questions about problems	4. What's the matter with . . . ?
5. Questions about suggestions	5. What . . . suggest . . . ?
6. Questions about opinions	6. What . . . think of . . . ?

Questions About Time

These questions ask when an event or activity takes place. Some time questions ask about frequency or duration. Time questions can be asked in several ways:

- *When . . . ?*
- *How often . . . ?* (frequency)
- *At what time . . . ?*
- *How long . . . ?* (duration)

The answer choices are times of day, parts of the day, days of the week, dates, years, amounts of time, and so on. Often, one or more of the distractors are mentioned in the conversation but do not answer the question. And sometimes the correct answer is not mentioned directly by the speakers.

Sample Item: Time Question

Man: We don't have any reservations. Is it still possible for us to get a table for two?

Woman: You're in luck — a party of two just cancelled their reservations. We can seat you in about fifteen or twenty minutes.

Man: Great! I was worried, but I guess this is our lucky night!

Q. How long will they have to wait for seats?

(A) A couple of minutes

● Less than twenty minutes

(C) A half hour

(D) Two hours

> The woman says that she can seat them "in about fifteen or twenty minutes." Therefore, answer (B), "Less than twenty minutes," is the correct answer.

Questions About Reasons

These questions ask why someone does something, why someone feels a certain way, why an event occurs, and so on.

These are typical reason questions:

- *Why did . . . happen?*
- *Why is the man/woman going to . . . ?*
- *Why does the man/woman want to . . . ?*
- *Why is the man/woman upset/happy/puzzled?*

Some reason questions are negative questions:

- *Why did . . . not happen?*
- *Why does he/she not want to . . . ?*

Man: We don't have any reservations. Is it still possible for us to get a table for two?

Woman: You're in luck — a party of two just cancelled their reservations. We can seat you in about fifteen or twenty minutes.

Man: Great! I was worried, but I guess this is our lucky night!

Q. Why was the man worried?

● He didn't have any reservations.

(B) He reserved the seats too late.

(C) He didn't know if this was a good restaurant.

(D) He thought he might be late for a party.

> The man says he doesn't have reservations and that he "was worried."

Exercise 3.5

Focus: Answering detail questions dealing with time and reasons.

Directions: Listen to the conversation. Read the question about the conversation and then choose the one option — (A), (B), (C), or (D) — that best answers the question.

 Now start the audio program.

1. Why is Mr. Maras leaving?

   (A) To talk to a client

   (B) To go to his office

   (C) To board an airplane

   (D) To meet his wife

2. When will the office open again?

   (A) This weekend

   (B) On Monday

   (C) On Tuesday

   (D) On Wednesday

3. At what time will the man see the movie?

   (A) At 7:30

   (B) At 7:40

   (C) At 9:00

   (D) At 9:10

4. Why does Carlos congratulate Eva?

   (A) She'll be making a lot more money.

   (B) She found a better job.

   (C) She's been promoted.

   (D) She likes the region where she'll be working.

5. When did Frank start working here?

   (A) In 2003

   (B) In 2004

   (C) In 2005

   (D) In 2006

6. When does Patrick hope to come to work?

   (A) At lunchtime

   (B) This afternoon

   (C) Tomorrow morning

   (D) Tomorrow afternoon

7. Why did the man NOT take the shuttle bus?

(A) He wanted to save time.

(B) He wanted to impress someone.

(C) It left without him.

(D) There was no room on it.

8. Why is Dan upset?

(A) He lost his new coffee mug.

(B) He could not attend the conference.

(C) He did not get any coffee this morning.

(D) He could not find some important papers.

9. How long was Ms. Shearson out of the country?

(A) For a few days

(B) For a month

(C) Exactly a year

(D) Just over a year

10. Why is Jim NOT going to the trade fair?

(A) The distribution manager will not permit it.

(B) He is too busy.

(C) The trip is too expensive.

(D) He does not want to attend.

Questions About Plans

These questions ask what a person intends to do in the future. They can be phrased in a number of ways:

- *What is the man/woman planning to do?*
- *What does the man/woman plan to do next?*
- *What plan has been suggested?*
- *What does the man/woman want to do?*

The answer choices are four plausible plans. One or two of the distractors may be discussed in the conversation but are incorrect because the plan or plans are changed or rejected.

Sample Item: Plan Question

1st woman:	Good Morning, National Office Supplies — Customer Service Department. Janice Nelson speaking.
2nd woman:	Hello, Janice, this is Ms. Tupton. I'm calling about an order I just received. There were twenty packages of blue paper, but we ordered white paper. I believe we spoke last week about a similar situation. And this time, my manager's upset!
1st woman:	I'm really sorry, Ms. Tupton — I'll take care of the problem right away. Give me the invoice number on the shipment, and I'll get an order of white paper out to you later this afternoon.

Q. What is Ms. Nelson planning to do?

(A) Make a copy of the invoice

(B) Speak to her manager

(C) Call Ms. Tupton later today

● Send a new order

> Ms. Nelson says, "I'll get an order of white paper out to you later this afternoon." This means that she is planning to send a new order with the correct color of paper.

These questions ask about some difficulty that one or both of the speakers experience. There are several ways to phrase these questions:

- *What is the problem here?*
- *What is wrong with . . . ?*
- *What is the man/woman concerned about?*

- *What is the man's/woman's problem?*
- *What is bothering the man/woman?*
- *What is the man/woman worried about?*

The answer choices are four possible problems. One or more of the choices may be mentioned but are not the problem being asked about.

Sample Item: Problem Question

1st woman: Good Morning, National Office Supplies — Customer Service Department. Janice Nelson speaking.

2nd woman: Hello, Janice, this is Ms. Tupton. I'm calling about an order I just received. There were twenty packages of blue paper, but we ordered white paper. I believe we spoke last week about a similar situation. And this time, my manager's upset!

1st woman: I'm really sorry, Ms. Tupton — I'll take care of the problem right away. Give me the invoice number on the shipment, and I'll get an order of white paper out to you later this afternoon.

Q. What is the problem?

(A) The new shipment has not arrived.

● The wrong order was delivered.

(C) The company sent too many packages.

(D) The invoice number was incorrect.

> Ms. Tupton's manager is upset because they received a shipment of blue paper, but they had ordered white paper.

Exercise 3.6

Focus: Answering detail questions that deal with plans or problems.

Directions: Listen to the conversation. Read the question about the conversation and then choose the one option — (A), (B), (C), or (D) — that best answers the question.

 Now start the audio program.

1. What is the problem with the bicycle?

   (A) It is very old.

   (B) There is no key for the lock.

   (C) It has been stolen.

   (D) There is no air in one tire.

2. What is Mr. Neufield's immediate plan?

   (A) To postpone the meeting with Mr. Utsumi

   (B) To meet with the chief engineer

   (C) To talk with Mr. Utsumi

   (D) To make several phone calls

3. What does Mary plan to do?

   (A) Change her field

   (B) Go on vacation

   (C) Start her own business

   (D) Go to graduate school

4. What is the problem here?

   (A) The CD is damaged.

   (B) The woman dislikes the music.

   (C) The CD player is out of order.

   (D) The man can't find the CD.

5. What does Ms. Powers plan to do before hiring Katie?

   (A) Interview her again

   (B) Write her a letter

   (C) Give her a test

   (D) Contact her references

6. What plan does the second speaker suggest?

   (A) Traveling to Manila

   (B) Asking Mr. Quizon to visit

   (C) Changing their place of operations

   (D) Offering Mr. Quizon another position

7. Why is the woman concerned about the documents?

   (A) They have been lost.

   (B) They contain many mistakes.

   (C) They are not in the proper order.

   (D) They have not been read.

8. What is wrong with the apartment?

   (A) It is too big for him.

   (B) It does not have enough rooms.

   (C) It is too expensive.

   (D) It is not in the right location.

9. What is the problem?

   (A) The flowerpot is broken.

   (B) The glass cannot be replaced.

   (C) The table has not been set.

   (D) The tabletop was damaged.

10. What does Mr. Dufour plan to do?

    (A) Become an artist

    (B) Buy some art

    (C) Hire more advisors

    (D) Study art

Questions About Suggestions

These questions ask what advice one speaker gives to another person (usually the other speaker). These questions can be phrased in various ways:

- What is the man's/woman's suggestion?
- What suggestion is made?
- What does the man/woman advise . . . to do?

- What is the man/woman suggesting?
- What is the man's/woman's advice?

Woman: It must be a big change to go from being a marketing manager to a product designer. So, are you enjoying the job?

Man: Not as much as I thought I would. I didn't think I'd have to work so late to meet the deadlines.

Woman: Well, give it a chance — you've only been in this position for a month. It took me a year of on-the-job training to adjust to the pace around here.

Man: Oh, I intend to. I'm not a quitter. I actually enjoy challenges.

Q. What advice does the woman give?

● To stay on the job

Ⓑ To take a risk

Ⓒ To apply for another position

Ⓓ To give someone a present

> The man indicates that he doesn't like working there very much. The woman tells him to "give it a chance" — in other words, to stay on the job for now.

Questions About Opinions

These questions ask how a speaker feels about something or someone. These questions can be phrased in a number of ways:

- What is the man's/woman's opinion of . . . ?
- How does the man/woman feel about . . . ?
- What does the man/woman think about . . . ?

Sample Item: Opinion Question

Woman: It must be a big change to go from being a marketing manager to a product designer. So, are you enjoying the job?

Man: Not as much as I thought I would. I didn't think I'd have to work so late to meet the deadlines.

Woman: Well, give it a chance — you've only been in this position for a month. It took me a year of on-the-job training to adjust to the pace around here.

Man: Oh, I intend to. I'm not a quitter. I actually enjoy challenges.

Q. What does the man think about his job?

Ⓐ It isn't challenging enough for him.

● He doesn't like the long hours.

Ⓒ He wants to quit immediately.

Ⓓ It doesn't provide any options.

> The man says that he doesn't like the job very much because he has to work "late to meet the deadlines." If he is working late, this means he is working long hours.

Exercise 3.7

Focus: Answering detail questions involving suggestions and opinions.

Directions: Listen to the conversation. Read the question about the conversation and then choose the one option —
(A), (B), (C), or (D) — that best answers the question.

 Now start the audio program.

1. What is Mr. Lo's advice?

   (A) That the woman bring her child to the party

   (B) That the woman contact his wife

   (C) That his wife take care of the woman's child

   (D) That the couple stay home

2. What suggestion is made?

   (A) To cut prices

   (B) To reduce the number of workers

   (C) To get some good advice

   (D) To bring in fewer consultants

3. What did the man think of the play?

   (A) It was boring.

   (B) He liked it better than the woman did.

   (C) He did not see it.

   (D) It lasted too long.

4. How does the man feel about Arlene's job?

   (A) It provides many opportunities.

   (B) It takes up too much of her time.

   (C) It does not pay well enough.

   (D) It is interesting work.

5. What does Hans suggest?

   (A) That she go out for a meal

   (B) That she work in her room

   (C) That she have food delivered

   (D) That she go to sleep now

6. What does she think they should do?

   (A) Have the copier repaired

   (B) Buy some antique furniture

   (C) Replace the copier

   (D) Get some more copies made

7. What does the first man think of the plan?

   (A) It will never be adopted.

   (B) It may save money.

   (C) It will not impress customers.

   (D) It is a waste of time.

8. What does she suggest the man do?

   (A) Go to a nearby café

   (B) Wait for Ms. Bauer

   (C) Go to the meeting

   (D) Come back another day

9. How does Donna feel about the building?

   (A) It is not warm enough.

   (B) It has too many windows.

   (C) It is too stuffy.

   (D) It is not safe.

10. What does the woman suggest the man sell?

    (A) His business

    (B) His automobile

    (C) His exercise equipment

    (D) His health club membership

C. Inference Questions

The answers for inference questions are not directly stated in the conversations. Instead, you have to draw a conclusion — called an inference — based on the information that is presented by the speakers. In other words, you have to interpret what the speakers are implying.

Inference questions can be phrased in various ways:
- *What does the man/woman imply?*
- *What is the man/woman saying about . . . ?*
- *What can be said about . . . ?*
- *What is known about . . . ?*

- *What can be inferred from the conversation?*
- *What does the man/woman mean?*
- *What is probably true about . . . ?*

Sample Item: Inference Question

1st woman: Good Morning, National Office Supplies — Customer Service Department. Janice Nelson speaking.

2nd woman: Hello, Janice, this is Ms. Tupton. I'm calling about an order I just received. There were twenty packages of blue paper, but we ordered white paper. I believe we spoke last week about a similar situation. And this time, my manager's upset!

1st woman: I'm really sorry, Ms. Tupton — I'll take care of the problem right away. Give me the invoice number on the shipment, and I'll get an order of white paper out to you later this afternoon.

Q. What can be inferred from this conversation?

(A) The problem has already been taken care of.

(B) There is no blue paper in stock at present.

● Ms. Tupton's manager wasn't upset last time.

(D) Janice Nelson is a new employee.

> Although the information in choice (C) is not stated directly, it can be inferred. Ms. Tupton says, "And this time, my manager's upset!" "This time" implies a change from last time. Her manager was not upset last time.

Exercise 3.8

Focus: Answering inference questions.

Directions: Listen to the conversation. Read the question about the conversation and choose the one option — (A), (B), (C), or (D) — that best answers the question.

 Now start the audio program.

1. What can be inferred about their situation?

(A) They are having dinner by candlelight.

(B) The electricity is not on.

(C) They are examining something with a flashlight.

(D) It is the middle of the day.

2. What can be said about the situation?

(A) They are not at home.

(B) The sky is seldom clear here.

(C) The smell is unpleasant.

(D) They have just walked for miles.

3. What does the woman imply?

(A) She cannot go sailing tomorrow.

(B) Her decision depends on the weather.

(C) There will not be enough wind for sailing.

(D) She enjoys this kind of weather.

4. What is probably true about Natalie?

(A) She makes her own clothing at home.

(B) She does not need any new clothes.

(C) She has worked there only for a few weeks.

(D) She no longer works as a clerk.

5. What is the man implying?

(A) He just started playing the piano.

(B) He would like to take lessons from the woman.

(C) He has never taken lessons.

(D) He does not play as well as the woman.

6. What is known about the security system?

(A) It is generally on in the morning.

(B) It is an unusual system.

(C) It was broken when the man arrived.

(D) It was recently installed.

7. What can be inferred about the climate where they live now?

(A) It has four seasons.

(B) It is always warm.

(C) It is usually cool and brisk.

(D) It is nicest in the autumn.

8. What can be inferred about these two?

(A) They do not have to work today.

(B) They have to attend a meeting.

(C) They wrote the memo.

(D) They are not new employees.

D. Three-Way Conversations

One conversation in Part 3 will be among three speakers and feature two men and a woman, or two women and one man. It is important to distinguish between the two male or female speakers who will often be referred to by their names. Question types for three-way conversations are similar to other questions in this section. They may appear as overview, detail, or inference questions. Possible question types are:

• *Where most likely is the conversation taking place?*
• *What does Amy think about the news?*
• *What does the man say to Carl?*

1st woman:	I have some interesting travel packages for you to choose from today.
Man:	Oh, great! We're really looking forward to a nice vacation. What do you have?
1st woman:	I found a nice package tour to Bali where you can stay at a three-star resort hotel.
Man:	Wow! Sounds good. What do you think about going to Bali, Sandra?
2nd woman:	I've always wanted to go there, Mike. But isn't it on the expensive side?
1st woman:	Actually, it's very reasonable. Less than two-thousand dollars for both of you.
Man:	Well, then. Tell us more.

Q. Where most likely is the conversation taking place?

(A) At an airport check-in counter

(B) At a hotel front desk

(C) At an international festival

● At a travel agency

> The first woman says, "I have some interesting travel packages for you to choose from today" and continues to speak about travel. So she must be a travel agent working at a travel agency.

Q. What does Sandra ask about the travel package?

(A) The destination

● Its price

(C) The accommodations

(D) Its availability

> Sandra asks the first woman, "But isn't it on the expensive side?"

Q. What will Sandra and Mike most likely do next?

● Listen to an explanation

(B) Book a trip

(C) Pay for a tour

(D) Show their passports

> The conversation ends with Mike saying, "Well, then. Tell us more."

Exercise 3.9

Focus: Understanding and answering questions about a conversation among three speakers.

Directions: Listen to the conversation. Read the three questions about each conversation and then choose the best option — (A), (B), (C), or (D) — for each question.

1. Where is the conversation most likely taking place?

   (A) At a conference center

   (B) At a construction site

   (C) In an office building

   (D) In an office cafeteria

2. What does Nora say about construction at the downtown office?

   (A) She doesn't know much about it.

   (B) She isn't very interested in it.

   (C) She participated in its planning.

   (D) She will ask a manager about it.

3. When will the construction begin?

   (A) On March 10

   (B) On March 11

   (C) On April 12

   (D) On April 13

4. What most likely is the woman's job?

   (A) A restaurant waiter

   (B) A restaurant chef

   (C) A food critic

   (D) A restaurant cashier

5. What problem did the speakers have with their food?

   (A) It was too cold.

   (B) It was too expensive.

   (C) It was too spicy.

   (D) It was too salty.

6. What does the woman offer the men?

   (A) An apology from the chef

   (B) A replacement dinner

   (C) Free beverages

   (D) A meal discount

7. What most likely is Candace Brown's job?

   (A) Website creator

   (B) Employment director

   (C) Marketing manager

   (D) Personnel clerk

8. What does Maria say about Candace?

   (A) She is a new employee.

   (B) She will take a vacation.

   (C) She is retiring soon.

   (D) She does good work.

9. What will the speakers probably do next?

   (A) Go to lunch

   (B) Discuss the website

   (C) Have some coffee

   (D) Conduct an interview

10. What will Luke and Sandra do in the near future?

    (A) Work for a new company

    (B) Start their own business

    (C) Move to a new location

    (D) Have another child

11. What does Sandra prefer in a rental property?

    (A) A single bedroom

    (B) A large garage

    (C) Outdoor space

    (D) A convenient kitchen

12. What will the speakers most likely do next?

    (A) Negotiate rental prices

    (B) Discuss rental properties

    (C) Review a rental contract

    (D) Go to view a rental property

E. Intention Questions

The answers for intention questions are not directly stated in the conversations. Instead, you have to draw a conclusion about the intention or meaning of a phrase based on the information that is presented by the speakers. In other words, you have to interpret what the speakers are implying.

Intention questions can be phrased in the following ways:
- *Why does the speaker say, ". . ."?*
- *What does the speaker mean when she says, ". . ."?*
- *What does the man mean when he says, ". . ."?*
- *What does the woman imply when she says, ". . ."?*

Sample Item: Intention Question

Woman: We need to choose a dessert for Betsy Chandler's retirement party. Do you have any ideas about what people like?

Man: You're the expert. I'll leave that decision completely up to you.

Woman: All right. Give me a few minutes to come up with a good idea.

Q. What does the man mean when he says, "You're the expert"?

(A) He congratulates the woman on her retirement.

(B) He thinks the woman is an excellent cook.

(C) He hopes the woman will lead a discussion.

● He believes the woman should make the decision.

> After stating, "You're the expert" the man says, "I'll leave that decision completely up to you." The woman follows up with, "All right. Give me a few minutes to come up with a good idea."

Exercise 3.10

Focus: Understanding and answering questions about intention and meaning.

Directions: Listen to the conversation. Read the question about the conversation and then choose the one option — (A), (B), (C), or (D) — that best answers the question.

 Now start the audio program.

1. What does the woman imply when she says, "Well, you're in luck today"?

   (A) The man can change a reservation.

   (B) The man has been hired.

   (C) The man has won a prize.

   (D) The man may make a purchase.

2. What does the man mean when he says, "I sure have"?

   (A) He agrees with the woman.

   (B) He has completed a job.

   (C) He will attend an event.

   (D) He will go home soon.

3. What does the man mean when he says, "I'm exhausted"?

(A) He has exercised a lot.

(B) He has worked hard.

(C) He has travelled far.

(D) He has given a speech.

4. Why does the man say, "Well, the survey data tells a different story"?

(A) To disagree with a statement

(B) To recommend an employee

(C) To offer a substitute

(D) To suggest a solution

5. What does the woman mean when she says, "Clients are waiting"?

(A) She wants the man to join her meeting.

(B) She will wait for people to arrive.

(C) She doesn't have much time to talk.

(D) She will ask her customers to wait.

6. What does the man mean when he says, "I'm not sure about that"?

(A) He may go on a business trip.

(B) He hasn't heard about a plan.

(C) He disagrees with the woman.

(D) He might not meet a deadline.

7. Why does the woman say, "Is that all right"?

(A) To inquire about a payment

(B) To ask for permission

(C) To change an order

(D) To show concern

8. What does the woman mean when she says, "I'll just try again later"?

(A) She will send an email.

(B) She will visit an office.

(C) She will make a phone call.

(D) She will apply for work.

9. What does the man mean when he says, "They couldn't have been any better"?

(A) Records were discovered.

(B) New products were introduced.

(C) Sales were outstanding.

(D) Profits have been stable.

10. Why does the man say, "Oh, of course"?

(A) He remembers an obligation.

(B) He gives permission.

(C) He suggests a plan.

(D) He requests payment.

11. What does the woman mean when she says, "I have the same problem as you"?

(A) She is late for work.

(B) She wants to speak to her boss.

(C) She would like some coffee.

(D) She is in a hurry.

12. What does the man mean when he says, "People are struggling to get in"?

(A) The restaurant is very popular.

(B) The restaurant's entrance is narrow.

(C) The restaurant is expensive.

(D) The restaurant's parking lot is small.

F. Graphic-Based Questions

The answers for graphic-based questions are not directly stated in the conversations. Instead, you have to draw a conclusion based on the information that is presented by the speakers *and* what is shown in the graphic.

Graphic-based questions always have the same preface ("Look at the graphic."). The second part of the question can be phrased in a variety of ways:

- *Look at the graphic. What time will the concert be held?*
- *Look at the graphic. Where is the post office?*
- *Look at the graphic. Which number should Ms. Colbert call?*
- *Look at the graphic. Who should Mr. Roberts contact?*

Sample Item: Graphic-Based Question

Woman:	Hello, sir. May I take your order now or would you like more time to think about it?
Man:	I'm ready to order now. I'd like the Herb Chicken and an iced tea.
Woman:	Oh, I'm sorry. We're all out of that already. It was very popular tonight.
Man:	Alright. Then how about the Bison Burger?
Woman:	I'm sorry again. The only dish still available is at the bottom of the Special Menu.
Man:	I see. Well, I'll have that one, then.

Today's Special Menu	
Sautéed Salmon	$18.64
Bison Burger	$20.46
Herb Chicken	$16.77
Pasta Primavera	$12.95

Q. Look at the graphic. What will the man most likely have to eat?

Ⓐ Sautéed Salmon

Ⓑ Bison Burger

Ⓒ Herb Chicken

● Pasta Primavera

> The man orders the Herb Chicken, but the woman says, "We're all out of that already." Then the man asks for the Bison Burger and the woman says, "The only dish still available is at the bottom of the Special Menu."

Exercise 3.11

Focus: Understanding and answering graphic-based questions.

Directions: Listen to the conversation. Read the question about the conversation, look at the graphic, and then choose the one option — (A), (B), (C), or (D) — that best answers the question.

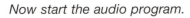 *Now start the audio program.*

Name	Comment
Paul Flowers	Clerk was impolite
Gail Sanders	Floor was dirty
Leo Watson	Music was loud
Pauline Mann	Store was crowded

1. Look at the graphic. Who will the woman most likely contact?

(A) Paul Flowers

(B) Gail Sanders

(C) Leo Watson

(D) Pauline Mann

Watt's Home Center
15% Discount Coupon

Good on purchases throughout the store.

Expires: September 10

Minimum purchase: $50

---

2. Look at the graphic. Why can't the man use the coupon?

(A) It is good only for particular items.

(B) It has already expired.

(C) It requires a minimum purchase.

(D) It can only be used with a credit card.

Building Directory

Floor	Section
5th	Management
4th	Accounting
3rd	Advertising
2nd	Sales
1st	Reception

3. Look at the graphic. In which section does Ms. Tracy Burton most likely work?

(A) Management

(B) Accounting

(C) Advertising

(D) Sales

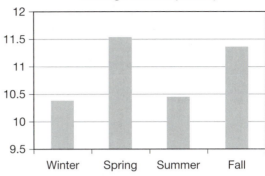

Average Rainfall (inches)

4. Look at the graphic. When does the man suggest holding the event?

(A) In the winter

(B) In the spring

(C) In the summer

(D) In the fall

Warning

Do not place near flame or heat. Doing so will damage this product. Do not store above 50° Centigrade.

For more information, call 555-1649

---

5. Look at the graphic. What most likely happened to the blender?

(A) It was exposed to fire.

(B) It was stored outdoors.

(C) It was kept near heat.

(D) It was overused.

Office Directory

Room	Employee
201	Brad Ferguson
202	Sheri Rice
203	Monica Sanchez
204	Lauren Lee

6. Look at the graphic. Where is the woman calling from now?

(A) Room 201

(B) Room 202

(C) Room 203

(D) Room 204

Directions: Listen to the conversations. Read the three questions about each conversation and then choose the best option — (A), (B), (C), or (D) — for each question.

 Now start the audio program.

1. Where are the people most likely speaking?

    (A) In a business's Accounting Department

    (B) In a company's Personnel Section

    (C) At the main office of a corporation

    (D) At an employment agency

2. What does Julia say about Naomi?

    (A) She is new to the area.

    (B) She is new to the company.

    (C) She has won a prize.

    (D) She had been a manager.

3. What will the speakers most likely do together?

    (A) Go to a business meeting

    (B) Meet a client

    (C) Attend a conference

    (D) Have lunch

4. Who is the first speaker?

    (A) An airline attendant

    (B) A travel agent

    (C) A tour guide

    (D) Ms. Simmon's boss

5. Why is Ms. Simmons going to Bangkok?

    (A) To attend a conference

    (B) To go sightseeing

    (C) To work on an engineering project

    (D) To promote a new product

6. What is famous?

    (A) The tour

    (B) The hotel

    (C) The conference

    (D) The temple

7. Who is the man?

    (A) An elevator repair person

    (B) A salesman

    (C) A reporter

    (D) A safety inspector

8. When will the man go to the downtown office building?

    (A) Later today

    (B) Tomorrow

    (C) The day after tomorrow

    (D) In three days

9. How does the woman feel about what the man says?

    (A) She is anxious.

    (B) She is glad.

    (C) She is surprised.

    (D) She is angry.

10. Where are they?

(A) At a police station

(B) In a bank

(C) At a driver's license bureau

(D) In a supermarket

11. What is Mr. Lee doing?

(A) Paying some bills

(B) Exchanging some merchandise

(C) Getting a new passport

(D) Changing money

12. What can be inferred about Mr. Lee?

(A) He doesn't have any identification with him.

(B) He will have to pay an extra service charge.

(C) He makes this transaction frequently.

(D) He didn't realize the transaction was free.

13. What does Dennis think about the restaurant?

(A) The music is too loud.

(B) The service is very slow.

(C) People are talking too loudly.

(D) It's too expensive.

14. Why does the woman NOT want to leave?

(A) The waiter was very attentive.

(B) It is her favorite place.

(C) They have already ordered.

(D) She likes the music.

15. What will the woman do next?

(A) Leave the restaurant

(B) Ask the man to sit down

(C) Cancel the order for dinner

(D) Talk to the waiter

16. Who is Marcus Kolb?

(A) A real estate investor

(B) An architect

(C) A resident of Market Street

(D) An office worker

17. What can be implied about the tower?

(A) It was built a long time ago.

(B) It is smaller than the neighboring buildings.

(C) It is like all the other buildings on Market Street.

(D) It is quite modern.

18. What is the woman's opinion of the tower?

(A) She is unimpressed with it.

(B) She is unsure about it.

(C) She feels that it suits the neighborhood.

(D) She thinks it is a wonderful building.

19. What does the woman say about the bid?

(A) It was accepted.

(B) It did not arrive on time.

(C) It was misplaced.

(D) It was not clearly written.

20. How did the man send the bid?

(A) By email

(B) By messenger service

(C) By express mail

(D) By fax

21. What does the man mean when he says, "Are you sure"?

(A) He is surprised about a price.

(B) He is worried about a mistake.

(C) He is unsure about a statement.

(D) He is not sure about an arrival.

22. What are they discussing?

   Ⓐ Their future plans

   Ⓑ New jobs

   Ⓒ Places to live

   Ⓓ Their families

23. Where are they?

   Ⓐ In Nancy's apartment

   Ⓑ In a car

   Ⓒ At the office

   Ⓓ On a bus

24. What can be inferred about the speakers?

   Ⓐ They live in the same building.

   Ⓑ They are sisters.

   Ⓒ They both want to move.

   Ⓓ They don't work together.

25. Who is the second speaker?

   Ⓐ A repair person

   Ⓑ A painter

   Ⓒ A sales representative

   Ⓓ A programmer

26. What are they discussing?

   Ⓐ An elevator

   Ⓑ A heater

   Ⓒ An air conditioner

   Ⓓ A computer

27. Why does the second man say, "Well, don't count on that"?

   Ⓐ He expects to leave the location early.

   Ⓑ He doubts that he will finish by tomorrow.

   Ⓒ He wants the customer to stop a machine.

   Ⓓ He cannot give the customer an estimate.

28. Which of the following decreased?

   Ⓐ Market share

   Ⓑ Labor costs

   Ⓒ Profits

   Ⓓ Taxes

29. What will most likely happen next quarter?

   Ⓐ The cost of labor will be lower.

   Ⓑ The financial market will decline.

   Ⓒ They will buy shares in a new company.

   Ⓓ Taxes will decrease rapidly.

30. How does the man feel about their company's future performance?

   Ⓐ He is disinterested.

   Ⓑ He is uncertain.

   Ⓒ He is depressed.

   Ⓓ He is optimistic.

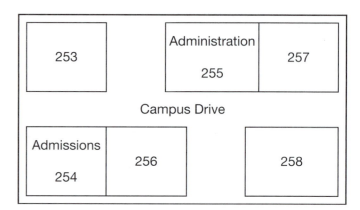

31. Look at the graphic. In which building is the English Department located?

   Ⓐ 253

   Ⓑ 256

   Ⓒ 257

   Ⓓ 258

32. What problem do the speakers have?

   Ⓐ They have parked in the wrong space.

   Ⓑ They forgot to submit papers.

   Ⓒ They are late for an event.

   Ⓓ They have lost their tickets.

33. What will the speakers most likely attend?

(A) A job interview

(B) An admissions lecture

(C) A musical performance

(D) A writing seminar

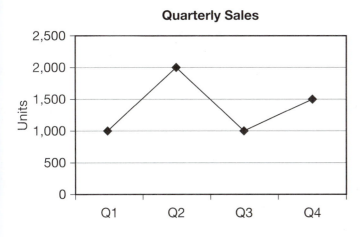

Quarterly Sales

34. When does the man want to hold a meeting?

(A) Tuesday morning

(B) Tuesday afternoon

(C) Thursday morning

(D) Thursday afternoon

35. Look at the graphic. Which quarter would the man like to focus on during the meeting?

(A) The first

(B) The second

(C) The third

(D) The fourth

36. What does the man ask the woman to do?

(A) Order coffee

(B) Contact customers

(C) Prepare photocopies

(D) Analyze a graph

Order Form	
Item	**Quantity**
Staples	25 boxes
Photocopy paper	12 boxes
Binders	8
Large folders	22

37. What problem does the woman have?

(A) A product was mislabeled.

(B) An item was misspelled.

(C) A schedule was mistaken.

(D) Documents weren't completed.

38. Look at the graphic. Which department most likely filled out the order form?

(A) Accounting

(B) Marketing

(C) Sales

(D) Personnel

39. What will the man do next?

(A) Contact colleagues

(B) Order some supplies

(C) Speak with his boss

(D) Make an appointment

Lesson 4 Short Talks

Format — Part 4

In Part 4, you will hear ten talks on the audio program. There are three questions for each talk. The questions are written in your test booklet. There are four answer choices following each question. You have to choose the best answer to the question based on the information that you hear in the talk. Before each of the talks, there is an introductory statement.

Examples of introductory statements:
Questions 80 through 82 are based on the following announcement:
Questions 95 through 97 refer to the following lecture:

Following each talk, you'll hear the questions without the answer choices, with eight-second pauses between each question. (You do not have to wait to hear the questions to answer them.)

Because this part of the test consists of both spoken material on the audio program and written questions and answer choices, it tests both listening and reading skills.

1. **The talks:** The talks are all monologs — that is, they are delivered by one speaker. They are fairly short — most are one to two minutes long.

2. **The questions:** Four main types of questions are asked about the talks: **overview questions, detail questions, inference questions,** and **intention questions.**
   - **Overview questions** require a general understanding of the lecture or of the situation in which it is given. Overview questions ask about the main idea or purpose of the lecture, or about the speaker, the audience, or the location where the talk is given. Some typical overview questions:
   Who is speaking?
   What is the purpose of the talk?
   What kind of people would probably be interested in this talk?
   What is happening in this talk?
   Where is this announcement being made?

- **Detail questions** relate to specific points in the talk. They begin with question words: *who, what, where, why, when, how, how much,* and so on. Some are **negative** questions; they ask what was *not* mentioned in the talk: *Which of the following is NOT true about . . . ?*

- **Inference questions** require you to make a conclusion based on the information provided in the talk. These questions often contain the word *probably* or forms of the verbs *imply* or *infer*:
  What is probably true about . . . ?
  What does the speaker imply about . . . ?
  What can be inferred from this talk?

- **Intention questions** require you to make a conclusion about the intention or meaning of a speaker's phrase based on information provided in the talk. Some typical intention question forms are:
  Why does the speaker say, ". . ."?
  What does the man mean when he says, ". . ."?
  What does the woman imply when she says, ". . ."?

3. **The answer choices:** All the answer choices are plausible answers to the questions. In many cases, the distractors are mentioned in the talk. Just because you hear an answer choice mentioned in the talk does not mean it is the correct answer for a particular question.

Tactics   Part 4

1. Listen carefully to the introductory announcement that is given before each talk. It will tell you what kind of talk you are going to hear (an announcement or a commercial, for example) as well as which questions to look at during that talk.

2. While listening to each talk, keep your eyes on the corresponding set of three questions and answer choices. Do not look away or close your eyes in order to concentrate on the spoken material. You must focus on both the talk and the written questions.

3. Because the questions are written out, you can use them to focus your listening for particular information.

4. Do not mark your answer sheet while the talk is going on, even if you know the answer. The act of answering a question may cause you to miss the information you need to answer the question or questions that follow.

5. Do *not* wait for the speaker on the audio program to read the questions. Begin answering as soon as the talk is over, and answer all three questions as soon as you can. If you have a few seconds left before the next talk begins, preview the next three questions in your test booklet.

6. Never continue working on the questions about one talk after another talk has begun.

7. If you are not sure of an answer, eliminate unlikely choices and then guess.

8. Always answer each question. Never leave any blanks.

Start the audio program and read along as the directions are read.

Directions: During this part of the exam, there are a number of brief talks. These talks are not written out and are spoken only once, so you must listen carefully.

There are three questions about each of the talks. Following the questions are four possible answers — (A), (B), (C), and (D). You must decide which of these best answers the question and then mark the correct answer.

1. What does the speaker mean when he says, "Your cooperation is appreciated"?
   - (A) He wants people to consider taking public transportation.
   - (B) He wants people to stay away from temporary construction areas.
   - (C) He would like drivers to pay attention to airport rules.
   - (D) He would like drivers to avoid the short-term parking structure.

2. Which of these is NOT permitted?
   - (A) Leaving a vehicle unattended
   - (B) Unloading suitcases
   - (C) Letting passengers out of a vehicle
   - (D) Stopping for a short period

3. Where is long-term airport parking available?
   - (A) In front of the terminal
   - (B) In the airport parking structure
   - (C) At a parking lot downtown
   - (D) At the Jones Road facility

4. What kind of weather is predicted for the weekend?
   - (A) Rapidly changing
   - (B) Cloudy and cooler
   - (C) Rainy or snowy
   - (D) Warm and sunny

5. During what season is this forecast probably being given?
   - (A) Spring
   - (B) Summer
   - (C) Autumn
   - (D) Winter

6. What does the speaker suggest people do on Wednesday?
   - (A) Listen to the weather forecast
   - (B) Dress warmly because it will be cold
   - (C) Carry umbrellas in case of rain
   - (D) Go out to the countryside

7. Where is the announcement probably being given?
   - (A) At a pharmacy
   - (B) At a sporting event
   - (C) At a department store
   - (D) At a gas station

8. What has been found?
   - (A) A black briefcase
   - (B) A piece of paper
   - (C) A pair of glasses
   - (D) Some medicine

9. Look at the graphic. Where does the speaker imply that the lost item can be found?

STORE LAYOUT

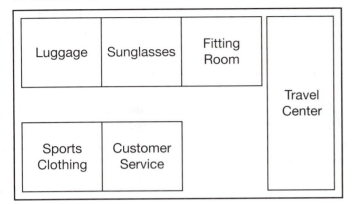

(A) Next to the Luggage section

(B) Next to the Travel Center

(C) Across from the Sports Clothing section

(D) Across from the Sunglasses section

---

10. Who is Elizabeth Bryce?

(A) An employee in the shipping department

(B) A supervisor in the shipping department

(C) The winner of the employee of the year award

(D) An assistant to the CEO

11. Which of the following is NOT true about Elizabeth Bryce?

(A) Her suggestion may save the company money.

(B) She can park next to the CEO this month.

(C) She will get a promotion.

(D) Her evaluations were very good.

12. What does the employee of the year receive?

(A) A small bonus

(B) The CEO's parking place

(C) Thousands of dollars a year

(D) A new car

13. Who would be most interested in what is being offered in this advertisement?

(A) Business travelers

(B) University students

(C) Language teachers

(D) International tourists

14. Which of these courses is NOT presently available?

(A) Japanese

(B) Spanish

(C) English

(D) Russian

15. How many DVDs are enclosed in each kit?

(A) One

(B) Two

(C) Four

(D) Eight

Testing Points and Skill-Building Exercises

The talks that you will hear on the audio program during Part 4 concern many different topics and are given in a variety of situations. However, most of the talks can be classified into one of the categories presented in this section. In each part of this section, a different type of talk and the questions about it are briefly analyzed. Then there are exercises involving four or five talks of that type.

A. Public Announcements

These talks are brief informational messages like those given to groups of people in public places. Among the most common are announcements made on board airplanes or in airports. Others are given at stores, at sporting events, and in other similar situations.

Sample Items: Public Announcement

Woman: Attention, shoppers: someone has just turned in a pair of prescription sunglasses in a black leather case. They were found on the floor of the sporting goods department. If these glasses are yours, please come to the customer service counter to claim them. We would like to remind shoppers to check that their personal belongings are secure at all times.

Q. Where is the talk probably being given?

- (A) At a pharmacy
- (B) At a sporting event
- ● At a department store
- (D) At a gas station

> This is an overview question about the location where the talk is given. A number of key words and phrases provide clues to the location: *shoppers*, *sporting goods department*, and *customer service counter*. These words and phrases point to the conclusion that the talk is given in a department store.

Q. What has been found?

- (A) A black briefcase
- (B) A piece of paper
- ● A pair of glasses
- (D) Some medicine

> The speaker says that the lost item is a pair of prescription sunglasses in a black leather case.

Q. What is it that shoppers should do?

- ● Watch their possessions
- (B) Check out the sale on the first floor
- (C) Get ready for closing time
- (D) Make use of customer service

> The speaker reminds shoppers to check that their personal belongings are secure at all times.

Exercise 4.1

Focus: Understanding and answering questions about public announcements.

Directions: Listen to the talks, and then answer each of the three questions about them by marking the correct choice — (A), (B), (C), or (D).

 Now start the audio program.

1. Where is this announcement being made?
   - (A) On an aircraft
   - (B) In a store in Glasgow
   - (C) At an airport
   - (D) On a shuttle bus

2. Why is Mr. Kim being paged?
   - (A) There's a message for him.
   - (B) His flight has been delayed.
   - (C) Someone has found his ticket.
   - (D) There is an emergency.

3. Where are the white telephones located?
   - (A) On board the aircraft
   - (B) At the ticket counter
   - (C) All over the airport
   - (D) At an information booth

4. Who is the audience for this talk?
   - (A) People at a cafeteria
   - (B) Shoppers at a grocery store
   - (C) Guests at a party
   - (D) People who want to go fishing

5. What is being offered at a special price?
   - (A) Meat
   - (B) Bread
   - (C) Charcoal
   - (D) Fish

6. How long is the special price being offered?
   - (A) One day
   - (B) Two days
   - (C) One week
   - (D) One month

7. Where is this announcement being made?
   - (A) On an airplane
   - (B) At a shopping center
   - (C) Aboard a ship
   - (D) In a seaside restaurant

8. Who is Nicholas?
   - (A) A lost child
   - (B) A waiter
   - (C) Someone's father
   - (D) The purser

9. What problem is mentioned?
   - (A) High waves
   - (B) Strong winds
   - (C) Long delays
   - (D) High prices

10. What will people see on the tour?
    - (A) A skyscraper
    - (B) A national monument
    - (C) A cavern
    - (D) A factory

11. How long does the tour last?

    (A) Fifteen minutes

    (B) Two hours

    (C) Four hours

    (D) All day

12. At what age must someone purchase a full-price ticket?

    (A) Four

    (B) Six

    (C) Twelve

    (D) Thirteen

13. What is the destination of this flight?

    (A) Los Angeles

    (B) The Grand Canyon

    (C) Flagstaff

    (D) Denver

14. When will this plane be landing?

    (A) In a few minutes

    (B) In around twenty minutes

    (C) In about two hours

    (D) In around nine hours

15. What will probably be served on this flight?

    (A) Breakfast

    (B) Lunch

    (C) Dinner

    (D) Late-night snack

B. News, Weather, and Public Service Bulletins

These talks are similar to ones you might hear on radio and television, especially on news programs. Questions usually ask what is being reported and about details given in the talk.

Sample Items: News, Weather, and Public Service Bulletins

Woman: It looks as though our warm, sunny, summer-like weather will continue at least through Saturday and Sunday, so this weekend will be the perfect time to go out to the countryside to view the colorful fall foliage. On Monday, though, it appears we're in for a change. It should be a little cooler with cloudy conditions, and there's a chance of rain. The long-range forecast shows a few snow flurries coming our way by Wednesday of next week. And you can expect to see the temperatures drop to around 22 degrees Fahrenheit that day — that's minus 5 degrees Celsius, folks, so you'd better get out those winter coats.

Q. What kind of weather is predicted for the weekend?

(A) Rapidly changing

(B) Cloudy and cooler

(C) Rainy or snowy

● Warm and sunny

> The speaker says that the weather will be warm and sunny through the weekend. Choice (B) refers to the prediction the speaker makes for Monday.

Q. During what season is this forecast probably being given?

(A) Spring

(B) Summer

● Autumn

(D) Winter

> The speaker says that the weather will be "summer-like." This indicates that the weather will be warm, as it is in the summer. The speaker also forecasts cool and cloudy conditions for Monday. However, it is clear from the mention of "colorful fall foliage" (leaves) that it is autumn.

Q. What does the speaker suggest people do on Wednesday?

(A) Listen to the weather forecast

● Dress warmly because it will be cold

(C) Carry umbrellas in case of rain

(D) Go out to the countryside

> The speaker says snow is predicted for next Wednesday, so the temperature will be getting much colder. Therefore, the speaker suggests that people dress in their winter coats to stay warm.

Exercise 4.2

Focus: Understanding and answering questions about news, weather, and public service bulletins.

Directions: Listen to the talks, and then answer each of the three questions about them by marking the correct choice — (A), (B), (C), or (D).

Now start the audio program.

1. What caused the delay in the launch?

   (A) Bad weather

   (B) The failure of the rocket engines

   (C) Scheduling problems

   (D) Computer problems

2. How do new-generation space shuttles differ from older shuttles?

   (A) They have more powerful engines.

   (B) They can stay in space longer.

   (C) They are not affected as much by the weather.

   (D) They have far more sophisticated computers.

3. When will the shuttle *Pathfinder* probably be launched?

   (A) This afternoon

   (B) Tonight

   (C) Tomorrow

   (D) The day after tomorrow

4. What is the purpose of this bulletin?

   (A) To warn residents of a damaging storm

   (B) To indicate that there is no danger

   (C) To report on the destruction

   (D) To ask for listeners' help

5. Where is the hurricane now moving?

   (A) Towards the open ocean

   (B) To the southeast

   (C) Towards the Eastern Seaboard

   (D) Over Bermuda

6. How fast were the winds predicted to be?

   (A) 80 miles per hour

   (B) 100 miles per hour

   (C) 120 miles per hour

   (D) 200 miles per hour

7. What is the purpose of this talk?

   (A) To sell more balloons

   (B) To invite parents to a special event

   (C) To discuss a potential danger

   (D) To introduce a new type of balloon

8. Which of these may present a danger to children?

   (A) An inflated balloon

   (B) The gas inside a balloon

   (C) The sound of a popping balloon

   (D) A piece of popped balloon

9. Which of the following would the speaker NOT approve of for safety reasons?

   (A) Allowing young children to blow up balloons

   (B) Using balloons at an adult's birthday party

   (C) Tying strings to balloons

   (D) Popping balloons with a pin

10. Where is the speaker?

    (A) In a radio station

    (B) In a helicopter

    (C) On the side of the road

    (D) In a truck

11. How did the truck cause a delay?

    (A) It dropped its cargo.

    (B) It collided with a car.

    (C) It broke down.

    (D) It ran out of fuel.

12. Which of the following does the speaker recommend for northbound drivers?

    (A) Interstate 74

    (B) The Valley Expressway

    (C) Lake Avenue

    (D) Route 8

C. Commercial Messages

These talks resemble the advertisements that you hear on radio or television. They attempt to sell listeners goods or services. Questions about commercial messages often ask what product is being advertised, what kind of people would be interested in the product, and, sometimes, how much the product costs.

Sample Items: Commercial Message

Man: Are you frustrated because you need to know a language for business reasons but you're just too busy to take classes? Then order a language kit from Translingua. Watch our DVDs and work from our CD-ROM in the comfort of your home. Learn in a natural way by listening to native speakers in business situations and then responding to them in your own words. Courses now available in English, Spanish, and Japanese. Courses in French and Russian will be available in the next few months. Each kit contains four workbooks, two DVDs, and one CD-ROM. Call Translingua today.

Q. Who would be most interested in what is being offered in this talk?

- ● Business travelers
- Ⓑ University students
- Ⓒ Language teachers
- Ⓓ International tourists

> The advertisement begins by discussing the problem businesspeople face in learning another language. It also mentions that the course involves "native speakers in business situations." This course would probably be of most interest to business travelers.

Q. Which of these courses is NOT presently available?

- Ⓐ Japanese
- Ⓑ Spanish
- Ⓒ English
- ● Russian

> According to the speaker, courses in English, Spanish, and Japanese are currently available. The course in Russian will not be available for a few months.

Q. How many DVDs are enclosed in each kit?

- Ⓐ One
- ● Two
- Ⓒ Four
- Ⓓ Eight

> According to the talk, there are two DVDs in each language kit.

Exercise 4.3

Focus: Understanding and answering questions about commercial messages.

Directions: Listen to the talks, and then answer each of the three questions about them by marking the correct choice — (A), (B), (C), or (D).

Now start the audio program.

1. Which of the following is NOT available at the time this talk is being given?

   (A) Water sports
   (B) Golf
   (C) Skiing
   (D) Fishing

2. Which of the following people would be most interested in the festival held in June?

   (A) People who enjoy jazz
   (B) Artists and craftspeople
   (C) Classical music fans
   (D) Beginning skiers

3. How do summer hotel rates compare to winter rates?

   (A) They are twice as high.
   (B) They are slightly higher.
   (C) They are the same.
   (D) They are half as high.

4. Which of these products is especially for international use?

   (A) The radio
   (B) The clock
   (C) The iron
   (D) The briefcase

5. What claim is NOT made of these products?

   (A) They are attractive.
   (B) They are very durable.
   (C) They are lightweight.
   (D) They are inexpensive.

6. Where would you NOT be able to purchase these products?

   (A) Europe
   (B) North America
   (C) Asia
   (D) South America

7. What advantage does this magazine have over other business magazines?

   (A) It is more interesting and readable.
   (B) It is available in more locations.
   (C) It offers more up-to-date news.
   (D) It covers more international business.

8. How often is this business magazine published?

   (A) Once a month
   (B) Once a week
   (C) Five times a week
   (D) Seven times a week

9. How much does the guide mentioned in the talk cost?

   (A) It's free if the order is for two or more subscriptions.
   (B) It's free if the subscription is ordered today.
   (C) It's three dollars per copy if you subscribe today.
   (D) It's thirty dollars for each additional copy.

10. What is being offered?

    (A) Message delivery
    (B) Package design
    (C) Coffee products
    (D) Baked goods

11. What claim does the speaker make about the products?

    (A) They can be made to suit special occasions.
    (B) They are sold at discount prices.
    (C) They are available twenty-four hours a day.
    (D) They can be found all over the world.

12. Which of the following is NOT mentioned as an occasion to use these products?

    (A) Retirements
    (B) Weddings
    (C) Birthdays
    (D) Meetings

D. *Business Talks*

These talks are similar to introductions or remarks made at business meetings, or to announcements made in work settings. Questions about these talks often focus on the location, the speaker, or the audience, as well as on details brought up in the talks.

Sample Items: Business Talk

Woman: And now, ladies and gentlemen, I'd like to present the award for employee of the month to Elizabeth Bryce from the shipping department. She not only received top evaluations from her supervisor, she also submitted a suggestion that could save the company thousands of dollars a year in shipping costs. Besides a small bonus in next week's paycheck, Ms. Bryce gets a reserved parking place for a month — the one right next to the CEO's spot. She also becomes eligible for the employee of the year award, and as you know, the employee of the year wins a new car.

Q. Who is Elizabeth Bryce?

- ● An employee in the shipping department
- (B) A supervisor in the shipping department
- (C) The winner of the employee of the year award
- (D) An assistant to the CEO

> The speaker is presenting the employee of the month award, and she mentions that Elizabeth Bryce works in the shipping department of this firm.

Q. Which of the following is NOT true about Elizabeth Bryce?

- (A) Her suggestion may save the company money.
- (B) She can park next to the CEO this month.
- ● She will get a promotion.
- (D) Her evaluations were very good.

> Only choice (C) is not mentioned.

Q. What does the employee of the year receive?

- (A) A small bonus
- (B) The CEO's parking place
- (C) Thousands of dollars a year
- ● A new car

> According to the speaker, the employee of the year is awarded a new car.

Exercise 4.4

Focus: Understanding and answering questions about business talks.

Directions: Listen to the talks, and then answer each of the three questions about them by marking the correct choice — (A), (B), (C), or (D).

 Now start the audio program.

1. When is this talk being given?
   - (A) During a party
   - (B) Before a sales presentation
   - (C) After a celebration
   - (D) At a meeting

2. What had the speaker probably told the audience last month?
   - (A) That the sales figures had increased
   - (B) That a celebration was being planned
   - (C) That they should try to increase sales
   - (D) That they must prepare an agenda

3. Whose sales figures increased the most in the previous month?
   - (A) Jane's
   - (B) Rob's
   - (C) Nina's
   - (D) Tom's

4. What is the woman's purpose in giving the talk?
   - (A) To request some information about satellites
   - (B) To introduce her firm's products
   - (C) To thank her colleagues for doing a good job
   - (D) To suggest a merger between the two firms

5. Why is the speaker NOT passing out information booklets now?
   - (A) She wants the audience to give their full attention to the presentation.
   - (B) She needs to give herself time to review the materials.
   - (C) She wants the people in the audience to take notes before they see the booklets.
   - (D) She has discovered some inaccurate information in the booklets.

6. What will the woman do next?
   - (A) Give a multimedia presentation
   - (B) Examine a new product
   - (C) Take a short break
   - (D) Answer some questions

7. Where are the shots being given?
   - (A) In the nurse's office
   - (B) In the lunchroom
   - (C) At the health department
   - (D) At a clinic

8. How much will the shots cost?
   - (A) Nothing
   - (B) Ten dollars
   - (C) Twenty-five dollars
   - (D) Forty dollars or more

9. Why is the company offering these shots?
   - (A) The health department requires it.
   - (B) The workers have demanded it.
   - (C) The firm doesn't want workers to miss work.
   - (D) The flu has been especially severe this year.

10. What is the speaker's purpose?
    - (A) To propose changes in a schedule
    - (B) To welcome some visitors
    - (C) To discuss some technical matters
    - (D) To introduce new members of the board

11. What is the occasion of this talk?
    - (A) A meeting of the executive board
    - (B) A conference in Singapore
    - (C) A tour of the facilities
    - (D) An informal social gathering

12. What will they be doing two days from now?
    - (A) Sightseeing in the city
    - (B) Riding on a the famous sky train
    - (C) Taking a charter bus tour
    - (D) Sailing in the harbor

E. Recorded Messages

These talks are similar to the recorded messages you might hear on the telephone and in other situations. Questions about these talks usually concern the situation in which the talk is given, the audience, and details given in the recording.

Sample Items: Recorded Message

Man: Your attention, please. Stopping momentarily in front of the airport terminal buildings is permitted only for the unloading of passengers and baggage. This applies to all passenger vehicles and taxis. Airport buses are required to use the special loading zone on Level D. Short-term parking is available at the airport parking structure, and long-term parking is available at the facility on Jones Road. Do not leave your vehicle unattended for any reason. Unattended vehicles will be ticketed and towed to the police lot downtown. Your cooperation is appreciated.

Q. What type of vehicle must use the Level D loading zone?

(A) Motorcycles

● Airport buses

(C) Taxi cabs

(D) Airport shuttles

> The speaker says that airport buses are required to use "the special loading zone on Level D."

Q. Which of these is NOT permitted?

● Leaving a vehicle unattended

(B) Unloading suitcases

(C) Letting passengers out of a vehicle

(D) Stopping for a short period

> The speaker says, "Do not leave your vehicle unattended for any reason." The other activities are allowed.

Q. Where is long-term airport parking available?

(A) In front of the terminal

(B) In the airport parking structure

(C) At a parking lot downtown

● At the Jones Road facility

> The speaker says that the long-term parking facility is on Jones Road.

Focus: Understanding and answering questions about recorded messages.
Directions: Listen to the talks, and then answer each of the three questions about them by marking the correct choice — (A), (B), (C), or (D).

 Now start the audio program.

1. Why is the caller unable to speak to anyone?
   (A) It is after business hours.
   (B) The representatives are talking to other people.
   (C) The airline's phone system is out of order.
   (D) The airline has gone out of business.

2. Which of the following is NOT an available online service?
   (A) Information on international arrival times
   (B) Confirmation of existing reservations
   (C) Information on domestic departure times
   (D) Change of reservations

3. What is the caller told to do?
   (A) Stay on the phone
   (B) Use another number
   (C) Call back later
   (D) Answer a question

4. Who is listening to this announcement?
   (A) Passengers on an airplane
   (B) Visitors to an amusement park
   (C) Passengers on a train
   (D) Tourists entering a national park

5. What are listeners told to do in an emergency?
   (A) Wait for assistance
   (B) Pull up the safety bar
   (C) Get away quickly
   (D) Call the park personnel

6. Why is this announcement being given?
   (A) To request assistance
   (B) To warn of an emergency
   (C) To explain a delay
   (D) To provide safety information

7. Which of the following does Woodland Gear probably NOT sell?
   (A) Hiking boots
   (B) Tents and sleeping bags
   (C) Vacation tours
   (D) Outdoor clothing

8. What should a caller press if he or she did not receive goods ordered last month?
   (A) ★ 1
   (B) ★ 2
   (C) ★ 3
   (D) ★ 4

9. When can customers place phone orders with this company on Sundays?
   (A) Any time of the day
   (B) From 7:00 a.m. to 6:00 p.m.
   (C) From 10:00 a.m. to 4:00 p.m.
   (D) Any time after 6:00 p.m.

10. Which of these movies has the latest starting time?
    (A) *Neon Streets*
    (B) *Daisy*
    (C) *Rico's Revenge*
    (D) *Star Voyage*

11. To which of these would someone go to see a family comedy?
    (A) Cinema 1
    (B) Cinema 2
    (C) Cinema 3
    (D) A special showing

12. How much is admission to the first showing of all the movies?
    (A) $3.00
    (B) $4.00
    (C) $5.00
    (D) $8.00

F. Intention Questions

The answers for intention questions are not directly stated in the talks. Instead, you have to draw a conclusion about the intention or meaning of a phrase based on the information that is presented by the speaker. In other words, you have to interpret what the speaker is implying.

Intention questions can be phrased in the following ways:
- *Why does the speaker say, ". . ."?*
- *What does the speaker mean when she says, ". . ."?*
- *What does the man mean when he says, ". . ."?*
- *What does the woman imply when she says, ". . ."?*

Sample Item: Intention Question

Woman: Hello, Mr. Garcia. This is Kelly Roberts from Fairfield Printing. I have a question about the invitation order you placed with us yesterday. Something just doesn't add up. Your order form indicates that you would like seventy-five printed invitations but only fifty envelopes to put them in. You may have a reason for this, but I'd like to check whether this is correct before we start printing. If you give me a call by five o'clock this evening, we can still deliver them to you by Friday.

Q. Why does the woman say, "Something just doesn't add up"?

- (A) The dates on an invitation are incorrect.
- ● The quantity of an order may not be correct.
- (C) She hesitates to increase an order.
- (D) She wants to correct the price on an order.

> After the phrase "Something just doesn't add up" the speaker says, "Your order form indicates that you would like seventy-five printed invitations but only fifty envelopes to put them in."

Exercise 4.6

Focus: Understanding and answering questions about intention and meaning.

Directions: Listen to the talk. Read the question about the talk and then choose the one option — (A), (B), (C), or (D) — that best answers the question.

 Now start the audio program.

1. What does the woman mean when she says, "I'm totally lost"?
   - (A) She has lost her office key.
   - (B) She has misplaced a report.
   - (C) She cannot find her way home.
   - (D) She cannot understand a document.

2. Why does the speaker say, "Well, it's not getting any earlier"?
   - (A) He wants to get started.
   - (B) He wants to revise a schedule.
   - (C) He wants to close the business.
   - (D) He wants to go home.

3. What does the speaker mean when she says, "Size isn't the only thing we do well"?
   - (A) Their location is also excellent.
   - (B) Their clerks recently won an award.
   - (C) They also carry imported goods.
   - (D) They also offer good prices.

4. What does the man imply when he says, "They certainly know what they're doing"?
   - (A) Salespeople will deliver a presentation.
   - (B) Salespeople have been successful lately.
   - (C) Their sales staff has had an average quarter.
   - (D) Managers will require salespeople to work more.

5. What does the woman mean when she says, "History is being made while we watch"?
   - (A) A documentary is being filmed.
   - (B) A new facility will open.
   - (C) An accident has taken place.
   - (D) An election is being held.

6. Why does the speaker say, "I think you'll be very happy to hear this"?
   - (A) His company made a large profit.
   - (B) His company will open a new branch.
   - (C) His company will hire Mr. Sial.
   - (D) His company will promote Mr. Sial.

7. What does the speaker mean when she says, "After all, they were the natural choice"?
   - (A) She wants to hire new employees.
   - (B) She congratulates co-workers.
   - (C) She hopes to plan a business trip.
   - (D) She agrees with a decision.

8. What does the man imply when he says, "I don't think you have anything to worry about"?
   - (A) Business papers are in order.
   - (B) Taxes will not increase.
   - (C) Bank statements will arrive.
   - (D) An order has been located.

9. What does the woman mean when she says, "They just don't stay on the shelves very long"?
   - (A) Products fell off the shelves.
   - (B) Workers forget to stock items.
   - (C) A product is selling well.
   - (D) Prices should be reduced.

10. Why does the speaker say, "You've got to tell me its name again"?
    - (A) To ask about a restaurant
    - (B) To change a schedule
    - (C) To invite someone to dinner
    - (D) To recall the name of a dish

11. What does the speaker mean when she says, "Take advantage while you can"?
    - (A) Parking will be free.
    - (B) A sale will end soon.
    - (C) Service is excellent.
    - (D) Coupons are valuable.

12. What does the man imply when he says, "In fact, I don't think they could have been any better"?
    - (A) Products have good quality.
    - (B) New employees performed well.
    - (C) Business results are excellent.
    - (D) Employees are efficient.

G. Graphic-Based Questions

The answers for graphic-based questions are not directly stated in the talks. Instead, you have to draw a conclusion based on the information that is presented by the speaker *and* what is shown in the graphic.

Graphic-based questions always have the same preface ("Look at the graphic."). The second part of the question can be phrased in a variety of ways:
- *Look at the graphic. When will the event be held?*
- *Look at the graphic. Who should Mr. Brown speak to?*
- *Look at the graphic. What is the incorrect quantity of chairs?*
- *Look at the graphic. Where will hikers NOT be able to go today?*

Sample Item: Graphic-Based Question

Woman: Hello, this is Judith Nguyen calling from The HBC Trading Company. I'd like to inform you that we have received your home furnishings shipment from Singapore ahead of schedule. We've inspected the merchandise and everything seems to have survived the journey undamaged. However, the number of dining chairs in the container doesn't match the invoice that the manufacturer included with the shipment. Could you please have a look at the document I sent you and confirm whether it's correct?

Shipping Invoice

Item	Quantity
Leather sofas	12
Coffee tables	16
Dining tables	20
Dining chairs	83

Q. Look at the graphic. Which quantity on the invoice is incorrect?

Ⓐ 12

Ⓑ 16

Ⓒ 20

● 83

> The speaker says, "However, the number of dining chairs in the container doesn't match the invoice that the manufacturer included with the shipment."

Exercise 4.7

Focus: Understanding and answering graphic-based questions.

Directions: Listen to the talk. Read the question about the talk, look at the graphic, and then choose the one option — (A), (B), (C), or (D) — that best answers the question.

 Now start the audio program.

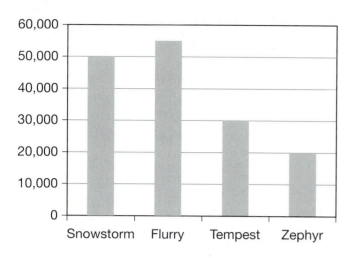

1. Look at the graphic. Which product is the speaker most concerned with?

(A) Snowstorm

(B) Flurry

(C) Tempest

(D) Zephyr

2. Look at the graphic. Which office does the speaker tell Mr. Tanaka to go to?

(A) Personnel

(B) Marketing

(C) Finance

(D) Sales

Law Office of Rios and Bates	
Section	**Room Number**
Personnel	4001
Marketing	4002
Finance	4003
Sales	4004

3. Look at the graphic. Which ingredient does the man express concern about?

(A) Total fat

(B) Cholesterol

(C) Sodium

(D) Carbohydrates

Nutrition Facts	
8 servings per container	
Serving size: 2/3 cup (55 grams)	
Amount per 2/3 cup	
Calories	**230**
Total Fat	8 grams
Cholesterol	18 grams
Sodium	160 milligrams
Carbohydrates	37 grams

Employee	Rating
Olivia Park	83
Robert Hughes	82
Brent Wallace	86
Jenifer Vasquez	84

4. Look at the graphic. Which employee is the speaker talking about?

(A) Olivia Park

(B) Robert Hughes

(C) Brent Wallace

(D) Jenifer Vasquez

Smart Value Supermarket
Discount Coupon

Good for the following discounts on purchases of $40 or more:

Food products —	$5
Paper products —	$7
Beverages —	$10
Medicines —	$12

5. Look at the graphic. What discount does the speaker offer?

(A) $5

(B) $7

(C) $10

(D) $12

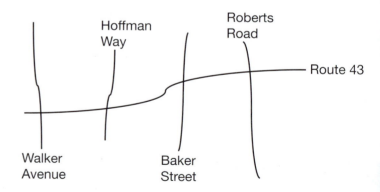

6. Look at the graphic. Which road will drivers be unable to drive on from May 2nd to May 3rd?

(A) Walker Avenue

(B) Hoffman Way

(C) Baker Street

(D) Roberts Road

Directions: Listen to the talks, and then answer each of the three questions about them by marking the correct choice — (A), (B), (C), or (D).

 Now start the audio program.

1. What is one disadvantage of a rowing machine?

    (A) It is not easy to assemble.

    (B) It is extremely expensive.

    (C) It exercises only half of the body.

    (D) It cannot be used by a beginner.

2. What do exercise experts claim?

    (A) Four months is all that is needed to get into shape.

    (B) One should exercise each muscle system separately.

    (C) Exercising only the upper body is dangerous.

    (D) It is best to exercise both body halves at one time.

3. What does the speaker mean when he says, "Not at all"?

    (A) He avoids a purchase.

    (B) He criticizes advertising.

    (C) He agrees with a proposal.

    (D) He disagrees with a proposition.

4. Why would someone rent a car from this agency?

    (A) To impress someone

    (B) To save time

    (C) To rent the newest models

    (D) To save money

5. Where is the rental agency located?

    (A) At the airport

    (B) On Marshall Boulevard

    (C) At a downtown hotel

    (D) In the Oxford Mall

6. Which of the following is NOT serviced by the free shuttle?

    (A) The airport

    (B) Downtown hotels

    (C) Airport hotels

    (D) North and South Port ferries

7. What is the speaker doing?

    (A) Introducing a new topic

    (B) Agreeing to a change in plans

    (C) Disagreeing with another speaker

    (D) Requesting more information

8. What does the speaker imply will take a lot of time?

    (A) Teaching temporary employees to do the job

    (B) Finding financial resources for the next project

    (C) Convincing the employees to work overtime

    (D) Scheduling workers for the Shannon project

9. With which of these statements would the speaker agree?

    (A) The Shannon project should not be completed.

    (B) Future projects will be delayed.

    (C) Jim's plan will save time and money.

    (D) Temporary workers should not be hired.

10. Who is the speaker?

(A) A newspaper journalist

(B) A fire chief

(C) An owner of a warehouse

(D) A television reporter

11. Why does the speaker say, "Chief, would you step over here for a moment, please?"

(A) To give him an award

(B) To assist him

(C) To interview him

(D) To ask for his advice

12. What was the cause of the fire?

(A) The owners refuse to say.

(B) It was an electrical explosion.

(C) It was an act of arson.

(D) The cause is still unknown.

13. Who is the speaker?

(A) A host of a radio show

(B) A university professor

(C) A guest on a television program

(D) A weather forecaster

14. Why should corn be harvested in the morning?

(A) It contains more vitamin C.

(B) It tastes sweeter.

(C) It contains more water.

(D) It is easier to pick.

15. What will probably be heard right after this talk?

(A) An advertisement for seeds

(B) More information about vitamins

(C) A discussion of plant parasites

(D) Some tips for cooking vegetables

16. What kind of business is APG?

(A) A home appliance store

(B) A news station

(C) A loan agency

(D) An electrical power company

17. What service is APG mainly discussing in this message?

(A) Home safety inspection

(B) Compensation for lost services

(C) Storm warning reports

(D) Their new website

18. How long should a customer wait before calling to receive this service?

(A) Twenty-four hours

(B) Forty-eight hours

(C) Thirty days

(D) Sixty days

19. What can be inferred about the location of the properties?

(A) It is warm throughout the year.

(B) It is still undeveloped.

(C) It has a dry, desert climate.

(D) It is on an island in the middle of a lake.

20. What is a short distance from the properties?

(A) Golf facilities

(B) Waterfalls

(C) Shops

(D) Villas

21. What will the speaker probably do next?

- (A) Show pictures of the property
- (B) Present information on other properties
- (C) Discuss how a property can be purchased
- (D) Install computer equipment for the demonstration

22. Who will be relocated?

- (A) The speaker
- (B) The Park Service Department
- (C) The Recreation Department
- (D) The employees at 10 Plaza Street

23. Who is responsible for the changes to the department?

- (A) The mayor
- (B) The office manager
- (C) The park rangers
- (D) Department of Motor Vehicle workers

24. What does the speaker imply when he says, "There's no need to pack up your things, though"?

- (A) Employees will be able to keep their jobs.
- (B) All personnel may keep working at their current desks.
- (C) A moving company will help workers move their belongings.
- (D) Changes at the company might be cancelled.

25. What type of event is the speaker mainly talking about?

- (A) A birthday party
- (B) A retirement party
- (C) An awards ceremony
- (D) A wedding party

26. What does the speaker say about balloons?

- (A) They must be kept inside.
- (B) They come in four colors.
- (C) They cannot be used.
- (D) They must be replaced.

27. Look at the graphic. Which quantity on the purchase order does the speaker recommend increasing?

- (A) 1
- (B) 2
- (C) 42
- (D) 150

Davis Party Supplies	
Purchase Order	
Customer: Terry Lopez	
Item	**Quantity**
3 x 10 Banner	1
Colored balloons	150
Table decorations	42
Welcome poster	2

Sources of Revenue

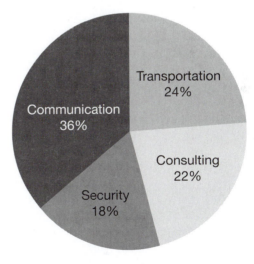

28. What can be said about the meeting?

- (A) It will last an hour.
- (B) It was called suddenly.
- (C) It is open to the public.
- (D) It is held regularly.

29. Who does the speaker say is responsible for the high revenue from Communication software?

(A) The business office

(B) The top management

(C) The sales team

(D) The advertising department

30. Look at the graphic. What does the speaker want listeners to concentrate on most?

(A) Communication

(B) Transportation

(C) Consulting

(D) Security

Reading

Guide to Reading

This section of the TOEIC® test consists of three parts, each with its own directions and format:

    Part 5: Incomplete Sentences   30 items
    Part 6: Text Completion   16 items
    Part 7: Reading Comprehension   54 items

When the test was revised in 2016, the number of items in different parts of this section was changed, and several new types of items were added to Parts 6 and 7.

Although ETS calls this entire section Reading, Part 5 is actually a test of grammar and vocabulary. Part 6 combines reading comprehension and grammar/vocabulary. Part 7 is a test of a number of reading comprehension skills.

Timing is an important factor in the Reading section. Your goal is to finish all the items and leave yourself a few minutes to go back to items that you found difficult.

Part 7 is the most time-consuming because it takes time to read the passages and answer the comprehension questions. You may be able to go through the items in Parts 5 and 6 more quickly, but you don't want to go so fast that you make mistakes. You may work on these parts in any order that you want. You may want to begin with Part 7 before working on Part 5 or Part 6.

This part of the *Guide* is divided into three lessons, each concerning one part of the test. These lessons familiarize you with the kinds of problems you will encounter on the test and provide exercises to prepare you for each type of problem.

Lesson 5 Incomplete Sentences

Format   Part 5

This part of the TOEIC® test consists of thirty sentences, each missing one or more words. Below each sentence are four words or phrases. Your job is to decide which of these four choices produces a complete, grammatical, and logical sentence when it is put into the sentence.

Tactics   Part 5

1. Begin by reading each item carefully. Try to guess what word or words are missing. Look for these words or similar words among the answer choices.

2. The most common testing point in Part 5 is vocabulary. Use the context of the sentence to help you choose the answer, and look for any grammar clues that help you eliminate distractors.

3. The second most common type of item in Part 5 involves word form. You can recognize these items because the answer choices are all forms of the same word. Use the endings of the words to determine which choice is correct in the context of the sentence.

4. Verb problems are the third most common item type in Part 5. The answer choices for these items are four forms of the same verb. Look for time words and other clues.

5. If the correct choice is not obvious, eliminate choices that are clearly incorrect and guess. Put a mark by items that you found difficult so that you can come back to them if you have time. Never leave any items unanswered.

6. Never spend too much time on any one item.

7. As soon as you finish Part 5, go on to Part 6.

Directions: This part of the test consists of incomplete sentences. Beneath each sentence, four words or phrases appear. Mark the answer choice — (A), (B), (C), or (D) — that best completes the sentence.

Look at the example

Mr. Morales read over the contract with great _____.

(A) interesting

● interest

(C) interested

(D) interestingly

This sentence should correctly read "Mr. Morales read over the contract with great interest." Therefore, the answer is (B).

---

1. Most of the firm's products are sold to wholesalers, but it does operate _____ small retail outlets.

   (A) a number of

   (B) a little

   (C) an amount of

   (D) few

2. The company could save money if it bought a fleet of more _____ vehicles.

   (A) economize

   (B) economic

   (C) economics

   (D) economical

3. The cafeteria begins serving lunch at noon and stays open _____ three.

   (A) at

   (B) by

   (C) until

   (D) within

4. I believe that Ms. Stathos took my flash drive by mistake and left _____ plugged into the computer.

   (A) her

   (B) herself

   (C) hers

   (D) she

5. The shift manager _____ everyone go home a half-hour early on Friday afternoon.

   (A) allowed

   (B) let

   (C) told

   (D) got

6. The Sherman Hotel has very reasonable _____ for single rooms.

   (A) rates

   (B) fares

   (C) fees

   (D) bills

7. Marbelis is looking for a job in _____ advertising or public relations.

   (A) both

   (B) or

   (C) neither

   (D) either

8. We are planning _____ out to dinner tonight.

   (A) taking our clients

   (B) our clients going

   (C) our clients will go

   (D) to take our clients

9. Jerry made his children _____ on Saturday.

(A) do some chores

(B) some chores were done

(C) to do some chores

(D) they did some chores

10. Anna _____ in this department since January.

(A) have been working

(B) works

(C) has worked

(D) has been worked

Testing Points and Skill-Building Exercises

Part 5 is a test of grammar, usage, and vocabulary. There is a range of testing points; however, certain patterns appear again and again. Most Part 5 items on a given TOEIC® test fit into one of the seven testing-point categories given in this guide.

A. Vocabulary

Vocabulary problems are the most common type of item in Part 5. Usually, around 40% to 50% of all items involve vocabulary. This part of the lesson discusses four types of vocabulary problems:
- Function words
- Words with similar meanings
- Words with unrelated meanings
- Items involving grammar clues

Function Words

The answer choices for this type of item are four function words (words used primarily to show grammatical relationships).

Sample Item: Function Words

Most of the firm's products are sold to wholesalers, but it does operate _____ small retail outlets.

● a number of

(B) a little

(C) an amount of

(D) few

Choices (B) and (C) are used with noncount nouns, not count nouns such as "outlets". Choice (D) "few" has a negative emphasis. It means "almost no outlets." However, the idea of this sentence is that there are some outlets. The best answer is Choice (A), because it has a positive emphasis and it can be used with count nouns. (Note that "a few" has a positive emphasis, and that "a few" would be a good answer as well.)

Certain function words are closely related and often appear as answer choices in the same items. Following is a list of some of these expressions with sentences that illustrate their use and explanatory notes.

> **enough** I don't have *enough* money to buy that sweater now. Besides, I don't think it's big *enough* for me.
> **too** It's *too* expensive to buy right now.
> **so** The suitcase was *so* heavy that I could barely lift it.
> **such** It was *such* a heavy suitcase that I could barely lift it.

- *Enough* is used to indicate that there is the correct amount of something needed to accomplish a certain goal.
- *Too* is used to indicate that there is more than the correct amount.
- *So* is used before an adjective (*so heavy*).
- *Such* is used before an adjective and a noun (*such a heavy suitcase*).
- Both *enough* and *too* are generally used with infinitives (*to buy that sweater*). *So* and *such* are generally used with *that* clauses (*that I could barely lift it*).

> **most** *Most* people enjoy music.
> **most of the** *Most of the* people at the concert seemed to enjoy it.
> **almost** *Almost* all the parking spaces were taken.
> **the most** This is *the most* exciting book I have read in a long time.

- *Most* means "the majority." It is used to speak of a large, generalized group (*most people*).
- *Most of the* is used to speak of a specific group (*most of the people at the concert*).
- *Almost* means "nearly." *Almost all the parking spaces* means "nearly all of them."
- *The most* is used with the superlative form of some adjectives (*the most exciting*).

> **yet** I don't think Henrik has arrived *yet*.
> **still** You're right, he is *still* not here.
> **anymore** Trisha does not live in that apartment complex *anymore*.
> **already** She has *already* found another place to live.

- *Yet* and *still* both mean "up to now." *Yet* is used chiefly in questions and negative statements, and usually comes at the end of a clause. It is sometimes used before infinitives. "Henrik has yet to arrive" has the same meaning as "Henrik has not arrived yet."
- *Still* is used in all types of sentences: questions, statements, and negative statements.
- *Anymore* is used to indicate that something is not happening now. It occurs in questions and negative statements, and usually comes at the end of a clause.
- *Already* is used to indicate that something has happened before now. It is used in statements and questions.

> **any** Do you have *any* change?
>   No, I don't believe I have *any*.
> **some** Can I have *some* soup?
>   Sure, there's *some* in the pot.

- *Any* is used in questions and negative statements.
- *Some* is used in questions and affirmative statements.

> **ever** Have you *ever* gone skydiving?
>   No, and I do not *ever* plan to go.
> **never** I have *never* been skydiving either, but I would like to give it a try.

- *Ever* is used in questions and negative statements. It means "at any time."
- *Never* is used in affirmative statements. It means "not ever."

> **no** There was *no* coffee in the pot.
> **none** There was *none* left.
> **not** This is *not* coffee — it's tea.
>   I do *not* want any tea.

- *No* is used before nouns (*no coffee*) and certain comparative words (*no sooner, no longer*).
- *None* means "not any" or "not one."
- *Not* is a function word that makes almost any word or words negative.

> **after** We will go to dinner *after* the theater.
>   We will go to dinner *after* the play is over.
> **afterwards** We will go to the theater first and to dinner *afterwards*.

- *After* is used as a preposition before nouns (*after the theater*) or as an adverb-clause marker before a clause (*after the play is over*).
- *Afterwards* is an adverb and is usually used at the end of a clause.

> **much** Will the trip take *much* time?
> **many** Yes, it will be *many* hours before we arrive.
> **a little** There is *a little* money in the wallet.
> **a few** There are *a few* dollars.
> **little** There is *little* chance you will find a job in that field.
> **few** There are *few* opportunities in that field.
> **amount** There is a large *amount* of work that has not been done.
> **number** There are a *number* of jobs that must be done.

- The terms *much, a little, little,* and *amount* are used with noncount nouns (*time, money, chance,* and *work* above).
- The terms *many, a few,* and *number* are used with countable nouns (*hours, dollars,* and *jobs* above).
- *A little* and *a few* have positive meanings. "A little money" means "not much money, but some." "A few dollars" means "not many dollars but some."
- *Little* and *few* have negative meanings. "Little chance" means "almost no chance." "Few opportunities" means "almost no opportunities."

> **alike** Field hockey and soccer are *alike* in many respects.
> **like** *Like* soccer, field hockey is a fast-paced game.
>   Field hockey, *like* soccer, is a fast-paced game.
>   Field hockey is *like* soccer in that both are fast-paced.
> **similar (to)** Your leather coat and mine are *similar*.
>   Your leather coat is *similar to* mine.
> **the same (as)** Your leather coat and mine are nearly *the same*.
>   Your leather coat is *the same* size *as* mine.

- *Alike* is used in the pattern "A and B are alike."
- *Like* is used in these patterns: "Like B, A . . . ," "A, like B, . . . ," and "A is like B. . . ."
- *Similar* is used in the patterns "A and B are similar" and "A is similar to B."
- *Similar to* cannot begin a sentence or clause.
   - "*Similar to* Spanish, Italian is derived from Latin." (INCORRECT)
   - "*Like* Spanish, Italian is derived from Latin." (CORRECT)
- *The same* is used in the patterns "A and B are the same" and "A is the same as B."
- *Alike* can also be used in this pattern: "Adults and children *alike* can enjoy this movie." This means "Both adults and children can enjoy this movie."

> **between** Relations *between* the two countries are friendly.
> **among** The man divided his estate *among* his four children.

- *Between* is used to refer to two entities.
- *Among* is used to refer to more than two.

Exercise 5.1

Focus: Vocabulary problems with function words.

Directions: Underline the word in parentheses that best completes each sentence.

1. The bill for lunch was (so / such) high that I decided to put it on my credit card rather than pay cash.

2. Mr. Ridgeway decided to invest (any / some) money in hotels in Eastern Europe.

3. There was not (enough / too much) tape to seal the package properly.

4. I had (such / so) a bad flight that I (ever / never) intend to fly on that airline again.

5. (Most / Almost) of the rice grown in this country is exported.

6. We have sold (many / much) computer chips to that firm.

7. I intend to see that movie eventually, but I have not had a chance to see it (still / yet).

8. (Less / Fewer) people attended the conference this year.

9. Betina does not work here (still / anymore).

10. (Like / Similar to) Miami, Los Angeles has a mild climate.

11. After its merger with Global Airlines, Europa Airways will (no / not) longer use its old corporate logo.

12. The Malay language and the Indonesian language are (like / alike) in (almost / most) every respect.

13. There aren't (some / any) apartments available in that price range.

14. There is (too much / enough) wind today to fly a kite — it feels like a hurricane out there.

15. The (amount / number) of classified advertising in newspapers has declined, while the (amount / number) of classified ads that appear on the Internet has rapidly increased.

16. (Alike / Like) most professionals, doctors work long hours.

17. Mr. Olowu has (already / still) returned to Nigeria.

18. The capital city has (such / so) a large, rapidly growing population that city officials have (no / not) been able to solve the problem of waste disposal there.

19. (Among / Between) (most / the most) impressive buildings in the city of Hanoi is the Opera House.

20. (Little / Few) research has been done in that field (anymore / yet).

21. Hyde Park is a popular spot with Londoners and visitors (like / alike).

22. Mr. Moon was (too / so) busy last week that he had to eat lunch at his desk every day.

23. (A few / Few), if any, games are more difficult to master than the Asian game Go.

24. Ms. Renaldi is (no / not) longer on Facebook.

25. There's still (little / a little) gasoline left in the tank, but not (much / many).

Words with Similar or Unrelated Meanings

Some items involve not function words but content words — usually nouns, verbs, and adjectives — with similar or unrelated meanings. This may be the most difficult type of Part 5 item to prepare for, because it is impossible to know in advance what words will be tested. The best way to improve your vocabulary is to read, read, and read. Keep a dictionary handy, or use your phone to make a list of "likely" words — words that you think might appear on the test — and try to learn five to ten words a day.

Sample Item: Words with Similar Meanings

The Sherman Hotel has very reasonable _____ for single rooms.

● rates
(B) fares
(C) fees
(D) bills

> The four answer choices are all nouns with related definitions; they all deal with the idea of payment or cost. *Fares* are payments for transportation. *Fees* are payments for certain services. *Bills* are written statements of charges. *Rates* are used for the cost of rooms at hotels.

Sample Item: Words with Unrelated Meanings

The value of large diamonds is sometimes difficult to _____.

(A) replace
(B) develop
(C) authorize
● assess

> The word *assess* means to evaluate, to estimate how much something is worth. It is the only word that logically fits into the blank. The other words are not close in meaning to the word *assess*.

Exercise 5.2

Focus: Completing sentences involving content words with similar or unrelated meanings.

Directions: Decide which of the expressions on the right best completes each sentence on the left, and write the letter of that expression in the blank. For each set of items, there is one expression on the right that will not be used. After you complete the exercise, look up words that you are unfamiliar with in a dictionary.

1. I am going to _____ a vacation in late August.

2. Let's _____ lunch at Alfredo's Restaurant tomorrow.

3. Before you _____ a decision, consider all the facts.

A. keep

B. take

C. make

D. have

4. Ms. Dos Santos paid the _____ for dinner with the corporate credit card.

5. You must pay a _____ to enter the national park.

6. My plane _____ to Los Angeles was quite reasonable.

A. bill

B. payment

C. fee

D. fare

7. After twenty-five years with the firm, Mr. Osumi _____.

8. Gary was _____ because he was constantly late for work.

9. The company _____ the salaries of some of its executives in order to cut its expenses.

A. reduced

B. dismissed

C. retired

D. dropped

10. Ice cream and other frozen foods are located in the next _____.

11. We have to turn left at the next intersection, so you should get in the left _____.

12. I had to stand in _____ for fifteen minutes.

A. line

B. row

C. lane

D. aisle

13. To be a defensive driver, you must be able to _____ what other drivers will do before they actually do anything.

14. The olive branches on the flag of the United Nation _____ world peace.

15. At first, Mr. and Ms. Henderson wanted to _____ their kitchen themselves, but then they decided to hire a contractor to do the work.

A. signify

B. adapt

C. renovate

D. anticipate

16. Sylvie bought a _____ of French bread to make sandwiches.

17. I would like a _____ of butter on my toast.

18. There is just a _____ or two of orange juice left.

A. loaf

B. drop

C. pat

D. crumb

19. The Ironman Triathlon is an _____ competition that involves running, biking, and swimming long distances.

20. When Mr. Tobing was offered a transfer to the company's branch in Ireland, he was _____ to accept, but now he is happy that he did.

21. When applying for a new job, it is certainly _____ if you have some experience in that field.

A. reluctant

B. efficient

C. arduous

D. advantageous

22. Mr. Rizal began working here when he was in his _____ twenties.

23. At the peak of the flood, the water in the streets was as _____ as the water in the shallow end of a swimming pool.

24. Temperatures tomorrow are expected to be in the _____ thirties.

A. deep

B. high

C. late

D. far

25. The doctor _____ the emergency surgery under very adverse conditions.

26. When Ms. Gautier accepted the award for her designs, she said that she had _____ success through lots of hard work and a little good luck.

27. For some reason, Agnes _____ as though she didn't know us.

A. acted

B. performed

C. accomplished

D. achieved

28. Of course, the transmission on my car had to be replaced just weeks after the _____ had expired.

29. She has a _____ for being quite an aggressive negotiator, but I found her quite willing to compromise.

30. At first, his proposal received a rather chilly _____, but eventually, everyone decided that it was the best plan of action.

A. reception

B. precedent

C. reputation

D. warranty

Grammar Clues

In some vocabulary problems, grammar clues can indicate the correct answer, or at least help you eliminate distractors.

Sample Item: Grammar Clues

The shift manager _____ everyone go home a half-hour early on Friday afternoon.

(A) allowed

● let

(C) told

(D) got

The verb *let* has the same meaning as *allowed*. However, only *let* is used with the simple form of the verb (*go*). The verbs *allowed*, *told*, and *got* are all followed by a full infinitive (*to go*).

Exercise 5.3

Focus: Using grammar clues to complete vocabulary problems.

Directions: Underline the form that correctly completes the sentence. (See the Answer Key for an explanation of the grammar clues.)

1. The boss (said / told) that I had to work late.

2. (Visitors / Guests / Tourists) to the site should sign in here.

3. The new computer is (two / twice / double) as fast as the old one.

4. Nelson's uncle (proposed / suggested / advised) him to study management information systems.

5. The (shipment / merchandise / goods) are stored in the warehouse.

6. Suyarat was (looking / seeing) out the window of the plane.

7. Do you want to (pay / purchase / buy) for this with your debit card?

8. If I (say / tell) you a secret, do you promise not to talk to anyone about it?

9. My new apartment is (close / near / nearby) to the Medical Center.

10. The King James Hotel has set (standards / models / samples) for excellence in the hospitality industry.

11. Mr. Zamora is (regarded / considered) as an expert in the field of biotechnology.

12. Nancy (listened / heard) the governor's speech on the radio.

13. According to a recent survey, one out of three women in France (wears / has / puts) perfume every day.

14. Ms. Hracec received an important (mail / message) this morning.

15. How do you (account / explain) for this discrepancy?

Exercise 5.4

Focus: Reviewing and practicing all types of vocabulary problems in the Part 5 TOEIC® test format.

Directions: Decide which of the choices — (A), (B), (C), or (D) — best completes the sentence.

1. Investments in genetic engineering firms _____ down slightly in the last quarter.

    (A) went

    (B) declined

    (C) reduced

    (D) jumped

2. Our products are carefully _____ before they are shipped to wholesalers.

    (A) displaced

    (B) inspected

    (C) originated

    (D) provided

3. As _____ as I know, Doctor Cimbura is still planning to leave tomorrow.

    (A) long

    (B) far

    (C) well

    (D) much

4. Penelope auditioned for a _____ in the play, but she did not get it.

    (A) role

    (B) character

    (C) piece

    (D) line

5. This video demonstrates several tactics for _____ with common problems that managers encounter.

    (A) coping

    (B) handling

    (C) sharing

    (D) managing

6. The process _____ about an hour to complete.

    (A) has

    (B) spends

    (C) takes

    (D) was

7. Smoking is allowed only in specially _____ areas.

    (A) designated

    (B) restored

    (C) conducted

    (D) determined

8. The money can be paid in monthly installments or in a _____ sum.

    (A) lump

    (B) mass

    (C) full

    (D) whole

9. Art in public places is _____ to anyone who passes by.

    (A) present

    (B) there

    (C) attracted

    (D) accessible

10. Ms. Yoosten has _____ finished preparing the financial statement.

    (A) more or less

    (B) little or no

    (C) more and more

    (D) sooner or later

11. Entering this area without an identification badge is _____ forbidden.

- (A) highly
- (B) strictly
- (C) evenly
- (D) merely

12. The nurse took a blood _____ from Mr. Galindo.

- (A) sample
- (B) example
- (C) model
- (D) selection

13. During the "Midnight Madness" sale this weekend, downtown stores will not _____ until 2 a.m.

- (A) finish
- (B) end
- (C) complete
- (D) close

14. In order to start the machine, _____ this key to the right.

- (A) spin
- (B) cross
- (C) turn
- (D) press

15. The president of NFX Media Corporation is a _____ professional soccer player.

- (A) once
- (B) previous
- (C) former
- (D) past

B. Word Forms

In Section A of this lesson, you looked at problems in which the answer choices consisted of four different words. In this section, you will see items in which the answer choices consist of four forms of the same base word. In some of these items, each answer choice represents a different part of speech: noun, verb, adjective, or adverb. In other items, there is more than one form of a noun, verb, or adjective.

Sample Item: Word Forms

The company could save money if it bought a fleet of more _____ vehicles.

- (A) economize
- (B) economic
- (C) economics
- ● economical

All four choices are forms of the same base word. Choice (A) is a verb, choice (C) a noun. Choices (B) and (D) are both adjectives. An adjective is required to modify the noun *vehicles*. The adjective *economic* means "related to an economy;" *economical* means "efficient and inexpensive."

To answer these questions, you should be able to identify the forms that are given as adjectives, nouns, verbs, or adverbs, and to recognize which best fits into the blank in the sentence.

Nouns

Nouns name persons, places, things, and concepts. Concrete nouns refer to physical things, and abstract nouns refer to qualities and concepts. Most of the nouns that are tested in Part 5 are abstract nouns.

Some common noun endings:

-tion	information	-ery	recovery
-dom	freedom	-ship	friendship
-ence	experience	-tude	solitude
-ance	acceptance	-ism	industrialism
-ity	creativity	-cracy	democracy
-hood	brotherhood	-logy	biology
-ness	happiness	-ment	experiment

Common endings for nouns that refer to persons:

-er	writer	-ee	retiree
-or	governor	-ic	comic
-ist	psychologist	-ian	technician

Verbs

Verbs may be action verbs or linking verbs.
>She *exercises* every day. (action verb)
>They *seem* upset. (linking verb)

Common verb endings:

-ize	sanitize	-ify	notify
-en	lengthen	-ate	incorporate
-er	recover		

Adjectives

Adjectives modify nouns, noun phrases, and pronouns. Most adjectives tested in Part 5 refer to abstract qualities.
* Adjectives are used before nouns.
    >a *prosperous* business
    >a *common* occurrence
* Adjectives are used after the verb *to be* and other linking verbs.
    >That song is *sad*.
    >She looks *sleepy*.
    >That doesn't seem *important*.

Common adjective endings:

-ate	moderate	-y	sunny
-ous	ominous	-ic	economic
-al	normal	-ical	logical
-ing	interesting	-ial	remedial
-ed	bored	-ory	sensory
-able	comfortable	-less	hopeless
-ible	sensible	-ive	competitive
-ish	sluggish	-ly	friendly
-ile	fertile	-ful	colorful

Most of the adverbs seen in word-form problems are adverbs of manner. These adverbs are formed by adding the suffix -*ly* or -*ally* to an adjective. (The -*ally* suffix is used when the adjective ends in the letter *c*.)

    quickly   reasonably   precisely   enthusiastically

- Adverbs are most often used to modify verbs. They may come before or after the main verb, or at the end of the sentence.
  He *eagerly* accepted the challenge.
  Ms. Isgaard spoke *forcefully* to the audience.
  Wilson met his sales quota *quickly*.

- Some adverbs are used to modify adjectives and occur before those adjectives.
  His Internet business has been *moderately* successful.
  This bulletin is *slightly* out-of-date.

- A few adverbs have the same form as adjectives.
    fast   hard   high
  He was driving too *fast*. (adverb)
  His sports car is quite *fast*. (adjective)

- The adverb form of *good* is *well*.
  José did a *good* job on the contract. His boss congratulated him for doing so *well*.

Exercise 5.5

Focus: Completing sentences with the correct word form.

Directions: Decide which of the expressions on the right best completes each sentence on the left, and write the letter of that expression in the blank. For each set of items, there is one expression on the right that will not be used.

1. What do you _____ me to do?

2. You should ask Paul for some _____.

3. Do you really feel that changing jobs at this time is _____?

    A. advice
    B. advise
    C. advisor
    D. advisable

4. What this country needs is a few more honest _____.

5. I make it a point never to discuss _____ at dinner.

6. Anne Toshira won the election even though she did not have as much _____ experience as her opponent.

    A. politics
    B. political
    C. politicians
    D. politically

7. Is your insurance company going to reimburse you for your _____?

8. When did you _____ your phone?

9. I was unable to retrieve the _____ data.

    A. lost
    B. losing
    C. lose
    D. loss

10. Who is going to _____ for your cat while you are out of town?

11. _____ drivers often cause accidents.

12. Follow the directions _____, or you will make a mistake.

A. care

B. carefree

C. careless

D. carefully

13. You can _____ yourself with this issue by reading these briefs.

14. _____ with coding can help you get a job.

15. I am not _____ with that account.

A. familiar

B. familiarly

C. familiarize

D. familiarity

16. Economists fear that the recession may _____ next year.

17. She was _____ offended by his unkind remark.

18. Divers without their own supply of air can descend to a maximum _____ of around 100 feet.

A. deep

B. deepen

C. depth

D. deeply

19. My _____ specializes in working on European cars.

20. I cannot fix this machine; I'm not _____ inclined.

21. The train crash was due to human error, not _____ failure.

A. mechanic

B. mechanism

C. mechanical

D. mechanically

22. I cannot afford a new tablet computer, so I am looking for a good _____ one.

23. On a desert island, money would be _____.

24. _____ of this app find it very helpful.

A. uses

B. users

C. used

D. useless

Exercise 5.6

Focus: Reviewing and practicing word-form problems in the Part 5 format.

Directions: Decide which of the choices — (A), (B), (C), or (D) — best completes the sentence.

1. Mr. Uhl will _____ the technical manual into German.

(A) translate

(B) translation

(C) translator

(D) translatable

2. The fresh _____ grown on these farms is brought into the city by truck every morning.

(A) product

(B) production

(C) produce

(D) producing

3. This toy requires some _____ at home.

(A) assembled

(B) assemble

(C) assembler

(D) assembly

4. If a product is _____ packaged, it will get consumers' attention.

(A) attractively

(B) attraction

(C) attract

(D) attractive

5. There has been a lot of _____ about this new scheme.

(A) exciting

(B) excite

(C) excitable

(D) excitement

6. Mr. Fanconi has a lot of common _____.

(A) sensibility

(B) sensitivity

(C) sense

(D) sensation

7. Boston's Back Bay is a beautiful _____ containing many fine old houses.

(A) neighborhood

(B) neighbor

(C) neighboring

(D) neighborly

8. When can we expect _____ of those parts?

(A) delivery

(B) deliver

(C) deliverance

(D) deliverer

9. Tybalt Enterprises' environmental problems were revealed by a team of _____ journalists from a local television station.

(A) investigation

(B) investigate

(C) investigators

(D) investigative

10. Ms. Rhee _____ her point of view very well.

(A) defensive

(B) defendant

(C) defended

(D) defense

11. The personnel manager read all the _____ herself.

(A) applications

(B) applies

(C) applicants

(D) applicators

12. I went to a wonderful exhibit of _____ art at a gallery on Drew Street.

(A) photographer

(B) photography

(C) photograph

(D) photographic

C. Verbs

Answer choices of this type of problem consist of four forms of the same verb. The verb forms may be main verbs or auxiliary verbs plus main verbs.

Sample Items: Verbs

Anna _____ in this department since January.

- (A) have been working
- (B) works
- ● has worked
- (D) has been worked

In choice (A), *have* does not agree with the singular subject, *Anna*. Choice (B) incorrectly uses the simple present tense; the phrase *since January* indicates that the present perfect is needed. Choice (D) incorrectly uses the passive form of the verb.

Cans of paint must be thoroughly _____ in order to mix the pigments and the liquid solvent.

- (A) shaking
- (B) shook
- ● shaken
- (D) shake

Choice A is an *–ing* form, which is used for progressive verbs. However, in this sentence, a passive verb (*be* + past participle) must be used. Choice B is the past tense, but the past participle is required. Choice D is the simple form of the verb; a past participle is needed. Choice C is correct because it completes a passive verb phrase (*must be . . . shaken*).

Correct answer choices in this section have the following characteristics:

Correct Tense

Time words in the sentences provide clues as to which tense to choose. In the first sample item, the phrase *since January* indicates that the present perfect should be used. Look at these sentences:

He (move) to Brazil *a month ago*.
She (study) ballet *since she was a child*.
Ali *always* (have) a cup of coffee as soon as he *gets* to work.

In the first sentence, the phrase *a month ago* indicates that a past-tense verb is needed (*moved*).
In the second, the clause *since she was a child* indicates that the present perfect tense is required (*has studied*).
In the third, the word *always* and the use of the present tense in the second clause (*gets*) suggest that the simple present tense should be used (*has*).

Correct Voice (Active or Passive)

You may have to choose between active and passive verb forms. In the first sample item, choice (D) incorrectly involves the passive because the subject (*Anna*) performs the action rather than receiving it. In the second sample item, the subject (*cans of paint*) receives the action rather than performing it, so a passive verb (*must be . . . shaken*) is correct. Sentences with *by* + noun often require a passive verb.

Agreement of Subject and Verb

Singular verbs (*is, has, was, does, walks,* and so on) must be used with singular subjects. Plural verbs (*are, have, were, do, walk,* and so on) must be used with plural subjects. In the first sample item, choice (A) is incorrect because the plural verb *have* does not agree with the subject.

Correct Form of Irregular Verbs

Verb-form problems often involve verbs with irregular forms, especially those with different past tense and past participle forms. In the second sample item, choice (B) is incorrect because the past tense is used after the auxiliary verbs *must be*.

In some verb-form problems, infinitives (*to* + the simple form), *-ing* forms, and past participles are incorrect choices because they are used in place of main verbs. Used alone, these forms can never function as main verbs. For example, in the second sample item, choice (A) is incorrect because the *-ing* form cannot serve as a main verb.

Many items require you to choose between simple forms of the verb, *-ing* forms, and past participles. Here are some hints for selecting the correct forms:

- **The simple form follows all modal auxiliaries.**

might be	can stay	should hurry
must know	could take	may sell

    (Certain similar auxiliary verbs require full infinitives.)
    ought to go   used to play   have to hurry

- **The simple form is used in *that* clauses after certain verbs and adjectives.**
    (This verb form is sometimes called the present subjunctive.)

Verbs:			**Adjectives:**	
ask	recommend		better	mandatory
advise	request		essential	necessary
demand	suggest		imperative	urgent
insist	urge		important	vital
propose				

    I insist that Bill *accompany* us.
    It's essential that everyone *work* overtime this week.

    The passive form is *be* + past participle.
    I recommend that Judith *be promoted*.

- **The past participle is used after a form of *have* in all perfect forms of the verb.**

has said	had called	should have gone
have run	will have read	could have decided

- **The *-ing* form is used after a form of *be* in all progressive forms of the verb.**

is sleeping	has been writing	should have been wearing
was studying	had been drawing	will be waiting

- **The past participle is used after a form of *be* in all passive forms of the verb.**

is worn	had been promised
is being considered	will have been missed
were told	might have been cancelled
has been shown	would have been lost

Exercise 5.7

Focus: Completing sentences with the correct tense or form of the verb.

Directions: Fill in the blanks with the correct form of the verb in parentheses.

1. At this time of year, the sun (rise) _____ at about 5:30 a.m.

2. The game of backgammon (play) _____ for many centuries.

3. I (watch) _____ television last night when the electricity suddenly went out.

4. Margot (just return) _____ from Bangkok when she had to leave for Tokyo.

5. I probably (finish) _____ around midnight tomorrow night.

6. Peter may (spend) _____ two weeks in Bali.

7. It (snow) _____ in the mountains last night.

8. Since 2014, David Michaels (own) _____ a financial consulting firm.

9. That memo (write) _____ by Sadashumi yesterday.

10. I suggest that you (discuss) _____ this matter with Inspector Hanson.

11. I should have (take) _____ a vitamin pill this morning.

12. This newspaper (publish) _____ since 1872.

13. Caroline (give) _____ the baby a bath right now — can she call you back in a few minutes?

14. It is important that this product (promote) _____ heavily.

15. You must have (drive) _____ all night in order to get here so soon.

Exercise 5.8

Focus: Completing sentences with the correct forms of irregular verbs.

Directions: Decide which of the expressions on the right best completes each sentence on the left, and write the letter of that expression in the blank. For each set of items, there is one expression on the right that will not be used.

1. This watch was _____ to me by my grandfather.

2. I _____ those files to Marta an hour ago.

3. Karl always _____ his wife a dozen roses for their anniversary.

    A. gave
    B. gives
    C. giving
    D. given

4. Last year I _____ over 150,000 miles.

5. This fighter plane was _____ on over forty missions during the war.

6. I will be _____ to Johannesburg early next week.

    A. flying
    B. flown
    C. flew
    D. fly

7. I _____ at some wonderful restaurants when I was in New Orleans last spring.

8. Jean seldom _____ lunch before one-thirty.

9. I have never _____ frog legs — have you?

    A. eats
    B. ate
    C. eaten
    D. eating

10. She _____ skiing in Zermatt, Switzerland, last winter.

11. Mr. Zhang said he might _____ to Los Angeles later this year.

12. Naomi had already _____ by the time I got to the office.

    A. go
    B. went
    C. going
    D. gone

13. I may _____ a new car this year.

14. Joel has been _____ a lot of mail.

15. A few years ago, we _____ a lot more foot traffic on this street.

    A. get
    B. got
    C. getting
    D. gotten

Exercise 5.9

Focus: Practicing and reviewing verb-form problems in the Part 5 format.

Directions: Decide which of the choices — (A), (B), (C), or (D) — best completes the sentence.

1. Portuguese is _____ in Brazil, the largest country in South America.

   (A) speaking
   (B) spoke
   (C) speak
   (D) spoken

2. The plane was _____ its final approach to the airport when it developed a problem with its landing gear.

   (A) made
   (B) making
   (C) make
   (D) makes

3. Tokyo's main shopping district _____ Ginza.

   (A) is called
   (B) calls
   (C) is calling
   (D) calling

4. Carol Bridwell has _____ a senior partner in the law firm of Mason and Woodford.

   (A) named
   (B) naming
   (C) been named
   (D) being named

5. Matthew _____ the CPA exam last month.

   (A) will pass

   (B) passing

   (C) have passed

   (D) passed

6. It's mandatory that passengers _____ their seat belts.

   (A) fasten

   (B) fastening

   (C) should fasten

   (D) have fastened

7. Right now, day care is not provided at the factory, but a new day care center _____.

   (A) is built

   (B) has built

   (C) is being built

   (D) has been building

8. We must _____ faster to keep up with the project schedule.

   (A) to work

   (B) working

   (C) work

   (D) worked

9. Work on the assembly line _____ because a key piece of machinery broke down.

   (A) was delaying

   (B) delayed

   (C) was delayed

   (D) delay

10. Mr. O'Dell insisted that the proposal _____.

    (A) rewrite

    (B) be rewritten

    (C) is rewritten

    (D) rewrote

11. Although people say that "seeing is believing," I still cannot believe that what I _____ last night was really a UFO.

    (A) seen

    (B) had seen

    (C) saw

    (D) might see

12. Ricardo _____ tennis since he was eight years old.

    (A) has been playing

    (B) playing

    (C) was playing

    (D) had played

13. They are still _____ for an explanation.

    (A) wait

    (B) waiting

    (C) waited

    (D) waits

14. You ought _____ a thank-you note to Ms. Velez.

    (A) send

    (B) sending

    (C) have sent

    (D) to send

15. I am afraid the train will _____ by the time you get to the platform.

    (A) leaving

    (B) have left

    (C) left

    (D) be left

D. Personal Pronouns

The answer choices for this type of item are four different forms of a personal pronoun or a possessive adjective. All of the four choices may be different forms of one pronoun (*I, my, mine, myself,* for example) or they may be forms of more than one pronoun (*he, them, himself, themselves,* for example).

Sample Item: Pronouns

I believe that Ms. Stathos took my flash drive by mistake and left _____ plugged into the computer.

(A) her

(B) herself

● hers

(D) she

The pronoun shows possession (the flash drive belongs to Ms. Stathos). Because it does not come before a noun, *hers* is the correct form. (*Hers* means *her flash drive.*)

The following chart lists all the forms of personal pronouns and possessive adjectives.

	Pronouns	Use	Examples
Subject Pronouns Singular Plural	I, you, he, she, it we, you, they	Subject of a sentence or a clause	*I* finished the project. *She* is an architect. *They* didn't understand the instructions.
Object Pronouns Singular Plural	me, you, him, her, it us, you, them	Object of a verb or a preposition	Paula helped *me* a lot. I didn't talk to *him*. He showed *us* the photograph.
Possessive Adjectives Singular Plural	my, your, his, her, its our, your, their	Used before a noun to show possession	That's *her* new car. The horse got out of *its* stall. Thanks to all of you for *your* help.
Possessive Pronouns Singular Plural	mine, yours, his, hers ours, yours, theirs	Used without a noun to show possession	That briefcase is *hers*. She's a friend of *mine*. That's not our car, but it sure looks like *ours*.

	Pronouns	Use	Examples
Reflexive Pronouns Singular Plural	myself, yourself, himself, herself, itself ourselves, yourselves, themselves	Used as an object when the subject and the object are the same person*	I sent *myself* a copy of the e-mail. He cut *himself* shaving. All of you should be proud of *yourselves*.

*Reflexive pronouns have several other uses. They can be used with the word *by* to mean "alone" or "with no one else":
    I went to the party by *myself*.

Sometimes the reflexive pronoun can have this meaning without the word *by*:
    Since your friends can't help you, you'll have to do it *yourself*.

They are used for emphasis (to make an idea or a point stronger):
    The president of the corporation *himself* thanked her for her work.

They are also used with certain verbs, especially *enjoy*:
    We enjoyed *ourselves* when we went to the beach.

"Help —self" means "serve —self":
    Help yourself to a sandwich.

"Clean up after —self" means that the person who made the mess must do the cleaning:
    The painters did a good job painting the living room, and then they *cleaned up after themselves*.

Exercise 5.10

Focus: Completing sentences with the correct form of personal pronouns.

Directions: Fill in the blanks in the following sentences with the correct pronoun.

1. The pilot instructed the passengers to buckle _____ seatbelts and to keep _____ fastened until the plane had landed.

2. Our friends, the Andersons, remembered to bring _____ folding chairs to the outdoor concert, but _____ left _____ at home.

3. We can mail this check to you and _____ can deposit it _____, or _____ can deposit it directly into _____ account.

4. Ms. Szabo left _____ passport on the train, but fortunately, another passenger found _____ and returned _____ to _____.

5. I don't consider _____ an astronomer, but _____ do enjoy looking at the stars through _____ telescope.

6. The nurse told the couple that _____ had to have a child safety seat in the backseat of _____ car, and that she would check to see that _____ was properly installed before _____ would let _____ take _____ baby home from the hospital.

7. Tourists who visit the Eiffel Tower often take pictures of _____ with _____ in the background.

8. The car I drive belongs to the company _____ work for, but the GPS equipment installed in _____ is _____.

9. I'm pleased that my roommates pay _____ share of the rent on time, but _____ wish _____ would clean up after _____ when _____ use the kitchen.

10. You two will have to share _____ office with the visiting executives when _____ arrive on Monday.

Exercise 5.11

Focus: Reviewing and practicing problems involving personal pronouns in the Part 5 format.

Directions: Decide which of the choices — (A), (B), (C), or (D) — best completes the sentence.

1. The type of clothing that people wear tells us a lot about who _____ are.

- (A) we
- (B) they
- (C) you
- (D) their

2. Reinforced concrete has metal bars embedded in _____.

- (A) them
- (B) its
- (C) their
- (D) it

3. Around 8,000 years ago, people began to use animals to transport _____ and their belongings.

- (A) themselves
- (B) they
- (C) theirs
- (D) them

4. Shortly after Ms. Yang bought stock in Aston Products, Inc., the price of _____ shares shot up.

- (A) them
- (B) its
- (C) they
- (D) it

5. Although I do speak a little Italian, I don't consider _____ fluent in the language.

- (A) me
- (B) mine
- (C) myself
- (D) my

6. The best way for children to learn science is for them to perform experiments _____.

- (A) theirs
- (B) them
- (C) their
- (D) themselves

7. Emeralds get _____ beautiful green color from aluminum and chromium impurities in the stone.

- (A) its
- (B) their
- (C) theirs
- (D) it

8. The actress told the interviewer that it still seemed odd to attend her own movies and to see _____ up on the big screen.

- (A) her
- (B) she
- (C) herself
- (D) hers

9. My parents taught my brothers and me to take care of _____ by exercising and eating healthy foods.

(A) ourselves

(B) us

(C) ours

(D) we

10. Small businesses often limit _____ operations to a single community or a group of neighboring communities.

(A) its

(B) theirs

(C) it

(D) their

E. Prepositions

Answer choices for this type of problem consist of four prepositions. You must choose the correct one, based on the context of the sentence.

Sample Items: Prepositions

The cafeteria begins serving lunch at noon and stays open _____ three.

(A) at

(B) by

● until

(D) within

> All four prepositions can be used to express relationships of time, but only (C) indicates that an action (*stays open*) continues up to a certain point (*three*).

The Mississippi River roughly divides the United States _____ eastern and western halves.

● into

(B) to

(C) on

(D) between

> After the verb *divide*, both *between* and *into* can be used. *Divide between* is used with two people. ("He *divided* the money *between* his two children.") *Divide into* is used with parts (*eastern and western halves*).

In some items, the key to choosing the correct preposition is the word that comes before the blank, because certain nouns, adjectives, and verbs are always followed by the same prepositions. (This is true in the first sample item.)

Following are lists of nouns, adjectives/participles, and verbs that are commonly paired with certain prepositions, along with a list of phrasal prepositions, which are prepositions that consist of more than one word.

Nouns + Prepositions

appointment with
approach to
cause of
combination of
contribution to
cure for
decrease in
demand for
development in (a field)
development of (something)
effect of (something that affects)
effect on (the thing affected)
example of
exception to
experience in (a field)
experience with (something)
idea for
impact on
improvement in
increase in

influence on
interest in
native of*
part of
participation in
price of
probability of
problem with
process of
quality of
reliance on
result of
rules for (doing something)
rules of (a game)
satisfaction with
search for
solution to
source of
supply of
variety of

Adjectives/Participles + Prepositions

accustomed to
acquainted with
afraid of
angry at (something or someone)
angry with (someone)
attached to
aware of
based on
capable of
close to
dependent on
different from
disappointed with/by
eligible for
essential to/for
familiar with
free from (control)
free of (impurities)
identical to

inferior to
made of (material)
married to (someone)
native to* (somewhere)
necessary for
next to
perfect for
pleased with
polite to
preferable to
related to
responsible for (something or someone)
responsible to (someone)
safe from
satisfied with
similar to
suitable for
superior to
surprised at/by

*Note that the noun *native* takes the preposition *of* (He's a *native of* Scotland), but the adjective *native* takes the preposition *to* (This plant is *native to* Hawaii).

Verbs + Prepositions

account for
agree to (a plan)
agree with (someone)
approve of
arrive at (an airport, a train station, a building)
arrive in (a city or country)
begin by (doing something)
begin with (something)
believe in
benefit from
caution against
chat with
compete with
concentrate on
consist of
consult with
contribute to
cooperate with
deal with
decide on
depend on
engage in
escape from
divide among (more than two people)
divide between (two people)
divide into (parts)

furnish with
grow into
interfere with
invest in
move into (a house or room)
move to (a city or country)
participate in
pay for
plan on
prepare for
prohibit from
recover from
rely on
replace with
respond to
result in
subscribe to
substitute for
succeed in
talk about (a topic)
talk to (an audience or a person)
talk with (a person)
wait for (someone or something)
wait on (a customer)
withdraw from

Phrasal Prepositions

according to
ahead of
along with
because of
by means of
due to
in charge of
in favor of

in spite of
instead of
on account of
on behalf of
prior to
regardless of
thanks to
together with

Exercise 5.12

Focus: Completing sentences with prepositions that follow nouns, adjectives, and verbs, or are part of phrasal prepositions.

Directions: Complete the following sentences with the correct prepositions. (If you are unsure of the answer, take a guess before you check the lists on the previous pages.)

1. As the quality _____ this product has improved, the demand _____ it has grown.

2. This suit made _____ wool is superior _____ the other one.

3. Diana is planning to move _____ the office next _____ mine.

4. If there are any more problems _____ this design, Ms. Yamada, who is _____ charge _____ the art department, can deal _____ them.

5. The explosion that occurred was the result _____ a combination _____ several factors.

6. This sports car might not be suitable _____ a family, but it is perfect _____ a single person.

7. After he gets his doctoral degree, Li-Ming hopes to contribute _____ the search _____ a cure _____ cancer.

8. The development _____ a good bookkeeping system was essential _____ modern business.

9. Mr. Ewool, a native _____ Ghana, moved _____ the United Kingdom fifteen years ago.

10. There are many rules _____ using prepositions, but, unfortunately, there are many exceptions _____ the rules.

11. Thanks _____ improvements _____ medical technology, doctors today are capable _____ making much more accurate diagnoses.

12. I made an appointment _____ Mr. Hilbert to talk _____ the upcoming merger.

13. Although you will not be eligible _____ retirement for many years, you should start to prepare _____ it now.

14. According _____ some experts, the long-term effect _____ pollution _____ people's health may be more serious than was once thought.

15. Zambia is the source _____ over 15% of the world's supply _____ cobalt.

16. Together _____ his aides, the chancellor arrived _____ the airport.

17. We have found a solution _____ part _____ the problem.

18. If we intend to compete _____ Rockwood Industries, we must take a new approach _____ distribution and marketing.

19. I agreed _____ George when he said that before we decide _____ a plan, we need to talk _____ someone who has a lot of experience _____ this area.

20. Instead _____ guessing blindly, you should make an educated guess _____ means _____ the process _____ elimination.

In some items, the key to the correct preposition is the word that follows the blank — the prepositional object — or an overall understanding of the sentence. Some uses of common prepositions are given here:

Using *In*

Time

in + century (in the twenty-first century)
in + decade (in the 1940s; in the nineties)
in + year (in 2017)
in + season (in the spring)
in + month (in October)
in + parts of the day (in the morning; in the
    afternoon; in the evening)
But: at night

In (or *within*) is also used with amounts of time:
I'll be home *in* (*within*) an hour.

Place

in the world
in + continent (in Africa)
in + body of water (in the Caribbean)
in + country (in Thailand)
in + state/province (in Massachusetts; in Ontario)
in + city (in Munich)
in + building (in the Empire State Building)
in + room (in the kitchen)

Other

in + clothing (in a gray suit)
in + language (in Japanese)
in + book (in *The Complete Guide to the TOEIC® Test*)
in + newspaper (in the *International Herald Tribune*)
in + magazine (in *Asia Week*)
in + department (in the legal department)
in + field (in computer science; in architecture)
in + a person's opinion (in my opinion)
in the past/future
in a car/taxi
in trouble
in danger (of)
in part (= partially)
in front of
in the middle of
in back of
in the rear
in the market (for) (= trying to buy something)
in line (= waiting for something)
in the process (of)

Using *On*

Time

on + date (on May 23)
on + day (on Friday)

Place

on the earth/the planet/the globe
on + street (on Wall Street)
on + coast (on the East Coast)
on + floor (on the 42nd floor)

Other

on a vehicle (on a bus; on a train; on a plane)
on foot
on the cover (of a book or magazine)
on a page
on a trip
on sale (= for sale at a reduced price)
on the market (= for sale)
on schedule
on + musical instrument (on the guitar)
on time (for)
on television/radio/the Internet
on the phone
on a farm
on a map
on the other hand
on purpose (= intentionally)
on line (= on the Internet)

Using *At*

Time	Other
at + time of day (at 9:20; at midnight)	at present
at night	at the moment (= now)
	at first/last
Place	at most/least
at + address (at 634 Sutter Street)	at times (= sometimes)
at + building (at the Prado Museum)	at once (= immediately)
at home	at a high/low price
	(not) at all

(Note: Both *in* and *at* can be used with buildings. *In* emphasizes that someone or something is *inside* the building.)

Using *By*

By is used before a point of time to indicate the latest possible time. *By*, in this case, means "no later than."
  I will be home *by* noon.

By can mean "next to."
  She's standing *by* her friend.

By is used after passive verbs to identify the agent (the "doer") of the action.
  This report was written *by* Paco.

By heart means "memorized."
  The actor learned his lines *by heart*.

By is used with means of transportation and communication.
  by car   by plane   by email

(Note: Both *by* and *in/on* are used before means of transportation or communication. *By* is used only before singular nouns without articles or other determiners. If the noun is plural, or if it is preceded by a determiner, *in* or *on* is used.)
  in my car   on the plane   in this email   in trucks

Other

by chance	by hand	by far
by check/credit card	by means (of)	

Using *For*

For is used with a period of time to show the duration of an action.
  Smythe has been living abroad *for* six months.

(Note: *Since* is used with points of time to show a similar relationship.)
  Smythe has been living abroad *since* January.

For is used to show purpose.
  He went to the store *for* milk and bread.

For can mean "in place of" or "on behalf of."
I asked Sally to work *for* me on Saturday.

Other

for free	for sale (= on the market)
for rent	for good (= permanently)
for the sake (of)	

Using *During*

During is used with periods of time.
It snows a lot in Montreal *during* the winter.
His company grew rapidly *during* the 1990s.

During is *not* used with dates or days of the week.
He went swimming *during* Thursday. (INCORRECT)

Using *With*

With is used to express the idea of accompaniment or ownership.
I went to the restaurant *with* Andrea.
The man *with* the briefcase is the vice-president.

With is also used to indicate the tool or instrument used to accomplish something.
He opened the door *with* his key.
He paid the bill *with* a credit card.

Other

with pleasure
with someone's permission

Using *Until*

Until is used with points of time to indicate that an action continues (or doesn't continue) up to that point.
Helen practiced the piano *until* ten-thirty.
They won't arrive *until* tomorrow.

Using *From/To* and *Between/And*

These phrases are used with starting points and ending points.
From 2010 *to* 2015, Mr. Nolan was in charge of the sales division.
Between 2010 *and* 2015, Mr. Nolan was in charge of the sales division.
Interstate Highway 90 runs *from* Boston *to* Seattle.
Interstate Highway 90 runs *between* Boston *and* Seattle.

Exercise 5.13

Focus: Completing sentences with prepositions that precede certain prepositional objects.

Directions: Fill in the blanks with the correct prepositions.

1. I met my friend Howard _____ chance _____ the lobby of the Raffles Hotel _____ Singapore.

2. There's a phone number _____ the newspaper that we can call _____ more information.

3. _____ Korea, it is considered bad luck to sign your name _____ a red-ink pen.

4. The plumber promised me he would be here _____ least _____ three, but he didn't arrive _____ five.

5. InterSystem's international sales increased _____ 21% _____ 2012 and 2017.

6. Mr. Poernomo asked me to meet him _____ his office _____ the third floor _____ two-thirty, so I need to leave _____ a few minutes.

7. Deborah got _____ trouble _____ her boss for illegally copying software.

8. I always shower _____ the morning, but my roommate showers _____ night.

9. Ms. Vu has been living _____ that apartment building _____ 2460 Vine Street _____ September, but her sister has been there _____ several years.

10. The oil industry is _____ far the most important industry _____ Saudi Arabia.

11. Mr. Demmings bought some property _____ the West Coast _____ the late 1990s.

12. _____ January, all of the office furniture at Office Works will be _____ sale _____ greatly reduced prices.

13. I will arrive _____ Orly Airport _____ Paris _____ around nine o'clock.

14. _____ present, there are no job openings _____ the design department, but there may be an opening _____ a month or two.

15. Some of the most fashionable and expensive stores _____ the United States are _____ Rodeo Drive _____ Los Angeles.

16. Textiles were made _____ hand _____ the invention of the power loom _____ the nineteenth century.

17. Her photo appeared _____ the cover of *Business Watch*, and there was a story about her _____ the magazine as well.

18. I commute to work _____ the city _____ train, but my friend always travels there _____ his own car.

19. Every year, people _____ Mexico celebrate their independence from Spain _____ September 16.

20. _____ 2010 to 2016, he lived _____ a small farm _____ Vermont.

Exercise 5.14

Focus: Reviewing and practicing preposition-choice problems in a format similar to that of Part 5 of the TOEIC® test.

Directions: Decide which of the choices — (A), (B), (C), or (D) — best completes the sentence.

1. Botswana is famous _____ its diamond mines.

   (A) for

   (B) of

   (C) with

   (D) by

2. Padang food is a style of Indonesian food that is eaten _____ one's fingers.

   (A) by

   (B) with

   (C) in

   (D) to

3. This package must be in Wellington at least _____ noon Tuesday.

   (A) on

   (B) at

   (C) for

   (D) by

4. Ms. Chadwick was disappointed _____ the results of the advertising campaign.

   (A) for

   (B) of

   (C) on

   (D) with

5. The cheapest way to move goods overseas is _____, but that is also the slowest way.

   (A) by ships

   (B) on ship

   (C) by ship

   (D) to ships

6. _____ the next few months, we hope to arrange a joint venture with a company in the Czech Republic.

   (A) Within

   (B) With

   (C) Since

   (D) At

7. Choudhuri was hired because he is familiar _____ the latest developments in biotechnology.

   (A) to

   (B) with

   (C) in

   (D) about

8. Most of the delegates arrived _____ limousines.

   (A) at

   (B) on

   (C) in

   (D) by

9. The store is open _____ nine to six.

   (A) from

   (B) at

   (C) by

   (D) between

10. Bonnie has been married _____ Steve for two years.

    (A) with

    (B) at

    (C) by

    (D) to

11. If Mr. Tyler had cooperated _____ us, we could have finished in a couple of hours.

(A) to

(B) of

(C) with

(D) from

12. This novel is based _____ part on a true story.

(A) in

(B) on

(C) by

(D) at

F. Connecting Words

Expressions that join words, phrases, and clauses sometimes appear as answers in Part 5.

Sample Items: Connecting Words

Marbelis is looking for a job in _____ advertising or public relations.

(A) both

(B) or

(C) neither

● either

> The correct pattern is *either A or B.*

_____ I knew she had worked in an insurance agency for a year, I did not realize that she was so knowledgeable about health insurance.

(A) However

● Although

(C) Despite

(D) Even

> Only the adverb-clause marker *although* correctly completes the sentence. (The marker *even though* would also be correct.)

This town is not on the map _____ I have.

(A) this

(B) whom

(C) where

● that

> The adjective-clause marker *that* must be used to refer to a thing (*map*).

This part of the lesson discusses the following types of joining words:

• Coordinate conjunctions
• Correlative conjunctions
• Noun-clause markers
• Adjective-clause markers
• Adverb-clause markers
• Prepositional expressions

Coordinate Conjunctions

These one-word conjunctions are used to join words, phrases, and independent clauses.

Coordinate Conjunction	Use	Example
and	Used for addition	He wore a red *and* white tie. Mr. Iachini works at home *and* at his office.
or	Used for alternatives	Do you want a sandwich *or* some soup?
but	Used for contrast	The house is large *but* in poor condition.
nor	Used for negative alternatives	Kent doesn't own a boat, *nor* does he intend to buy one.
so	Used for effect/cause; means "for this reason"	Ramona did a great job, *so* she was given a raise.

Correlative Conjunctions

These two-word conjunctions are also used to join words, phrases, and independent clauses.

Correlative Conjunction	Use	Example
both . . . and	Used for addition	There are vacancies at *both* the Imperial Hotel *and* the Hotel Europa.
not only . . . but also	Used for addition	She *not only* has a real estate license *but also* owns her own real estate company.
either . . . or	Used for alternatives	You can go *either* by car *or* by bus.
neither . . . nor	Used for negative alternatives	He had *neither* strong financial backing *nor* a sound business plan.

Exercise 5.15

Focus: Completing sentences with coordinate and correlative conjunctions.

Directions: Decide which of the expressions on the right best completes each sentence on the left, and write the letter of that expression in the blank. For each set of items, there is one expression on the right that will not be used.

1. My desk is usually cluttered with papers, _____ my co-worker's desk is always neat and clean.

2. I do not think we should discuss the proposal now, _____ do I think we should vote on it.

3. You can use the front door _____ the side door.

4. We ran out of copier paper, _____ we had to borrow some from another department.

    A. nor
    B. and
    C. or
    D. but
    E. so

5. The elevator is not working, _____ is the air conditioner.

6. Are you looking for a new car _____ a used one?

7. My parents understand a little English, _____ they cannot speak it very well.

8. The brakes on your bicycle are not working very well, _____ you had better be careful.

    A. so
    B. nor
    C. or
    D. and
    E. but

9. Michelle plans to buy _____ a minivan or a small truck.

10. Nicolai studied English not only in the United States _____ in the United Kingdom.

11. I visited _____ Houston and Dallas to see clients and make some new contacts.

12. Neither a tennis court _____ a racquetball court was available for Saturday morning.

    A. both
    B. either
    C. but also
    D. nor
    E. or

13. Gloria's report was _____ precise but also well-organized.

14. We would like the walls in the boardroom painted a neutral tone — either cream _____ light tan.

15. Despite his improved performance, Frank was _____ promoted nor given a raise.

16. Text messages are both a fast _____ convenient means of communication.

    A. neither
    B. not only
    C. and
    D. or
    E. but

These words are used to join noun clauses to main clauses.

Noun-Clause Marker	Use	Example
that	Used when the noun clause is formed from a statement	**Original sentence:** Mr. Kee's office is down the hall. **Sentence with noun clause:** I know *that* Mr. Kee's office is down the hall.
if/whether	Either of these words can be used when the noun clause is formed from a yes/no question	**Original sentence:** Is Mr. Kee's office down the hall? **Sentence with noun clause:** Do you know *if* (or *whether*) Mr. Kee's office is down the hall?
wh- words (*what, when, why, where, what size,* and so on)	Used when the noun clause is formed from an information (*wh-*) question	**Original sentences:** Where is Mr. Kee's office? What floor is Mr. Kee's office on? **Sentences with noun clauses:** I don't know *where* Mr. Kee's office is. He couldn't tell me *what floor* Mr. Kee's office is on.

Adjective-Clause Markers

These words join adjective clauses (also called relative clauses) to main clauses. They are sometimes called relative pronouns.

Adjective-Clause Marker	Use	Example
who	Used as the subject of an adjective clause; refers to people	The employees *who* were hired last month have completed their training program.
whom	Used as the object of a verb or a preposition in an adjective clause; refers to people	The woman *whom* you met is an executive secretary. You should speak to the man to *whom* the package was sent.
whose	Used to show possession; usually refers to people	The woman *whose* jewelry was stolen called the police.
which	Used to refer to things or concepts	Goods *which* last for more than four months are called durable goods. My new phone, *which* I just bought last month, has a much better camera than the one on my old phone. This is one process *by which* steel can be made.
that	Used in certain adjective clauses in place of *who* or *which*; refers to both people and things	The family *that* lives next door to us will be moving soon. The car *that* was stolen was recovered the following week.
when	Used to refer to time	This is the time of day *when* I often feel a little sleepy.
where	Used to refer to places	That's the site *where* the company plans to build a new storage facility.

Note: In Part 5 problems, you will **not** be asked to decide whether *whom* is used correctly in place of *who*, or whether *that* is used correctly in place of *which* or *who*.

Focus: Completing sentences with noun-clause markers or adjective-clause markers.

Directions: Decide which of the expressions on the right best completes each sentence on the left, and write the letter of that expression in the blank. For each set of items, there is one expression on the right that will not be used.

1. I am lost; can you tell me _____ I can get back to the Palace Hotel from here?

2. Did you know _____ Donna was once a golf pro?

3. I am not sure _____ Paul quit, but he must have had a good reason.

4. I cannot decide _____ I should buy a car or lease one.

    A. how
    B. where
    C. whether
    D. that
    E. why

5. Do you know _____ Jean-Marc is in his hotel room?

6. I am not sure _____ people were actually at the reception, but over 200 had been invited.

7. Angel told me _____ I would find the folder.

8. Did you see _____ that magician just did?

    A. if
    B. how much
    C. where
    D. what
    E. how many

9. The woman _____ is standing by the water cooler has just started working in the finance department.

10. The friendships _____ I made in college are some of the most valuable ones I have ever made.

11. We are going to spend our vacation in a small town in France _____ my wife once lived.

12. The artist _____ paintings are on the walls of the office building has won several awards for her work.

    A. which
    B. who
    C. where
    D. when
    E. whose

13. I believe it was around July 1 _____ the buy-out took place.

14. The sales agent with _____ you will be training is named Tony Covello.

15. Anyone _____ car is parked in a red zone will get a parking ticket.

16. This is the part of the factory _____ the actual production work takes place.

    A. whom
    B. which
    C. whose
    D. when
    E. where

These words are used to join adverb clauses (also called subordinate clauses) to main clauses. These words are also called subordinate conjunctions. The adverb clause can either precede the main clause or follow it. If the adverb clause comes first, it is set off by a comma.

Adverb-Clause Marker (Time)	Use	Example
before	Means "earlier than the time that"	The game started *before* I got to the stadium.
after	Means "later than the time that"	You can read this memo *after* I have read it.
since	Means "from a time in the past until now"	I have not seen Kevin *since* he returned from Europe.
until	Means "up to the time that"	Frieda watched television *until* her roommate came home.
once	Used to indicate that when one action occurs, another takes place	*Once* Gustav arrives, we will start the meeting.
as soon as	Used to indicate that when one action occurs, another takes place	*As soon as* we have had lunch, we will resume the discussion.
as	Means "at the same time that"	Martha arrived at the party just *as* we were leaving.
when	Means "at the same time that"	*When* I arrived at the office, there was an important message for me.
while	Means "at the same time that"; used when the action of the verb has duration (when it takes some time to complete)	*While* Belinda was talking on the phone, I waited outside her office.

Other Adverb-Clause Markers	Use	Example
because since	Used for cause/effect	Mikos joined a health club *because* (or *since*) he wanted to get in shape.
although though even though while	Used to show contrast or opposition	*Although* (or *Though* or *Even though* or *While*) he was late, he didn't miss his plane.
if	Used to introduce a conditional clause; the condition may be possible or impossible (contrary to fact)	**Possible condition:** *If* Sam and Janet invite us, we will go to their party. (They might invite us.) **Impossible condition:** *If* Juan were here, he would be upset. (Juan is not here.)
unless	Used to indicate a negative condition; means "if . . . not"	*Unless* we hurry, we will be late. (This means, "If we don't hurry, we will be late.")

Prepositional Expressions

These expressions have the same meaning as certain adverb-clause markers but are used before noun phrases rather than before clauses.

Prepositional Expression	Use	Example
because of due to	These expressions have the same meaning as *because.*	*Because of* (or *Due to*) the bad weather, the garden party was cancelled. (This means, "Because the weather was bad, the garden party was cancelled.")
despite in spite of	These expressions have the same meaning as *although.*	*Despite* (or *In spite of*) their loss, the team is still in first place. (This means, "Although they lost the game, the team is still in first place.")

Exercise 5.17

Focus: Completing sentences with conjunctive adverbs, adverb-clause markers, and prepositional expressions.

Directions: Decide which of the expressions on the right best completes each sentence on the left, and write the letter of that expression in the blank. For each set of items, there is one expression on the right that will not be used.

1. Neil is familiar with Malaysia _____ he lived there as a child.

2. _____ the attractive offer Drummund Industries made him, he decided not to accept the job.

3. _____ temperatures are quite high here at this time of year, the ocean breezes make it seem cooler than it actually is.

4. _____ the heavy fog, flights out of Seattle have been cancelled.

A. because of

B. although

C. despite

D. if

E. because

5. The pilot inspected the plane just _____ he took off.

6. _____ you begin working full-time, you will have less time for your hobbies.

7. Noriko has been acting differently _____ she became the manager.

8. I cannot go to the beach _____ I have finished this work.

A. since

B. once

C. while

D. until

E. before

9. _____ their best efforts, the firefighters were unable to save the building.

10. _____ the weather was cool, he was wearing only a thin summer shirt.

11. _____ our continued growth and success, our firm will be hiring a number of new employees in the near future.

12. _____ we had to respond to so many people, we used a form letter.

A. despite

B. since

C. even though

D. unless

E. because of

13. _____ you want to spend a fortune, I wouldn't eat dinner at Chez Alpes.

14. He was not elected _____ the scandal he had been involved in.

15. _____ the risk, he loves racing his motorcycle.

16. _____ I were you, I would get a lawyer's advice on this matter.

A. because of

B. until

C. despite

D. if

E. unless

Exercise 5.18

Focus: Reviewing and practicing all types of connecting-word problems in the Part 5 format.

Directions: Decide which of the choices — (A), (B), (C), or (D) — best completes the sentence.

1. _____ you return from Istanbul, you'll have to fill out a trip report.

   (A) So that

   (B) Once

   (C) Since

   (D) No sooner

2. Write down _____ your cell phone number and your number at the office.

   (A) either

   (B) not only

   (C) both

   (D) neither

3. It took some time for Piotr to realize _____ he had made a mistake.

   (A) that

   (B) if

   (C) because

   (D) so

4. In this light, I cannot tell if this suit is dark blue _____ black.

   (A) either

   (B) and

   (C) both

   (D) or

5. Architecture is a profession _____ has always interested me.

   (A) which

   (B) who

   (C) in which

   (D) whose

6. A preliminary investigation indicates that the accident occurred _____ pilot fatigue.

   (A) because

   (B) due

   (C) because of

   (D) since

7. _____ you have any problems with this product, please contact our customer service representative.

   (A) If

   (B) Unless

   (C) Would

   (D) That

8. This is the village _____ Gunther was born.

   (A) which

   (B) where

   (C) which in

   (D) in that

9. David wanted to know _____ he had not been invited.

   (A) because

   (B) why

   (C) who

   (D) due to

10. That author _____ books you enjoy so much is going to be on a talk show on television tomorrow.

   (A) whose

   (B) his

   (C) who

   (D) who his

11. The CEO has not decided _____ of the two strategies he should adopt.

(A) what

(B) that

(C) which

(D) who

12. The magazine has attracted many new readers _____ Marilyn Bixby became the managing editor.

(A) while

(B) since

(C) once

(D) if

13. _____ its conservative appearance, this sedan has plenty of power and handles almost like a sports car.

(A) Despite

(B) Although

(C) In spite

(D) Even

14. Some corporations realize the importance of golf to business, _____ they sponsor golf tournaments.

(A) so

(B) due to

(C) since

(D) because of

15. No one in the theater group is a professional actor, _____ their performances are always first-rate.

(A) moreover

(B) or

(C) unless

(D) but

16. Mr. McCormick has _____ a master's degree nor a bachelor's degree in business.

(A) either

(B) not only

(C) neither

(D) both

G. Gerunds, Infinitives, and Simple Forms

Correct answers to these problems are gerunds (*-ing* forms), infinitives (*to* + simple forms), or simple forms of the verb (the infinitive without *to*). Distractors often include one or both of the other two forms and full clauses (subjects + verbs).

Sample Items: Gerunds, Infinitives, and Simple Forms

We are planning _____ out to dinner tonight.

(A) taking our clients

(B) our clients going

(C) our clients will go

● to take our clients

> The verb *plan* is followed by an infinitive, not by a gerund, as in choices (A) and (B), nor by a clause, as in choice (C).

He succeeded by _____ hard.

(A) work

● working

(C) he worked hard

(D) to work

> After a preposition (*by*), a noun or a gerund must be used. Choice (A), *work*, might be a noun, but then the sentence would have to read *by hard work*. A preposition cannot be followed by a clause (C) or an infinitive (D).

Jerry made his children _____ on Saturday.

● do some chores

(B) some chores were done

(C) to do some chores

(D) they did some chores

> The verb *made* is followed by an object and a simple form ("made someone do something"). *Made* cannot be followed by an infinitive (C) or by clauses (B), (D).

Gerunds are verbal nouns ending in *-ing*. Gerunds may be the subjects of verbs, the objects of prepositions, or the objects of certain verbs. (See list, page 157.)

Swimming is good exercise. (Gerund as subject)

John gets his exercise by *jogging*. (Gerund as object of preposition)

I enjoy *playing* tennis. (Gerund as object of verb)

Infinitives can also be used as verbal nouns. Infinitives can be the subjects of verbs or the objects of certain verbs. (See list, page 157.) Infinitives cannot be used as the objects of prepositions.

To fly a small plane must be exciting. (Infinitive as subject)

My brother wants *to get* a pilot's license. (Infinitive as object of verb)

After certain verbs, a noun or pronoun object must be used before the infinitive.

My father advised my brother *to wait*.

Infinitives have quite a few other uses.

- To show purpose (why something happens):

    She went to the bank *to deposit* the day's receipts.

    He took lessons *to learn* how to sing.

- After certain adjectives (including *able, anxious, easy, good, important, common, nice, ready, difficult, strange, hard,* and others):

    I'm anxious *to learn.*

    It's nice *to see* you again.

- After nouns:

    The next person *to walk* through that door will win a prize.

    That's not a common sight *to see.*

Simple forms (sometimes called "bare infinitives" or "*to*-less infinitives") are used after a few verbs. (See list below.)

    The office manager let Bill *move* to another desk.

Verbs Followed by Gerunds

admit	delay	go[2]	practice
anticipate	deny	justify	risk
appreciate	discuss	keep	stop[3]
avoid	dislike	mind	suggest
can't help[1]	enjoy	miss	understand
consider	finish		

Verbs Followed by Infinitives

afford	ask	know (how)	stop[3]
agree	choose	learn (how)	vote
aim	decide	seem	would like
arrange	deserve		

Verbs Followed by Objects + Infinitives

allow	get[4]	persuade	teach (how)
ask	help[1]	prepare	tell
cause	instruct	need	use
choose	invite	remind	warn
convince	permit	require	would like

Verbs Followed by Simple Forms

have[4]	let	make[4]	would rather
help[1]			

Notes:

1. The verb *help* can be followed by an infinitive or simple form.

   > He helped me *to solve* the problem.
   > He helped me *solve* the problem.

   Notice that the verb phrase *can't help* (meaning "can't prevent" or "can't stop") is used with a gerund.

   > His jokes are so funny that I can't help *laughing* at them.
   > I couldn't help *overhearing* your comment.

2. The verb *go* is followed by the *-ing* form of many "activity verbs": *go shopping, go dancing, go skiing, go bowling,* and others.

3. The verb *stop* is followed by either a gerund or an infinitive, depending on meaning.

   > I stopped *smoking* (meaning "I no longer smoke").
   > He stopped *to light* his pipe (meaning "He stopped doing something else in order to light his pipe").

4. The verbs *get, have,* and *make* are known as "causative verbs" because they indicate that one person causes another person to do something. They are used in the following patterns:

   > We got Bob *to help* us.
   > We had Bob *help* us.
   > We made Bob *help* us.

   Get and *have* can also be followed by past participles.

   > I got my car *washed*.
   > I had my car *washed*.

   Some verbs (which are not listed) can take either infinitive or gerund objects.

   > I like *to eat* ice cream.
   > I like *eating* ice cream.

   Since both answers are correct, these verbs will seldom be tested in Part 5.

In addition to the listed verbs, all two- and three-word verbs are followed by gerunds rather than by infinitive objects.

> Are you thinking of *moving*?
> Don't count on *seeing* Mr. Thomas.

Gerunds are used even when the verb phrase contains the word *to*, as in *look forward to, object to, devote to,* or *be opposed to*.

> He devotes much of his time to *planning* for the future.
> I look forward to *seeing* you again.

Some verbs on the list that are followed by infinitives are often used in passive patterns.

> This tool is used *to open* cardboard boxes.
> He was asked *to join* the committee.

Exercise 5.19

Focus: Completing sentences with gerunds, infinitives, or simple forms.

Directions: Complete the sentences with the gerund, infinitive, or simple form of the verb in parentheses.

1. By (sign) _____ this contract, you are agreeing (deliver) _____ these goods to us by the end of the month, or you risk (pay) _____ a penalty.

2. The president of Pioneer Avionics decided (implement)_____ new cost-control measures.

3. I enjoy (cook) _____, but I dislike (clean up) _____.

4. These boots are perfect for (hike) _____.

5. A sudden noise made the golfer (miss) _____ his shot.

6. I need (practice) _____ (speak) _____ Spanish before I travel to Costa Rica.

7. Rattan, a close relative of bamboo, is ofted used (make) _____ chairs, tables, and other furniture.

8. Mr. Kim invited me (go) _____ (shop) _____ with him when I return to Seoul.

9. The clerk denied (take) _____ the money, but he could not convince the store manager (drop) _____ the charges against him.

10. When I have the mechanic (fix) _____ my brakes, I am going to get him (change) _____ my oil as well.

11. Gwendolyn's doctor told her (stop) _____ (drink) _____ so much coffee.

12. I do not have enough money (pay) _____ all my bills.

13. My boss lets me (work) _____ from home whenever possible, and she allows me (arrange) _____ my own schedule.

14. I am really looking forward to (go) _____ to Mexico next month.

15. I would rather (go) _____ (ski) _____ than (stay) _____ home this weekend.

Exercise 5.20

Focus: Reviewing and practicing problems involving gerunds, infinitives, or simple forms in the Part 5 format.

Directions: Decide which of the choices — (A), (B), (C), or (D) — best completes the sentence.

1. I enjoy _____ a walk in the park after lunch whenever I have time.

   (A) taking
   (B) go for
   (C) take
   (D) to have

2. The health department requires the operators of restaurants _____ sanitary conditions.

   (A) maintenance
   (B) maintaining
   (C) to maintain
   (D) maintain

3. The latest economic statistics seem _____ an upturn in the economy.

(A) pointing to

(B) a prediction

(C) to indicate

(D) demonstrating

4. It was necessary for the architect _____ a hard-hat when she visited the construction site.

(A) wear

(B) to wear

(C) wearing

(D) wears

5. My father taught _____ skeptical of claims made by advertisers.

(A) me to be

(B) to be

(C) my being

(D) for me to be

6. _____ here is not permitted.

(A) Park

(B) You can park

(C) Having parked

(D) Parking

7. Did you have your assistant _____ this report?

(A) edit

(B) editing

(C) an edition

(D) to edit

8. I intend to stop _____ after January 1.

(A) to smoke

(B) smoking

(C) smoke

(D) smokes

9. I need someone to help me _____ these boxes into the truck.

(A) load

(B) loading

(C) loads

(D) loaded

10. Atsuko is going to Vancouver _____ some of her clients.

(A) for to visit

(B) visiting

(C) to visit

(D) visit

11. Please complete the paperwork before _____ in line.

(A) to stand

(B) be

(C) wait

(D) getting

12. Henry got someone _____ his car.

(A) wash

(B) washed

(C) washing

(D) to wash

Directions: Decide which of the choices — (A), (B), (C), or (D) — best completes the sentence.

1. When Lubis was in college, he was a very _____ person.

   (A) student

   (B) study

   (C) studies

   (D) studious

2. _____ the warning, they failed to evacuate the area.

   (A) Despite

   (B) Although

   (C) Even so

   (D) In spite

3. California Brands offers not only a generous base salary _____ an excellent benefits package.

   (A) and

   (B) but also

   (C) as well

   (D) or else

4. Bubble gum was first _____ in 1928.

   (A) markets

   (B) in the market

   (C) marketing

   (D) marketed

5. Our flight to Atlanta was on time, but _____ was an hour late.

   (A) they

   (B) theirs

   (C) their

   (D) themselves

6. Ten countries _____ the trade agreement.

   (A) ratified

   (B) registered

   (C) assigned

   (D) notified

7. I do not mind taking a business trip now and then, but I dislike _____ too much time away from home.

   (A) to spend

   (B) that I spend

   (C) spent

   (D) spending

8. Current liabilities are debts that must be paid _____ a year.

   (A) by

   (B) within

   (C) with

   (D) until

9. A number of automobile _____ agencies are located on the lower level of the airport.

   (A) renting

   (B) rents

   (C) rental

   (D) rented

10. We have been working on the balance sheet _____ two days now.

    (A) since

    (B) for

    (C) in

    (D) until

11. I am not sure how _____ it is from here to the capital.

(A) far

(B) much

(C) long

(D) distance

12. Will you _____ me to your associates?

(A) introduction

(B) introduce

(C) introductory

(D) introducing

13. The unemployment rate has _____ in recent months.

(A) fallen

(B) fell

(C) falling

(D) fall

14. He is convinced that the team from his country _____ the next World Cup.

(A) has won

(B) will have won

(C) will win

(D) would win

15. Job descriptions allow both prospective and current employees _____ what is expected of them.

(A) to know

(B) and know

(C) knowledge of

(D) knowing

16. Obtaining a patent for an invention can be _____ process.

(A) a retracted

(B) a hardened

(C) a lengthened

(D) an extended

17. This dish _____ better if you use fresh herbs and garlic.

(A) will be tasting

(B) tastes

(C) would have tasted

(D) tasted

18. _____ most people in his department, he has a degree in engineering.

(A) Likely

(B) Likewise

(C) Alike

(D) Like

19. It was uncomfortably cold in the boardroom because someone had set the air conditioner _____ high.

(A) such

(B) too

(C) far

(D) much

20. This sports car is equipped with a _____ eight-cylinder engine.

(A) powerful

(B) powering

(C) power

(D) powerfully

21. I do not know _____ he can make enough money by working only ten hours a week.

(A) why

(B) how much

(C) that if

(D) how

22. Prices on the stock exchange have been _____ wildly all week.

(A) vibrating

(B) wavering

(C) intensifying

(D) fluctuating

23. Many _____ entrepreneurs are self-taught in the field of business.

(A) successful

(B) succeed

(C) success

(D) successfully

24. The tour _____ about an hour to complete.

(A) makes

(B) takes

(C) has

(D) spends

25. A buyer's market is a market _____ sellers are so eager to sell that they offer very favorable terms to buyers.

(A) which in

(B) in where

(C) in which

(D) which

26. The water treatment plant _____ by the flood.

(A) damaged

(B) was damaged

(C) damaging

(D) has damaged

27. I first visited New Delhi fifteen years _____.

(A) ago

(B) previous

(C) prior

(D) early

28. When I take a trip, I like to get an early _____.

(A) beginning

(B) start

(C) go

(D) leaving

29. Are you planning to talk to Ms. Petrov on the phone or meet with her _____ person?

(A) on

(B) to

(C) by

(D) in

30. We have been looking for a suitable location for a branch office in Santiago, but we _____ have not found one.

(A) yet

(B) still

(C) anymore

(D) already

Lesson 6 Text Completion

Lesson Outline

Format   Part 6

This part of the TOEIC® test consists of four short readings. These readings may be articles, letters, emails, announcements, or advertisements. They are similar to the passages you will see in Part 7. There are four blanks in each reading that must be filled with the correct word, phrase, or sentence.

Three of the sentences in each passage are incomplete. In these three sentences, the blank indicates that a word or phrase is missing. Four answer choices marked (A), (B), (C), and (D) are given. You must decide which of these four choices produces a complete, grammatical, and logical sentence.

The testing points for incomplete sentences in Part 6 are similar to those in Part 5, except that they occur in short passages instead of in individual sentences. Some of the questions test vocabulary and some test various points of grammar.

Clues to help you choose an answer to complete a sentence are mostly found in the sentence that the blank occurs in. However, at least one item in each passage requires you to look at more than one sentence in order to choose the correct answer. Usually, you will need to look in the previous or following sentence for the clues that you need.

One blank in each reading represents a complete sentence that is missing from the passage. Four sentence choices are given for each blank. To answer this type of item, you must use the context (the sentences that come before or after the blank) to choose a sentence that logically fits in the passage. You must also pay attention to the overall meaning of the passage and to details in other parts of the passage. Therefore, you must read the passage carefully.

Tactics   Part 6

1. Begin by reading the passages. Do not just skim the passage; read it carefully. This may help you answer the Sentence Addition item correctly.

2. Now look at the three incomplete sentences. Try to guess what word or phrase is missing. Then try to find the word or words that you guessed, or a similar expression among the answer choices.

3. The most common testing point is vocabulary. The four answer choices may have similar meanings or completely different definitions. Use the context of the sentence to help you choose the correct answer, and look for any grammar clues that can help you.

4. Another common testing point in Part 6 is word form. The answer choices consist of four forms of the same word. Use the endings of words to determine which choice is correct in the context of the sentence and the passage.

5. Verbs are also a common testing point in Part 6. The answer choices consist of four forms of the same verb. Look for time words and other clues to help you pick the right verb form.

6. Remember: At least one item in each passage requires you to look at more than one sentence to find the answer.

7. Every reading has one Sentence Addition item. You need to use the context of the nearby sentences and ideas throughout the entire passage to answer these items.

8. Never spend too much time working on any one item.

9. As soon as you finish Part 6, go on to Part 7.

Preview Test   Part 6

Directions: Read the passages on the following pages. Four words, phrases, or sentences have been replaced by blanks. Four answer choices are given for each blank. Mark the answer choice — (A), (B), (C), or (D) — that best completes the text.

Questions 1–4 refer to the following article:

Museums and art collectors can now _____ with a new team of detectives: art technicians who find
            1.

microscopic flaws in a masterpiece before they turn into serious damage. Members of Project VASARI (Visual Art System for Archiving and Retrieving Images) in Munich have developed new technology to evaluate some of the world's most famous paintings. This technology uses high-resolution digital imaging taken directly from paintings. This _____ it possible to replace photography as a recording method. The
            2.

digital images are more accurate in terms of color and do not age like standard photographic materials. VASARI technology was first employed after the Louvre Museum lent Leonardo da Vinci's most famous painting, *Mona Lisa*, to another museum. The painting had been packed in a heavily padded, air-conditioned, fireproof crate. _____ it still sustained potentially dangerous cracks while it was being moved
        3.

that were invisible to the naked eye. VASARI technicians were able to detect these flaws so that they could be repaired by art restorers. _____.
       4.

---

1. Ⓐ consult
   Ⓑ define
   Ⓒ instruct
   Ⓓ exchange

2. Ⓐ does
   Ⓑ takes
   Ⓒ has
   Ⓓ makes

3. Ⓐ Because
   Ⓑ However,
   Ⓒ Although
   Ⓓ Therefore,

4. Ⓐ The earliest use of VASARI technology was to take pictures of old paintings that made them look as if they had just been painted.

   Ⓑ Technicians realized that the *Mona Lisa* had suffered invisible damage because the crate itself was damaged.

   Ⓒ Art restorers are able to repair many flaws, but there are some problems that are impossible to fix.

   Ⓓ VASARI technology can also create images of old paintings that approximate the quality of that of the originals when they were new.

Gatewood Scientific

Subject: Congratulations!
Date: Thurs, 4 Nov 20--
From: "Carson, Marina" <Marina.Carson@GatewoodInstruments.com>
To: "Philip Legere" <legere_philip@Preswick.com.au>

Dear Mr. Legere:

Yesterday I got a call from my old friend, David Preswick. He told me about your recent _____ to chief of
5.

the Research and Development Department. Congratulations!

As you may know, while Gatewood Instruments is not currently an active supplier to the R&D
department at Preswick, our firm did have a sizeable contract with your department not many years ago.

_____ .
6.

As we at Gatewood continue to expand our capabilities, I believe we will be able _____ you some new
7.

technologies that you will find very interesting. I hope to have the opportunity of chatting _____ you
8.

soon. I plan to be in Melbourne in December and hope that we can meet while I am there.

Again, congratulations, and I wish you much success in your new position.

Best,

Marina Carson

Marina Carson
Sales Director
Gatewood Scientific Instruments, Inc.

5. (A) promote
   (B) promotion
   (C) promotional
   (D) promoter

6. (A) I guarantee that we can provide the same level
       of service that we did at your old company.
   (B) I hope that now there may be an opportunity
       for us to re-establish a partnership.
   (C) We'll be happy to continue filling your need for
       quality scientific instruments.
   (D) I'm certain that your new position will be both
       challenging and rewarding.

7. (A) to offer
   (B) offers
   (C) by offering
   (D) offer

8. (A) to
   (B) at
   (C) with
   (D) for

Questions 9–12 refer to the following information:

Traditionally, most companies have purchased office equipment _____ with cash or with bank loans.
                                                              9.

However, these days, many companies lease equipment. There are two main types of leases. One type of lease is known as an operating lease. You pay a flat fee, but when the terms of the lease are up, ownership reverts to the lessor. A capital lease, also called a lease-to-own agreement, resembles a home mortgage in that the payments that you make go toward purchasing the equipment, and the equipment is _____ at the end
                                                                                                    10.

of a set period. _____ Is the equipment you require likely to become obsolete soon? _____ lease it. You
                 11.   **12.**

should also lease expensive equipment such as copiers, digital projectors, and communication systems. However, before you decide to lease, remember that, in the long run, leasing generally costs more than buying.

9. Ⓐ neither
 Ⓑ whether
 Ⓒ either
 Ⓓ both

10. Ⓐ yours
 Ⓑ yourself
 Ⓒ you
 Ⓓ your

11. Ⓐ Which type of lease is better for you?
 Ⓑ Where can you get more information about leasing?
 Ⓒ How do you decide whether to lease or to buy?
 Ⓓ What sort of companies should lease?

12. Ⓐ And so,
 Ⓑ If so,
 Ⓒ Therefore,
 Ⓓ Whatever

Because the Canadian province of Prince Edward Island (PEI) is an island, ferries have been an important part of its history. Today, Northumberland Ferries departs about every hour from Caribou in Nova Scotia to Wood Islands on Prince Edward Island, connecting the two towns. You can enjoy a snack, lounge on the deck, and soak up sunshine and sea air. _____. The ferries, however, are vulnerable to weather-related delays, so
13.

plan accordingly. The ferry does not operate from the end of December until early May _____ heavy sea ice.
14.

Confederation Bridge provides year-round access. It links Prince Edward Island to the Canadian mainland, stretching from the town of Borden Carleton, PEI, to Cape Tourmantine, New Brunswick. A 13-kilometer engineering marvel that _____ in the 1990s, the Confederation Bridge is a quick, convenient, and fascinating
15.

way to arrive on the Island, with crossings taking approximately 10 minutes. _____ are collected upon leaving
16.

PEI and are calculated for the round trip, regardless of travelers' initial point of entry. A shuttle service is available for pedestrians and cyclists.

13. (A) The trip is relaxing and picturesque in good weather.
    (B) Stormy weather is not uncommon, and can cause disruptions.
    (C) Northumberland Ferries was established in 1946.
    (D) Passengers pay only on the return trip to Caribou, Nova Scotia.

14. (A) in spite of
    (B) because
    (C) in case of
    (D) on account of

15. (A) built
    (B) was built
    (C) building
    (D) is built

16. (A) Tolls
    (B) Costs
    (C) Prices
    (D) Fares

Testing Points and Skill-Building Exercises

Part 6 tests grammar, usage, and vocabulary and may require an understanding of the main idea and of details in the passage. There is a wide range of possible testing points. However, as in Part 5, there are some testing points that occur again and again.

A. Vocabulary

As in Part 5, vocabulary is the most common testing point. About one-half of all items in Part 6 test vocabulary.

There are two types of vocabulary items in Part 6, depending on the answer choices.
• Words with similar meanings
• Words with unrelated meanings

Some answer choices may involve content words — nouns, verbs, and adjectives — with similar or unrelated meanings.

Sample Item: Words with Similar Meanings

A 13-kilometer engineering marvel, the Confederation Bridge is a quick, convenient, and fascinating way to arrive on the Island, with crossings taking approximately 10 minutes. _____ are collected upon leaving PEI and are calculated for the round trip, regardless of travelers' initial point of entry. A shuttle service is available for pedestrians and cyclists.

● Tolls

(B) Costs

(C) Prices

(D) Fares

> These words all have similar meanings: they are all related to money. Choice (D), *fares,* refers to the money required to travel on planes, buses, trains, etc. The best answer, however, is (A), because it refers to the money required to use certain roads and bridges.

Sample Item: Words with Unrelated Meanings

Museums and art collectors can now _____ with a new team of detectives: art technicians who find microscopic flaws in a masterpiece before they turn into serious damage.

● consult

(B) define

(C) instruct

(D) exchange

> The four answer choices are not close in meaning. Only one—*consult*—fits logically and grammatically into the blank. (To *consult with* is to get advice or information from someone.)

For more information on vocabulary items, see Lesson 5, Section A, pages 114–123.

Exercise 6.1

Focus: Completing passages with vocabulary items.

Directions: Decide which of the four answer choices — (A), (B), (C), or (D) — best completes the sentences in the Part 6 passages below. (Note: On actual tests, there are only **four** blanks in each passage. However, to provide you with more practice, the following passages have more than four blanks.)

When deciding which personal computers to buy for your business, you should consider more than the _____
1.
of memory or the size of the screen. You also need a good warranty policy that guarantees repair of _____
2.
components. Generally, basic warranties are for a fairly short period of time. Some warranties have additional options. For example, several computer retailers offer warranty _____ that include the cost of having a
3.
technician come to your office to help set up the computers or repair them. Many computer companies have toll-free telephone numbers that you can call for help and advice or provide opportunities to talk "live" on the Internet with a representative. Most companies also offer the possibility of _____ the warranty.
4.
For an additional _____, you can lengthen the existing warranty by one or two years.
5.
When most companies are shopping for computers, they don't even consider buying used computer systems because they fear _____ repairs. Their _____ might be unnecessary. Many used computer systems, especially
6.   7.
those bought from retailers or brokers rather than from companies that are going out of business, are sold with warranties as good as those on new machines. For companies that are just _____ up, used computers
8.
could be a good _____.
9.

1. (A) digit
   (B) number
   (C) amount
   (D) part

2. (A) related
   (B) defective
   (C) additional
   (D) instrumental

3. (A) policies
   (B) remarks
   (C) instructions
   (D) references

4. (A) remitting
   (B) contracting
   (C) disputing
   (D) extending

5. (A) rent
   (B) price
   (C) profit
   (D) fee

6. (A) priceless
   (B) high
   (C) costly
   (D) vast

7. (A) warning
   (B) caution
   (C) attention
   (D) advice

8. (A) starting
   (B) beginning
   (C) establishing
   (D) founding

9. (A) advantage
   (B) position
   (C) option
   (D) agreement

Canadian Wood Crafts, Inc.

120 Crown Park
Boulevard Brampton
Ontario L6T 4T7

Diana Labozan, Chief Buyer
Harper Furniture Stores, Ltd., 426 Queen Street
Toronto, Ontario M3M 3L1

Mar. 19, 20--

Dear Ms. Labozan,

Only about two weeks remain until the annual furniture and accessories trade show at the Toronto Exhibition Center!
On April 4–6, you'll have the opportunity to see styles and fabrics that will be _____ furniture fashion news
                                                                                                        10.
during the _____ year. I know you'll be _____ by our gorgeous new designs for our wood, metal, and acrylic
                    11.   12.
chairs, beds, entertainment units, and bookcases. You'll also enjoy running your fingers over the thirty new
fabrics we will have on _____.
                                      13.
When you come by our booth (#1142), be sure to ask for our special full-colour catalogue I've set aside for you.
This catalogue is a souvenir edition, _____ our twenty-five years of designing and building fine furniture. It also
                                                    14.
features a historical _____ of the Canadian furniture industry. I'll be there each day between 10 a.m. and
                              15.
4 p.m. It will be a pleasure to show you our new products personally.

Regards,

Brian Nickerson

Brian Nickerson
CEO, Canadian Wood Crafts

10. (A) making
    (B) getting
    (C) doing
    (D) having

11. (A) future
    (B) turning
    (C) upcoming
    (D) important

12. (A) relaxed
    (B) impressed
    (C) invested
    (D) distracted

13. (A) showing
    (B) demonstration
    (C) revelation
    (D) display

14. (A) memorizing
    (B) celebrating
    (C) experiencing
    (D) concentrating

15. (A) overview
    (B) sight
    (C) outlook
    (D) turn over

A press release is an effective public relations tool that _____ your company free publicity and advertising. It

16.

usually consists of a page or two of newsworthy material (information that is of interest to readers or viewers) _____ any event that you want to publicize. The subject of your article may be the introduction of new

17.

products or services, the promotion or addition of a key employee, your firm's relocation to a new site, or details about an upcoming seminar. However, newsworthiness is only one _____ of a successful press release.

18.

Busy newspaper editors often want to publish your press release exactly as received, so your article must be well written. No matter how interesting the subject, a poorly written press release will probably be _____. Make points in a clear and logical manner, and _____ in mind that _____ repels an editor more than poor

19.   20.   21.

spelling and grammar.

16. (A) confirms
    (B) entails
    (C) reflects
    (D) affords

17. (A) remarking
    (B) announcing
    (C) telling
    (D) speaking

18. (A) grade
    (B) point
    (C) degree
    (D) aspect

19. (A) abandoned
    (B) discarded
    (C) disappeared
    (D) exported

20. (A) keep
    (B) stay
    (C) hold
    (D) remain

21. (A) something
    (B) anything
    (C) nothing
    (D) everything

B. Word Forms and Verbs

Word-Form Items

The answer choices for word-form items consist of four forms of the same base word. Usually the four words have four different suffixes (*beautiful, beautifully, beauty,* and *beautify,* for example). Sometimes one answer choice will be a noun, one a verb, one an adjective, and one an adverb. Sometimes there may be two forms of a noun (as in the Sample Item) or two forms of a verb. To answer these questions correctly, you need to decide what form of the word correctly completes the sentence.

Yesterday I got a call from my old friend, David Preswick. He told me about your recent _____ to chief of the Research and Development Department. Congratulations!

- (A) promote
- ● promotion
- (C) promotional
- (D) promoter

All of the answer choices are forms of the word *promote*. After the phrase *He told me about*, a noun is needed, so *promotion* is the correct choice. (*Promoter* is also a noun, but it is a person who promotes.)

For more information on word forms, see Lesson 5, Section B, pages 123–127.

Verb Items

The answer choices for verb items consist of four forms of the same verb. Choose the correct form of the verb by looking at clues in the sentence or other sentences in the passage. These clues may be auxiliary verbs, time words, or the main verbs in other sentences.

Sample Item: Verbs

A 13-kilometer engineering marvel that _____ in the 1990s, the Confederation Bridge is a quick, convenient, and fascinating way to arrive on the Island, with crossings taking approximately 10 minutes.

- (A) built
- ● was built
- (C) building
- (D) is built

Choice (A) is incorrect because a passive verb is needed. (Someone built the bridge; the bridge *was built*.) Choice (C) is incorrect; an *–ing* form of the verb with no auxiliaries can never be the main verb of a sentence or clause. Choice (D) is a passive verb, but the time phrase *in the 1990s* indicates that a past tense verb is needed in this sentence. Choice (B) is the correct past passive verb.

For more information on verb items, see Lesson 5, Section C, pages 128–132.

Exercise 6.2

Focus: Completing passages with word-form and verb items.

Directions: Decide which of the four answer choices — (A), (B), (C), or (D) — best completes each sentence in the Part 6 passages below. (Note: On actual tests, there are only **four** blanks in each passage. However, to provide you with more practice, the following passages have more than four blanks.)

The Caribbean Single Market and Economy (CSME) _____ the free flow of labor, goods, services, and _____
                                    1.   **2.**

among participating Caribbean Community (CARICOM) member nations. The _____ of this single market
                                                            3.

means that legal and _____ restrictions affecting trade, labor, and technology within the CARICOM region
                         4.

may become a thing of the past. One of the greatest advantages of the agreement is that it will encourage regional trade. Furthermore, it _____ CARICOM nations to negotiate as a single entity. This will provide them
                               5.

with a better opportunity to influence policies concerning global trade. Perhaps the region may soon _____ a
                                                                                       6.

force in world trade negotiations. The biggest question about the agreement is whether its existing businesses and workforce can _____ the increased competition when more companies that are successful _____ enter
                                       7.   **8.**

the local market.

---

1. (A) involves
(B) involving
(C) involve
(D) involved

2. (A) capital
(B) capitalize
(C) capitalist
(D) capitalization

3. (A) emerge
(B) emergent
(C) emergence
(D) emerged

4. (A) administration
(B) administrator
(C) administrative
(D) administrate

5. (A) was allowed
(B) allowed
(C) allow
(D) will allow

6. (A) become
(B) became
(C) becoming
(D) becomes

7. (A) survive
(B) survivor
(C) survival
(D) surviving

8. (A) international
(B) internationalize
(C) internationally
(D) internationalism

Questions 9–15 refer to the following article:

Several years ago, three Purdue University students entered a contest which was sponsored by the Indiana Soybean Council to develop new uses for soybeans. They molded oil from the beans into crayons. The council _____ these prototypes to a company in Florida that makes crayons. At that time, all crayons _____ from
9.   **10.**
petroleum-based paraffin wax. "Our director of marketing saw the potential for an environmentally _____
                                                                                                                              11.
crayon," said corporate representative Rick Joyce. After spending one year and $2 million to make the bean-based crayon firmer and less _____ than the prototype, the company also found that the new crayon made a
                                        12.
smoother, more solid line on paper than its petroleum-based _____ and was less prone to flaking. "We _____
                                                                                 13.   **14.**
up with a crayon that is not only good for the environment but also a better product," Joyce said. "This could
_____ increase our market share."
15.

9. (A) takes
   (B) has taken
   (C) took
   (D) had taken

10. (A) were making
    (B) were made
    (C) made
    (D) have been made

11. (A) friendship
    (B) friend
    (C) friendly
    (D) friended

12. (A) breaking
    (B) unbreakable
    (C) unbroken
    (D) breakable

13. (A) competitive
    (B) competitively
    (C) compete
    (D) competitor

14. (A) wound
    (B) winding
    (C) were wound
    (D) wind

15. (A) significance
    (B) significantly
    (C) significant
    (D) signify

Atlas Cleaning Solutions

Date: Mon, 14 May 20--
From: "Jennifer Sagrilla" <JenSagrilla@AtlasSolutions.com>
To: "Stewart Donaldson" <S_Donaldson@MastersonPropMgmnt.com>
Subject: Appointment to finalize cleaning contract

Hello Mr. Donaldson:

I want to let you know how much I appreciate your letting me meet with you and your associates on Monday. I _____ you have had time to look over our proposal to provide comprehensive cleaning services for the
16.
Linslade Office Complex that I _____ you on Monday. As I mentioned when we _____, we will take extra care
17. **18.**
to ensure that your office suites receive the finest services possible. Our team of supervisors _____ evaluate
19.
the products and techniques that we use and _____ the work done by our cleaning staff. What's more, they will
20.
check with your office tenants on a bi-weekly basis to make sure that the work is being done to their _____.
21.
Please feel free to check with anyone on the list of references that I provided you with. I am _____ that all our
22.
corporate clients are pleased with our work. I hope that I've convinced you that we have the talent and _____
23.
to vacuum, mop, wax, dust, and buff your complex cleaner than any other firm. I'd like to stop by with a contract
sometime later this week, if possible, so that we can start brightening the office environment at the Linslade Office
Complex on the first of next month. I am _____ forward to hearing from you soon!
24.

Best regards,
Jennifer Sagrilla

General Manager
Atlas Cleaning Solutions

16. (A) will hope
(B) hope
(C) hoped
(D) have hoped

17. (A) have brought
(B) brought
(C) am bringing
(D) will bring

18. (A) met
(B) meeting
(C) meet
(D) were met

19. (A) constant
(B) constancy
(C) constantly
(D) constants

20. (A) inspectors
(B) inspect
(C) inspection
(D) inspected

21. (A) satisfaction
(B) satisfactorily
(C) satisfied
(D) satisfactory

22. (A) certain
(B) certainty
(C) certainly
(D) ascertained

23. (A) enthusiastic
(B) enthused
(C) enthusiasm
(D) enthusiastically

24. (A) looking
(B) look
(C) looked
(D) to look

C. Sentence Addition

When the TOEIC® test was revised in 2016, a new type of Part 6 item was added: Sentence Addition. Rather than add a word or phrase to an incomplete sentence, you must fill a blank with one of four possible complete sentences — (A), (B), (C), or (D) — to complete the passage. Sometimes you can decide which of the four sentences is best by examining the sentence that comes just before or after the missing sentence.

Sample Item 1: Sentence Addition

Because the Canadian province of Prince Edward Island (PEI) is an island, ferries have been an important part of its history. Today, Northumberland Ferries departs about every hour from Caribou in Nova Scotia to Wood Islands on Prince Edward Island, connecting the two towns. You can enjoy a snack, lounge on the deck, and soak up sunshine and sea air. _____. The ferries, however, are vulnerable to weather-related delays, so plan accordingly.

- ● The trip is relaxing and picturesque in good weather.
- (B) Stormy weather is not uncommon, and can cause disruptions.
- (C) Northumberland Ferries was established in 1946.
- (D) Passengers pay only on the return trip to Caribou, Nova Scotia.

The sentence before the blank mentions activities that would be enjoyable in good weather (*lounging on the deck* and *soaking up sunshine and sea air*). The sentence following the blank talks about problems that can be caused by bad weather (*weather-related delays*). The word *however* in this sentence indicates a contrast with the previous sentence. Choice (A) expands on the idea in the previous sentence by describing a trip in good weather, and is in contrast with the idea in the following sentence. It is therefore the best answer. Choice (B) describes bad weather, and is not in contrast to the following sentence. Choices (C) and (D) are not about the weather at all, and would be out of place in this part of the passage.

Sometimes, you must use an idea that appears in another part of the passage to choose the best answer. This means that you must read the passage carefully in order to pick the best answer.

Sample Item 2: Sentence Addition

Museums and art collectors can now _____ with a new team of detectives: art technicians who find microscopic flaws in a masterpiece before they turn into serious damage. Members of Project VASARI (Visual Art System for Archiving and Retrieving Images) in Munich have developed new technology to evaluate some of the world's most famous paintings. This technology uses high-resolution digital imaging taken directly from paintings. This _____ it possible to replace photography as a recording method. The digital images are more accurate in terms of color and do not age like standard photographic materials. VASARI technology was first employed after the Louvre Museum lent Leonardo da Vinci's most famous painting, *Mona Lisa*, to another museum. The painting had been packed in a heavily padded, air-conditioned, fireproof crate. _____ it still sustained potentially dangerous cracks while it was being moved that were invisible to the naked eye. VASARI technicians were able to detect these flaws so that they could be repaired by art restorers. _____.

4.

4. (A) The earliest use of VASARI technology was to take pictures of old paintings that made them look as if they had just been painted.

(B) Technicians realized that the *Mona Lisa* had suffered invisible damage because the crate itself was damaged.

(C) Art restorers are able to repair many flaws, but there are some problems that are impossible to fix.

(●) VASARI technology can also create images of old paintings that approximate the quality of that of the originals when they were new.

> Choice (A) might seem to be a good answer if you have not read the passage carefully. But according to an earlier sentence, making old paintings look new was NOT the earliest use of the VASARI technology. "VASARI technology was first employed after the Louvre Museum lent Leonardo da Vinci's most famous painting, *Mona Lisa,* to another museum." Therefore, choice (D) is the best choice.

Exercise   6.3

Focus: Completing passages with sentences.

Directions: Decide which of the four sentences—(A), (B), (C), or (D)—best completes each short passage.

Question 1 refers to the following information:

Many of the laws and principles of statistics can be applied to business. An example of this is the Law of Large Numbers, which is especially important in the insurance industry. Imagine that an insurance company provides fire insurance for ten houses for one year. The company has no accurate way to predict how many of these ten houses will burn down in one year. Therefore, the company does not know how much to charge the homeowners for fire insurance. Now suppose that a company insures 100,000 homes for ten years. Over the years, this insurance company learns that, on average, 50 houses a year burn down. Now, thanks to the Law of Large Numbers, the insurance company knows how much to charge its customers. _____.

1.

1. (A) This statistic justifies the insurance company's decision to raise its home insurance rates.
(B) The more statistics about risks are available, the more accurate predictions about risks will be.
(C) Of course, in some years, fewer houses will burn down, and in some years more will burn down.
(D) The law indicates that a large insurance company faces more risk than a smaller insurance company.

Question 2 refers to the following article:

Aluminum can packaging is inexpensive. The cans themselves are cheap, they are easy to recycle, and they are durable and airtight. Most importantly, they can be filled very rapidly. The aluminum industry produces at least 125 billion cans a year, but there has not been an increase in production for three years. _____. The primary reason
                                                                                                    2.
for this has been consumers' positive response to packaging with innovative shapes and features. Manufacturers of some well-known beverages are featuring plastic bottles with interesting shapes that attract the attention of shoppers. Some smaller drink manufacturers have switched to glass packaging because its more exclusive look and feel appeals to their upscale customers. In response to the growing competition, aluminum can manufacturers are working on new features and shapes as well as exploring international markets.

---

2. Ⓐ Despite the advantages of aluminum cans, manufacturers are facing increased competition from the glass and plastic container industries.
　　Ⓑ This year, however, aluminum can manufacturers are expecting to increase their share of the market.
　　Ⓒ In fact, all container manufacturers, including those that produce plastic and glass containers, have seen no increase in sales.
　　Ⓓ Not only are there advantages for manufacturers of aluminum cans, there are also many positive aspects for consumers.

Question 3 refers to the following advertisement:

Virtual PO Box gives you a permanent street address at which to receive postal mail. This is important as many companies will not send mail to a conventional Post Office box. _____. New incoming mail is scanned and
                                                                                    3.
immediately available the same day it arrives. You can then decide whether to have the mail opened and the contents scanned by us, forwarded to you by mail, or thrown away. All mail content scanning requests are processed within 6 business hours. Managing your postal mail online with Virtual PO Box is so easy, you'll never want to handle mail the traditional way again.

---

3. Ⓐ We pick up your mail from the Post Office and send it on to you immediately.
　　Ⓑ We respect your privacy and would never read any of your personal mail.
　　Ⓒ We scan the unopened envelopes and send the scans in emails so you can see your mail online.
　　Ⓓ We sort your mail and keep only letters and packages which are important to you.

Question 4 refers to the following article:

African nations introduced Europe to the pleasures of tropical produce 40 years ago. But Southeast Asian, Caribbean, Central American, and South American countries have almost supplanted African fruit exporters in recent years. _____. They also need to build better transportation systems and more storage facilities and increase

4.

the variety of fruits and vegetables they can supply.

4. (A) The Netherlands, the United Kingdom, and Belgium are the leading direct importers of fresh fruit and vegetables from developing countries.

(B) To regain their share of the expanding European market, African exporters will have to improve their marketing research.

(C) Meanwhile, product innovations will result in fresher taste and will improve customer experience.

(D) Some of the most popular fruit imports include mangoes, figs, cherries, pineapples, plums, and melons, while popular vegetables include avocados, peppers, and snow peas.

Question 5 refers to the following article:

Sales at department stores have been falling since the early 2000s. Government figures show that they hit their peak in January 2001, when monthly sales came to $19.9 billion. In June of this year, that figure had dropped to $13.2 billion. Most big chains have had to close stores, sometimes hundreds of stores. With shoppers increasingly buying online or from discount stores, department stores are trying to rethink their business to keep up with consumers who want a different experience in stores from that which they find online or on their phones. _____.

5.

"It's all about creating an experience in the store," said one department store executive. "People will shop here. They'll eat here. They'll meet their friends here."

5. (A) That includes hiring more attentive sales staff and bringing in new types of services and merchandise.

(B) This is because buying goods online or by phone is simply more convenient and, in many instances, more economical.

(C) Many consumers prefer shopping in department stores because they can see what they are buying and can try on clothing before making a purchase.

(D) More and more, department stores have depended on big discounts to attract shoppers — a move that hurts profits.

D. Other Part 6 Testing Points

Here are some other items that will be tested in Part 6:

- Prepositions
- Connecting words
- Gerunds, infinitives, and simple forms
- Pronouns

Prepositions

Some answer choices consist of four prepositions. Look for clues in the passage to help you find the answer. The preposition may be paired with a noun, an adjective/participle, or with a verb. For example:

appointment with   afraid of   surprised by   chat with

The choice of preposition might also depend on the prepositional object (i.e. the noun that follows the preposition). For example:

in June   on Wednesday   by chance   since 2014

Sample Item: Prepositions

I hope to have the opportunity of chatting _____ you soon. I plan to be in Melbourne in December and hope that we can meet while I am there.

A) to

B) at

● with

D) for

> The verb *chat* (meaning "talk informally") takes the preposition *with*.

For more information on prepositions, see Lesson 5, Section E, pages 136–145.

Connecting Words

Many types of connecting words are tested in Part 6 items.

Coordinate conjunctions: *and, or, but, nor, so*
Correlative conjunctions: *both ... and, not only ... but also, either ... or, neither ... nor*
Noun-clause markers: *that, if/whether, what, when, why, how much,* etc.
Adjective-clause markers: *who, whose, whom, that, which, when, where*
Adverb-clause markers: *because, since, if, when, once, although, even though, unless, as, while,* etc.
Prepositional expressions (used with nouns): *despite, in spite of, because of, due to,* etc.
Conjunctive adverbs: These words are used to join sentences and clauses. The use of common conjunctive adverbs is explained in the following chart.

Conjunctive Adverb	Use	Example
therefore	cause/effect	George lost his watch. *Therefore,* he is often late.
nevertheless	contrast/opposition	Betina was not feeling well. *Nevertheless*, she went to work.
however	contrast	Britain is considered an island. *However*, Australia is considered a continent.
likewise	similarity	Some words in French come from English. *Likewise*, some words in English come from French.
Furthermore, moreover	addition	Mr. O'Dell is a successful engineer. *Furthermore*, he owns his own business. I found that movie boring. *Moreover*, I thought it was far too long.

In order to choose the correct conjunctive adverb, you will generally have to look at the sentence BEFORE the one with the blank and understand the relationship between them.

Sample Items: Connecting Words

The painting had been packed in a heavily padded, air-conditioned, fireproof crate. _____ it still sustained potentially dangerous cracks while it was being moved that were invisible to the naked eye.

(A) Because

● However,

(C) Although

(D) Therefore,

There is a contrast between the information in the two sentences. The painting was packed in a safe container, but it was damaged. The only one of the four choices that can show contrast between two sentences is choice (B). You cannot answer this item unless you look at the previous sentence.

Traditionally, most companies have purchased office equipment _____ with cash or with bank loans.

(A) neither

(B) whether

● either

(D) both

The correlative conjunction *either* is correctly paired with *or. Whether* is also used with *or* in some sentences ("I don't know whether to stay or to leave."), but it doesn't make sense in this sentence.

For more information on connecting words, see Lesson 5, Section F, pages 145–155.

Gerunds, Infinitives, and Simple Forms

The answer for this type of problem is a gerund (*doing, working, sleeping*), an infinitive (*to do, to work, to sleep*), or a simple form (*do, work, sleep*). Other verb forms may also be used as distractors.

Sample Item: Gerunds, Infinitives, and Simple Forms

As we at Gatewood continue to expand our capabilities, I believe we will be able _____ you some new technologies that you will find very interesting.

●   to offer

(B)   offers

(C)   by offering

(D)   offer

> With the word *able*, the infinitive *to offer* is needed, so choice (A) is correct.

For more information on gerunds, infinitives, and simple forms, see Lesson 5, Section G, pages 156–160.

Pronouns

The four answer choices for this type of problem may be four forms of one pronoun (*he, his, him, himself*) or they may be the same form of four different pronouns (*he, you, they, we*) or a combination of both of these (*it, itself, them, themselves*). Often, to find the correct answer for this type of problem, you must look in earlier sentences.

Sample Item: Pronouns

A capital lease, also called a lease-to-own agreement, resembles a home mortgage in that the payments that you make go toward purchasing the equipment, and the equipment is _____ at the end of a set period.

●   yours

(B)   yourself

(C)   you

(D)   your

> The possessive pronoun *yours* is correct here. The pronoun means "your equipment." (The word *your* also shows possession, but it must be used before a noun.)

For more information on pronouns, see Lesson 5, Section D, pages 133–136.

Exercise   6.4

Focus: Completing passages involving prepositions, connecting words, gerunds/infinitives/simple forms, and pronouns.

Directions: Decide which of the four answer choices — (A), (B), (C), or (D) — best completes the sentences in the reading passages. (Note: On actual tests, there are only **four** blanks in each passage. However, to provide you with more practice, the following passages have more than four blanks.)

Questions 1–13 refer to the following letter:

Computer Elements, Inc.
16 Grange Road London E14 7PL

B.P. Misuta
Director, IT Department
ITPI Media, Ltd.
15 Canada Square
London
E14 5AG

Dear Mr. Misuta,

_____ behalf of our interview team, I want _____ our appreciation for your participation _____ our market
1. **2.** **3.**
research effort. Your input was invaluable and gave us important information that will let us _____ better
4.
programs and products for our customers. And in a way, you've made it a little easier for yourself as well because,
_____ the future, we know what you expect from _____! The information _____ you provided will have a direct impact
5. **6.** **7.**
_____ a number of specific design decisions involving products we will be releasing in the next year _____ two. _____,
8. **9.** **10.**
it will allow us _____ our portfolio of products with our customers' wants and needs in mind. Again, thanks to you and
11.
to all the members of _____ organization _____ your ideas and opinions!
12. **13.**

Best regards,

Norma J. Baudo
Marketing Director
Computer Elements, Inc.

1. (A) In
   (B) On
   (C) For
   (D) By
2. (A) to convey
   (B) conveying
   (C) to be conveyed
   (D) convey
3. (A) on
   (B) from
   (C) with
   (D) in
4. (A) design
   (B) designing
   (C) to design
   (D) designed
5. (A) by
   (B) on
   (C) in
   (D) until

6. (A) us
   (B) our
   (C) ours
   (D) ourselves
7. (A) whom
   (B) that
   (C) about
   (D) with
8. (A) of
   (B) on
   (C) at
   (D) in
9. (A) so
   (B) and
   (C) or
   (D) although

10. (A) Moreover
    (B) However
    (C) Nevertheless
    (D) Although
11. (A) expansion
    (B) by expanding
    (C) expand
    (D) to expand
12. (A) you
    (B) yours
    (C) your
    (D) yourselves
13. (A) share
    (B) to share
    (C) for sharing
    (D) shared

Questions 14–21 refer to the following article:

By _____ a few large pistons _____ many small ones, an Australian inventor claims to have built an engine
     14.   **15.**
that minimizes the wear and tear _____ arises from the friction and vibration in conventional engines. The new
                              16.
design ensures that fuel is completely burned. _____ should produce virtually no toxic exhaust, _____can run
                                        17.   **18.**
on low-grade fuels such as coconut oil. The "split-cycle engine," as it is known, will next be tested _____
                                                                                          19.
independent researchers at several universities. The inventor, Rich Mayne, and his colleagues hope that a
leading car company will consider _____ the engine in a prototype "car of the future" that is being developed
                              20.
_____ the support of the Australian government.
 21.

14. (A) replacing
     (B) replaced
     (C) to replace
     (D) replaces

15. (A) by
     (B) with
     (C) to
     (D) as

16. (A) they
     (B) that
     (C) those
     (D) who

17. (A) They
     (B) There
     (C) He
     (D) It

18. (A) moreover
     (B) or
     (C) and
     (D) therefore

19. (A) by
     (B) with
     (C) from
     (D) at

20. (A) to use
     (B) using
     (C) it will use
     (D) used

21. (A) from
     (B) by
     (C) of
     (D) with

Arrowhead

To: "Michael Timmons" <TimmonsM@D&BAssociates.com>
Subject: Computer desks
From: "Valerie Bahta" <ValBahta@Arrowhead.com>
Date: Tuesday 6 June 20--

Dear Mr. Timmons,

I enjoyed _____ with you yesterday. After seeing your office space, I am certain _____ Arrowhead Office
      22.   **23.**
Products can furnish you _____ the type of computer desks that will fit comfortably into your offices and will
               24.
help _____ shoulder and back fatigue among your employees. As I mentioned, our policy is _____
   25.   **26.**
clients a discount of 20% on orders totaling $500 or more. You mentioned that you were interested _____
                                                              27.
purchasing six desks, which cost $500 each. The bill would come to $3,000. At 20% off, your price would be
$2,400. The desks you picked out are our most popular model. We have enough in stock to fill your requirements
_____ present, but I cannot guarantee the price _____ we run out and must reorder. Each time we receive
28.   **29.**
a new shipment, costs seem to jump. _____, I strongly urge you _____ your order as soon as possible.
                              30.   **31.**

Sincerely,
V. Bahta
Sales Manager
Arrowhead Office Products

22.
(A) meet
(B) to meet
(C) having met
(D) meeting

23.
(A) as
(B) that
(C) if
(D) so

24.
(A) with
(B) for
(C) to
(D) by

25.
(A) eliminating
(B) that eliminates
(C) eliminate
(D) has eliminated

26.
(A) give
(B) given
(C) to give
(D) gave

27.
(A) on
(B) in
(C) for
(D) to

28.
(A) in
(B) at
(C) on
(D) by

29.
(A) that
(B) since
(C) although
(D) if

30.
(A) Therefore
(B) Because
(C) However
(D) Whenever

31.
(A) to place
(B) place
(C) placing
(D) having placed

Directions: Read the passages on the following pages. A word, phrase, or sentence has been replaced by a blank in some of the sentences. Four answer choices are given. Mark the answer choice — (A), (B), (C), or (D) — that best completes the text.

Questions 1–4 refer to the following advertisement:

Choose ReefCo, International
For the Most Important Perishable of All!

Choose the wrong international refrigerated transport company and you're gambling with more than your valuable shipment of meat, fruit, or other perishables. _____. For superior and dependable transport service, the world
1.

turns to **ReefCo, International.** With a _____ expanded fleet of larger ships and new state-of-the-art refrigerated
2.

containers, **ReefCo, International** can handle the most demanding shipping challenges. _____, **ReefCo,**
3.

International sets the world standard for customer service. So . . . don't trust your good name to just _____.
4.

Ship with the company that you can count on.

Ship with **ReefCo, International**
— and ship with confidence

1. (A) Each vessel in our fleet is designed specifically for the type of cargo that it will be transporting.
   (B) Our ships are designed to make loading and unloading efficient while increasing cargo capacity.
   (C) And because your cargo is perishable, you can be sure our ships are among the fastest cargo ships in the world.
   (D) You're also putting your most valuable perishable of all at jeopardy: your reputation.

2. (A) lately
   (B) shortly
   (C) recently
   (D) nearly

3. (A) Furthermore
   (B) Although
   (C) Nevertheless
   (D) However

4. (A) everything
   (B) someone
   (C) something
   (D) anyone

Skyler Travel

To: Dhat721@earthweb.com

Subject: Skyler Travel Password

From: "Skyler Support Team" <no_reply@skyler.net>

Date: 19 Sept 20--

Dear User Dhat 721,

You have _____ a password reminder for your Skyler Travel account. As it is impossible for us to _____ your
     5.   **6.**

original password, we have generated a new one. Your new password is Ruk77epu. Please use this password to

log into Skyler next time. _____ you log in, you can change your password if you wish.
                           7.

_____. Please do not reply.
   8.

Best wishes,

Skyler Support Team

5. (A) asked
   (B) requested
   (C) inquired
   (D) questioned

6. (A) retire
   (B) retreat
   (C) retract
   (D) retrieve

7. (A) Once
   (B) Since
   (C) But
   (D) Afterwards

8. (A) The current password for your account is D721hat.
   (B) Note that this is an automatically generated email.
   (C) For all your travel needs, contact Skyler Travel.
   (D) Thank you again for contacting Skyler Travel.

Questions 9–12 refer to the following article:

Employment expert Teena Rose has some _____ for job-seekers: "Sell, don't tell." "Most candidates for jobs
    9.
basically just talk about their experience and background. They give a very one-dimensional, flat description of what
they do best instead of selling themselves to prospective employers by emphasizing the value they could bring to the
company," said Rose. "When your résumé is read next to those of other candidates with basically the same skills, you
need something to make yours _____ out. Simply describing your skills and accomplishments in a different way
    10.
will make an immeasurable impact on prospective employers," she said. Selling yourself is very different from merely
talking about how good you are, according to Rose. "Instead of saying that you're good at marketing, write on your résumé
or explain in the interview that your past experience shows that you are good at marketing, and back up this claim with
figures. That's a good example of selling _____," she explains. Why? _____.
            11.   12.

9. (A) advisor
   (B) advise
   (C) advisory
   (D) advice

10. (A) stand
    (B) standing
    (C) that stands
    (D) to stand

11. (A) itself
    (B) yourself
    (C) themselves
    (D) yourselves

12. (A) Because marketing involves not only selling products; it also involves selling yourself.
    (B) Because a strong résumé and good interviewing techniques are the best way to get the job you want.
    (C) Because most employers believe that your past experience is indicative of your future performance.
    (D) Because marketing is a skill that is best learned through experience rather than through discussion.

What if you went to work one day and your personal office was gone? That could happen if a new trend in business catches on. It's called *hoteling,* and here is how it works. Before you go into your office, you call ahead to someone _____ the "concierge" and make a reservation. When you arrive, you find all your personal belongings have

13.

been taken out of a locker and put at a workstation. It might be any workstation in the company's office. Only your phone extension remains the same. The space is _____ as long as you need it, but when you travel, your

14.

things are boxed and put away in a locker _____ you return. In large cities such as London, New York, or

15.

Hong Kong, office space is very expensive, and when those offices sit empty, the rent is wasted. _____. But for

16.

management consultants, for example, who may spend up to 90% of their time away from their home office, it may be an ideal situation.

13. (A) acknowledged
    (B) regarded
    (C) designated
    (D) figured

14. (A) yours
    (B) you
    (C) yourselves
    (D) your

15. (A) since
    (B) along
    (C) until
    (D) once

16. (A) Because it is unlikely that anyone will ever consider hoteling as desirable as having a permanent office.
    (B) Sometimes employees will make reservations just in case they need office space.
    (C) Even proponents of this scheme admit that it won't work for every business or for every employee.
    (D) Nevertheless, a permanent office represents stability, a way to express individuality, and a symbol of rank.

Lesson 7

Reading Comprehension

Lesson Outline

Format — Part 7

Part 7 is the longest part of the TOEIC® test. It's also the last part, so you may be getting tired. However, you need to stay focused on the test for a little while longer. (Of course, if you want, you may work on Part 7 before you work on Part 5 and Part 6.)

Part 7 consists of 7–10 single reading passages with a total of 29 questions. There are also two Paired Readings (each consisting of two related readings) with a total of 10 questions, and three Three-Part Readings with a total of 15 questions. There are four possible answer choices for each of the 54 questions. You must pick the correct answers based on information in the passages and then mark the answers on your answer sheet.

The Reading Passages

Most of the single reading passages are fairly short. Some are only three or four sentences in length. However, there are some longer passages. The longest passages may have up to 300 words. The passages deal with a wide variety of subject areas: business, travel, trade, entertainment, technology, and so on.

Most of the passages can be classified as one of these six types:

1. **Articles** similar to those in newspapers and magazines
2. **Business correspondence**, including letters, emails, and memos
3. **Advertisements** similar to those in newspapers and magazines
4. **Announcements and notices** about upcoming events, policies, performances, and so on
5. **Non-prose readings**, such as charts, schedules, business forms, graphs, maps, and so on
6. **Message chains**, which are a series of text messages or an Internet discussion

The Paired Readings and the Three-Part Readings usually consist of two or three different types of passages. For example, you may see a business form and an email, or an article, a letter, and an email.

There are two to five questions for each single reading passage, and there are five questions for each Paired and Three-Part Reading. There are six main types of questions asked:

1. **Overview questions**
2. **Detail questions**
3. **Vocabulary questions**
4. **Inference questions**
5. **Intention questions**
6. **Sentence addition questions**

- **Overview questions** occur after most of the passages. To answer overview questions correctly, you need a "global" (overall) understanding of the passage. The most common overview question asks about the purpose or the main topic of the passage:

  What does this article mainly discuss?
  What is the purpose of this letter?
  Why was this notice written?

  Other overview questions ask about the writer of the passage, the readers of the passage, or the place of publication:

  In what business is the writer of the passage?
  What is the author's opinion of _____ ?
  Who would be most interested in the information in this announcement?
  For whom is this advertisement intended?
  Where was this article probably published?

- **Detail questions**, the most common type of Part 7 question, ask about specific points in the passage. You will usually have to scan the passage to find and identify the information. Generally, the answer and the information in the passage do not look the same. For example, a sentence in a passage may read "This process is not nearly as simple as it once was." The correct answer may be "The procedure is now far more complex." Some typical detail questions are:

  What is indicated about _____?
  What is true about _____?
  Where will the sales meeting be held?
  What must _____ do in order to _____?
  What is reported about _____?
  When will the interview take place?

  Some detail questions are **negative questions**. These always include the word NOT, which is printed in UPPERCASE (capital) letters:

  Based on the information in the passage, which of the following is NOT true?

  Negative questions usually take longer to answer than other detail questions.

- **Vocabulary questions** ask about the meaning of a word or phrase in the reading passage. You can use the context (other words in the passage) to help you decide which one of the four answer choices is closest in meaning to the word in the passage. This is what vocabulary items look like:

  Which of the following is closest in meaning to the word _____ in paragraph 2, line 4?
  The word _____ in paragraph 2, line 4 is closest in meaning to

  You will see vocabulary questions only when there are five questions after a reading.

- A few questions in Part 7 are **inference questions**. The answers to these questions are not directly stated in the passage. Instead, you must draw a conclusion using the information that is given. Some typical inference questions are:

  Which of these statements is probably true?
  Which of the following can be inferred from this notice?
  What will _____ probably do next?

  There may also be **negative inference questions**:

  What is NOT suggested about _____?

- **Intention questions** ask what the author or someone else means by using a certain phrase in the reading:

    At 10:30 A.M., what does Mr. _____ mean when he writes, "_____"?

    You will generally see intention questions only after Message Chain readings. For more about intention questions, see Section F of this chapter.

- **Sentence addition questions** ask where a sentence that is NOT in the original passage should be added:

    In which of the positions marked [1], [2], [3], and [4] does the following sentence best belong?
    "_____."

Answer Choices

All are believable answers to the questions. Incorrect choices often contain information that is presented somewhere in the passage but does not correctly answer the question.

A Note About Vocabulary

Most of the vocabulary in the passages consists of relatively common English words and phrases, but there will probably be expressions that you do not know. However, you can understand most of a reading and answer most of the questions even if you don't know the meaning of all the words. Also, you can guess the meaning of many unfamiliar words in the passages through context. In other words, you can use the familiar words in the sentence to get an idea of what an unfamiliar word in the same sentence means.

Tactics Part 7

1. First, look at the passage quickly to get an idea of what it is about.

2. Next, read the questions about the passage. You should not read the answer choices at this time. Try to keep these questions in the back of your mind as you read the passage.

3. Read the passage. Try to read quickly, but read every word; don't just skim the passage. Look for answers to the questions that you read.

4. Answer the questions. For detail and inference questions, you will probably have to refer back to the passage. You can use the eraser-end of your pencil as a pointer to focus your attention as you look for the information needed to answer the question.

5. In the Multiple Readings section, remember that you must look at more than one reading to find the answer for at least one of the questions.

6. If you are unsure of the answer, eliminate answer choices that are clearly wrong, and then guess.

7. Don't spend too much time on any item. If you find a question or even an entire passage confusing, guess at the answer or answers and come back to these items later if you have time.

8. If you have not answered all the questions and only a few minutes are left, read the remaining questions without reading the passages, and choose the answers that seem most logical.

Preview Test Part 7

Directions: Questions in this part of the test are based on a wide range of reading materials, including articles, letters, advertisements, and notices. After reading the passage, decide which of the four choices — (A), (B), (C), or (D) — best answers the question and mark your answer. All answers should be based on what is stated in or on what can be inferred from the readings.

Look at the example

La Plata Dinner Theater announces the opening of *Life on the River*, a musical based on a book by Mark Twain. Dinner is served from 6:30 to 8:00, and the performance begins at 8:30 every evening.

What is opening?

(A) A bookstore

(B) An art exhibit

● A play

(D) A restaurant

> The reading states that *Life on the River* is a musical that is opening at La Plata Dinner Theater. You should choose (C).

Questions 1–5 refer to the following article:

Go ahead, have a cheeseburger, France's Constitutional Council said.

The agency that monitors the constitutionality of laws wasn't ruling on nutrition but on linguistics. –[1]– Its decision substantially weakens a law meant to stop the invasion of foreign words into the French language. That law banned the use of English in broadcasting, advertising, and science. –[2]– The government also sought to ban words such as "cash flow," "marketing," "software," and "air bag" from advertisements, broadcasts, menus, and books.

The nine-member Council ruled that the controversial law encroached on "the fundamental liberty of thought and expression" guaranteed by the French constitution. –[3]– The Council ruled that the government had no right to impose official French translations of foreign words on private citizens, companies, and the media. "Freedom of expression implies the right of citizens to choose the most appropriate terms to express their thoughts," the Council ruled. –[4]– Public authorities and nationalized companies other than radio and television stations must therefore continue to communicate in French.

1. What is this article mainly about?

   (A) The passage of a new bill

   (B) A breakthrough in research

   (C) A foreign invasion

   (D) The weakening of a recent law

2. Which of the following is closest in meaning to the word "monitors" in paragraph 2, line 1?

   (A) reviews

   (B) proposes

   (C) rejects

   (D) inspires

3. The members of the Council are probably experts in which of these fields?

   (A) Nutrition

   (B) Advertising

   (C) Law

   (D) Linguistics

4. In which of the positions marked [1], [2], [3], and [4] does the following sentence best belong?

   "It would have, for instance, forced restaurateurs to advertise 'hamburgers au fromage' instead of cheeseburgers."

   (A) [1]

   (B) [2]

   (C) [3]

   (D) [4]

5. Why did the Council make this decision about the law?

   (A) Because so many people objected to the law

   (B) Because the law was believed to violate the constitution

   (C) Because restaurant owners were unhappy with the law

   (D) Because the law did not have its intended effect

METRO LODGING REPORT: JULY

Location	Room Nights		Occupancy Percentage	Average Room Cost
	Occupied	Available		
AIRPORT	89,649	104,847	85.5%	$128.28
NORTH SUBURBAN	29,686	35,065	84.7%	$93.75
WEST SUBURBAN	46,279	50,950	90.8%	$97.78
MIDTOWN	29,681	37,851	78.4%	$89.70
DOWNTOWN	62,620	77,271	81.0%	$179.61

6. What does this report concern?

   (A) Apartment buildings

   (B) Hotels

   (C) Parking lots

   (D) Office buildings

7. Which area had the highest rate of occupancy in July?

   (A) North Suburban

   (B) Airport

   (C) West Suburban

   (D) Downtown

8. What does the chart indicate about Downtown?

   (A) On average, it had the most expensive rooms.

   (B) It had fewer empty rooms in July than Midtown did.

   (C) It had more rooms than any other area.

   (D) There were more rooms per building than in other areas.

Questions 9–10 refer to the following advertisement:

Owning a **franchise** *can be magical!*

The expanding children's service market offers an excellent return on your investment — and puts a little magic into your summer. Summer Magic Day Camps franchises provide door-to-door pick-up services for children (ages 6–13) and a wide variety of activities in parks and other locations. No need to invest in expensive camp facilities, as all activities are held off-premises. You can operate the business part-time and from home. We provide all the know-how and direction needed for start-up and day-to-day operations. Very reasonable franchise fees.

9. For whom is this advertisement intended?

   (A) People who want to operate their own business

   (B) Parents of young children

   (C) People who own summer camps

   (D) People who want to work as camp counselors

10. The company placing this advertisement would probably NOT provide information on which of the following?

   (A) Where to hold activities

   (B) What kind of activities to provide

   (C) How to attract campers

   (D) How to purchase a site for the camp

The Richmond Hotel
Chicago, Illinois

Warren Purcell, Convention Chair
American Association of Photoengravers
North Central District
Suite 28
621 Plum Street
Detroit, Michigan 48201

Dear Mr. Purcell:

Mr. Scarlotti, our general manager, passed on your letter requesting information regarding our convention facilities and asked me to respond. I am happy to comply.

As you can see from our brochure, we offer large meeting rooms for plenary sessions and display areas, and an ample number of small "breakout" rooms for workshops and concurrent meetings. Banquet facilities are also available. Our centralized location is convenient to other hotels, fine restaurants, and all the sights of downtown Chicago, as you can see from the map I've sent. I'm also enclosing a list of special room rates for convention attendees.

I think you will find the Richmond Hotel the perfect host for your convention. Our experienced and courteous staff really knows what it takes to make a convention run smoothly.

Please let me know if there is any other information or help I can provide.

Sincerely,

Diana Lockhurst

Diana Lockhurst, Convention and Banquet Manager

Encl: (3)

11. What is the main purpose of this letter?

(A) To ask for further information

(B) To respond to a request

(C) To confirm a reservation

(D) To explain the general manager's opinion

12. Which of the following is NOT enclosed?

(A) A schedule of events

(B) A publicity brochure

(C) A map of downtown Chicago

(D) A list of room rates

AMERICAN IMPRESSIONISM AND REALISM
A Landmark Exhibition from the Met

20 JAN 20-- TO 22 APR 20--
WAMA | TICKETED

Exclusive to the Western Australia Museum of Art in Perth is the exhibition "American Impressionism and Realism: A Landmark Exhibition from the Met." This exhibition presents 71 paintings by 34 artists from New York's Metropolitan Museum of Art. –[1]– Among them are some of the Met's best examples of paintings in the American Impressionist and Realist traditions, many of which have never before been displayed outside their home in New York.

Leading figures — such as Impressionists John Singer Sargent, Mary Cassatt, Childe Hassam, and William Merritt Chase, and Realists Robert Henri, John Sloan, and William Blackins — are represented by several works. –[2]– The exhibition considers how proponents of two styles that flourished around 1900 responded artistically to modern life in very different fashions.

More than 30 iconic Australian paintings from those two schools that also flourished in Australia during the early twentieth century are also to be included in the exhibition. –[3]– They include works by artists such as Tom Roberts, Charles Conder, and Frederick McCubbin.

"American Impressionism and Realism" includes light-filled landscapes and seascapes, magnificent portraits of women and children, and images that reflect many aspects of modern life. –[4]–

---

13. What is the main theme of this display?

(A) The range of contemporary painting in the U.S.

(B) The contrast between today's art and art in 1900

(C) A comparison between U.S. artists and Australian artists

(D) Differences between two important styles of art

14. What does the announcement suggest about some of the artists whose work is in this exhibition?

(A) They have only one piece of art that is being displayed.

(B) They are neither Realists nor Impressionists.

(C) They are neither Australian nor from the U.S.

(D) They have never had their paintings exhibited outside the U.S. before.

15. Which of the following artists is NOT considered a Realist?

(A) John Sloan

(B) Mary Cassatt

(C) William Blackins

(D) Robert Henri

16. In which of the positions marked [1], [2], [3], and [4] does the following sentence best belong?

"These works highlight how artists from our country responded to key artistic developments of the period."

(A) [1]

(B) [2]

(C) [3]

(D) [4]

Questions 17–18 refer to the following online chat session:

Moon, Ji-young [10:34]
Good morning, Rich, I hope you are having a good trip. Hey, I wonder if you can help us out—we're having a little problem here.

Palmer, Richard [10:35]
Morning, Ji-young. Sure, what's up?

Moon, Ji-young [10:35]
Ms. Poe needs to get into that old filing cabinet next to your desk. Do you know where the key is?

Palmer, Richard [10:37]
Well, I have one on my key ring here. I think there's another in the lock ... if not, look in the top drawer of my desk.

Moon, Ji-young [10:42]
No, it's not in the lock, and I don't see it in your drawer.

Palmer, Richard [10:42]
After my meeting with Mr. Delgado today, I could send it by express courier. It could be there by tomorrow.

Moon, Ji-young [10:42]
I'll ask Ms. Poe if that's what she wants you to do.

Poe, Diana [10:49]
Hi, Rich. It turns out that it wasn't actually locked. The filing cabinet drawers were just stuck. I gave the bottom drawer a good kick and it popped open. Thanks anyway.

Palmer, Richard [10:50]
Well, glad the problem is solved.

Poe, Diana [10:51]
See you next week. Hope you have a good meeting with Mr. Delgado. He's a tough negotiator.

---

17. Where is one of the keys to the filing cabinet?

(A) It's inside the filing cabinet lock.

(B) Mr. Palmer has it.

(C) It's in Mr. Palmer's desk drawer.

(D) Ms. Poe has it.

18. At 10:49, what does Ms. Poe mean when she writes, "Thanks anyway"?

(A) Mr. Palmer does not need to send her the key by express courier.

(B) She appreciates the fact that Mr. Palmer is meeting Mr. Delgado.

(C) She is happy that Mr. Palmer was able to help her locate the key.

(D) Mr. Palmer should leave the key in the office when he goes out of town.

Questions 19–23 refer to the following advertisement and email message:

Global Office Recruitment Services, Ltd.

Japanese + English Fluency `New!`
£30,000 + good benefits! Challenging role as office manager with varied duties. Responsible person with accounting experience. University graduate preferred. File #1231.

Russian-speaking personal assistant
£32,500 + top benefits in the business! Executive assistant for director of investment firm. Must be fluent in English. Knowledge of Czech, Polish, or Hungarian useful. You will look after director's schedule and organize appointments and meetings. File #942.

Bilingual French-English customer relations manager
£42,000 + benefits package. International trading company with offices in London, Paris, New York, and San Francisco seeks supervisor for customer relations department. Must have management experience and good interpersonal skills. Advanced computer skills needed. Relocation from the UK not required but must be available for frequent travel. File #1194.

German/French-speaking project manager
£45,000 + benefits. Project manager with minimum two years' experience needed. Make best use of your interpersonal, professional, and linguistic skills. Varied tasks. Mother-tongue fluency in German, French, and English necessary. Must be available to begin work immediately. File #1083.

Spanish/English Fluency `New!`
£23,000. Management trainee at lovely British-owned resort on the Costa Brava, Spain. No experience required. File #1321.

Contact Justina Birchmore at GORS, Ltd.
Russell House 60 Bedford Street London WC2E 9HP
Tel. 0147 372 8167 Fax 0147 372 9193 Email JTB@GORS.co.uk
Telephone 9–11 AM or 1–4 PM *or* Fax, mail, or email CV and cover letter
Include file number in all correspondence.

From: "Elizabeth Goodly" <elizgoodly@asu.edu>
To: "Justina Birchmore" <JTB@GORS.co.uk>
Subject: Employment position
Date: May 14, 20--
Attachment(s): 1

Ms. Birchmore,

I tried to call you yesterday morning about 10 your time but was unable to reach you. I wanted to let you know that I am quite interested in the position of Project Manager that you recently advertised.

My father is from the U.K. and my mother is French. My father worked in Germany and I spent three years there when I was in high school. Therefore, I am quite fluent in English, French, and German. As you can see from my résumé (attached), I have had two years' experience as a project manager in a government office and about a year as the manager of a large London bookstore. I want to work in an international environment and I believe I am well qualified for this position.

One problem: I am currently finishing my graduate business degree (MBA). I will not be available for employment until almost the end of this month.

I would very much like to further discuss this position with you. I will be in London by May 27 and will be available for an interview then. Please contact me by email or phone (1-480-555-6642).

Thanks,

Elizabeth Goodly

19. What do all the positions in the advertisement require?

(A) At least two years of experience

(B) The ability to relocate outside of the U.K.

(C) A university degree

(D) The ability to speak more than one language

20. What can be said about the position that Ms. Goodly is interested in?

(A) It has the best benefits.

(B) It is a new listing.

(C) It has the highest pay.

(D) It has already been filled.

21. What problem does Ms. Goodly mention in her email?

(A) She is unable to start work immediately.

(B) She is not free to come to an interview.

(C) She does not have fluency in one of the three required languages.

(D) She does not have enough experience as a project manager.

22. What instruction did Ms. Goodly fail to follow when contacting Justina Birchmore?

(A) She did not attach a copy of her résumé.

(B) She did not call GORS at the proper time.

(C) She did not include the file number in her email.

(D) She did not say which languages she can speak.

23. What other job listed in the advertisement might Ms. Goodly be qualified for?

(A) Office manager (File #1231)

(B) Personal assistant (File #942)

(C) Customer relations manager (File #1194)

(D) Management trainee (File #1321)

EAGLE RIVER SCHOOL DISTRICT
DEPT. OF LIFELONG LEARNING
REGISTRATION FORM: SUMMER I TERM, JUNE 11 TO JULY 16

NAME: _Jenny Bryant_   ADDRESS: _4277 Grant Avenue_

PHONE: _541-555-7447_   _Eagleton, Oregon 97623_

EMAIL: _jennB123@pxmail.com_   DATE: _May 23, 20--_

Register early! Classes fill up fast. And if you register before May 11, you are eligible for a 10% "early bird" discount.

Class Number	Class	Cost
A239	Portrait Photography	$200
A131	Grow Your Own Vegetables	$100
T023	Driver's Ed*	$150
T122	Fencing 2*	$150

Subtotal _$600_
Discount _____
Total payment due _$600_

Please register my son Peter Bryant for these two classes.

Payment: ___ Credit Card   ✔ Check
Credit Card Type: _____ Credit Card Number: _____ Expiration Date: _____

Receipt? ✔ Yes   ____ No (Receipts can be sent only if you provide an email address or a self-addressed, stamped envelope.)

If a class is full or is cancelled due to low enrollment, you will be notified by phone or email. If you need to cancel a class registration, you must do so by May 11 to receive a full refund (minus $10 processing fee). If a class is full or is cancelled by Lifelong Learning, a full refund will be issued.

EAGLE RIVER SCHOOL DISTRICT
DEPT. OF LIFELONG LEARNING

May 27, 20—

Dear Ms. Bryant,

We are pleased to inform you that you and your son have been registered for the following classes for the fall term:

Confirmed Registration	Class Number	Time	Location	Instructor
	A239	Mon. & Wed. 7–9 p.m.	West Ridge High School Art Room	Asuka Kunihara
✔	A131	Sat. 11 a.m. –1 p.m.	Eagleton High School Room 119	Donna Bartel
✔	T023	Sat. 1–3 p.m.	Meet in Eagleton High School Cafeteria	Mike Holland
✔	T122	Mon. & Wed. 7–9 p.m.	Mountain Shadows Middle School Gymnasium	Carlos Escobar

Sorry, we could not confirm your registration for the Portrait Photography course because that class is already full. Your refund is being processed and will be sent to you within a week.

Sincerely,

Monica Rajeesh

Monica Rajeesh
Asst. Director, Dept. of Lifelong Learning
Eagle River School District
(541)-555-6578
MRajeesh@ERSD.edu

May 28, 20—
To: MRajeesh@ERSD.edu
From: jennB123@pxmail.com

Dear Ms. Rajeesh,

Thank you for confirming classes for myself and Peter. I am disappointed that the Portrait Photography class is unavailable, as I am a long-time admirer of Ms. Kunihara's work and was looking forward to taking her class. For that reason, I am going to ask you not to return the check for tuition for that class, as I would like to enroll in her Tuesday and Thursday Nature Photography class. I know the tuition for the nature photography class is $25 higher than for the class I had originally signed up for, so on Monday I will call in and give you my credit card information to cover the extra cost of that class.

Thank you,
Jenny Bryant

---

24. Why did Jenny Bryant not receive a discount?

(A) She did not register for enough classes.

(B) She registered after June 11.

(C) She received her confirmation late.

(D) She did not register before May 11.

25. What is probably enclosed with Jenny Bryant's registration form?

(A) A schedule

(B) A self-addressed, stamped envelope

(C) A check

(D) A registration form for her son

26. How many classes is Jenny Bryant confirmed for as of May 27?

(A) None

(B) One

(C) Two

(D) Four

27. What will Peter Bryant learn to do on Saturdays?

(A) To fence

(B) To take photographs

(C) To drive

(D) To grow vegetables

28. What do the portrait photography class and the nature photography class have in common?

(A) They meet on the same evenings.

(B) They cost the same.

(C) They are taught by the same teacher.

(D) They are both unavailable.

Testing Points and Skill-Building Exercises

The readings in Part 7 cover a wide range of topics and represent many types of materials. However, most fit into the six categories described in Sections A-F of the lesson. Each section describes a type of passage, presents an analysis of an example, and offers an exercise.

A. Articles

Readings of this type resemble brief articles or parts of articles such as the ones found in newspapers or magazines, or on the Internet. Some concern business topics. Another common type is a report on a survey or study. You will probably see from one to three articles per test.

Overview questions about articles ask about the main point of the article. They may also ask you about the author's opinion or background. Some ask what type of reader would be interested in this article or where the article was probably published.

Detail and negative questions deal with specific points made in the article. Some questions ask you to interpret numbers that appear in the article.

Sample Items: Questions About Articles

Go ahead, have a cheeseburger, France's Constitutional Council said.

The agency that monitors the constitutionality of laws wasn't ruling on nutrition but on linguistics. –[1]– Its decision substantially weakens a law meant to stop the invasion of foreign words into the French language. That law banned the use of English in broadcasting, advertising, and science. –[2]– The government also sought to ban words such as "cash flow," "marketing," "software," and "air bag" from advertisements, broadcasts, menus, and books.

The nine-member Council ruled that the controversial law encroached on "the fundamental liberty of thought and expression" guaranteed by the French constitution. –[3]– The Council ruled that the government had no right to impose official French translations of foreign words on private citizens, companies, and the media. "Freedom of expression implies the right of Citizens to choose the most appropriate terms to express their thoughts," the Council ruled. –[4]– Public authorities and nationalized companies other than radio and television stations must therefore continue to communicate in French.

1. What is this article mainly about?

   (A) The passage of a new bill

   (B) A breakthrough in research

   (C) A foreign invasion

   ● The weakening of a recent law

> The article is primarily about a ruling of the French Constitutional Council that "substantially weakens a law."

2. Which of the following is closest in meaning to the word "monitors" in paragraph 2, line 1?

    ● reviews

    (B) proposes

    (C) rejects

    (D) inspires

> The word *monitors* means "reviews," "pays attention to," "watches."

3. The members of the Council are probably experts in which of these fields?

    (A) Nutrition

    (B) Advertising

    ● Law

    (D) Linguistics

> The article says that the Council is "The agency that monitors the constitutionality of laws."

4. In which of the positions marked [1], [2], [3], and [4] does the following sentence best belong?

    "It would have, for instance, forced restaurateurs to advertise 'hamburgers au fromage' instead of cheeseburgers."

    (A) [1]

    ● [2]

    (C) [3]

    (D) [4]

> The missing sentence connects with the previous sentence because it presents an example of a more general idea ("That law banned the use of English in broadcasting, advertising, and science"). It also connects with the following sentence, which provides examples other than the word *cheeseburger*. There are also grammatical clues. The pronoun *It* connects with the phrase *that law* in the previous sentence, and so does the connecting phrase *for instance*.

5. Why did the Council make this decision about the law?

    (A) Because so many people objected to the law

    ● Because the law was believed to violate the constitution

    (C) Because restaurant owners were unhappy with the law

    (D) Because the law did not have its intended effect

> According to the article, the Council ruled that the law "encroached on 'the fundamental liberty of thought and expression' guaranteed by the French constitution."

Sentence addition questions, such as Question 4, were introduced when the TOEIC was revised in 2016. You will typically see this type of question in question sets following articles and business correspondences, such as emails. This type of question presents a sentence that is not in the reading. You must decide where is the most logical place to add the sentence to the reading — in positions [1], [2], [3], or [4].

To answer these questions correctly, you must look for clues in the missing sentence and in the sentences that come before and after the four positions. There may be *content* clues. For example, the missing sentence in Question 4 is related to the prior sentence because it provides an example. The previous sentence states that the law banned the use of English in certain fields. The missing sentence gives an example of the effect of that law — it indicates that restaurateurs could not use the word *cheeseburgers* in their advertisements; instead, they must use the French equivalent. The missing sentence is also connected to the following sentence, which provides more examples of words that had been banned in French advertising — *cash flow*, *marketing*, etc.

You can also sometimes use clues from the vocabulary and grammar of the missing sentence or the sentences that come before or after the positions marked with numbers. These clues include:

- Pronouns and referents
- Linking words and phrases
- Synonyms
- The repetition of key words

In Question 4 above, the pronoun *It* connects with its referent. (A referent is the noun or noun phrase that a pronoun stands for. In this case, the referent of the pronoun is the phrase "that law.") The linking phrase "for instance" also connects the missing sentence to the previous one.

Here's another example pertaining to the same article:

In which of the positions marked [1], [2], [3], and [4] does the following sentence best belong?

"But the Council upheld the section of the law affecting government officials and employees, citing Article 2 of the constitution, which states that 'the language of the Republic is French.'"

(A) [1]   (C) [3]

(B) [2]   (D) [4]

The best position for this sentence is [4]. The first part of this paragraph states that the Council's decision allows the use of foreign words for "private citizens, companies, and the media" and that they can "choose the most appropriate terms to express their thoughts." The missing sentence, however, is in contrast with this idea. It introduces the idea that the Council's ruling does not apply to government officials and employees. The linking word *But* links the missing sentence to the previous one and shows this contrast. The sentence following position [4] shows a result of this part of the Council's decision. All public and nationalized companies, except for the media, must still use French. The linking word *therefore* in this sentence shows that this is a result of the ruling, and connects the following sentence to the missing sentence.

Here's an example from another reading in the Preview Test:

More than 30 iconic Australian paintings from those two schools that also flourished in Australia during the early twentieth century are also to be included in the exhibition. –[3]– They include works by artists such as Tom Roberts, Charles Conder, and Frederick McCubbin.

16. In which of the positions marked [1], [2], [3], and [4] does the following sentence best belong?

"These works highlight how artists from our country responded to key artistic developments of the period."

(A) [1]   (C) [3]

(B) [2]   (D) [4]

The phrase *These works* is a synonym for the phrase *Australian paintings* in the previous sentence. The repetition of the word *works* in the sentence following the position marked [3] also connects that sentence with the missing sentence.

Exercise 7.1

Focus: Understanding and answering questions about articles.

Directions: Read the passages, and then mark the best answers to the questions.

Questions 1–5 are based on the following article:

Every year, about 290 million tires — an average of almost one tire for every person in the United States — are discarded. –[1]– Currently, U.S. automobile manufacturers are turning 18 million pounds of tires each year into car parts: seals, air deflectors, and other parts not visible to consumers. –[2]–

Now, a new process that grinds tires into fine powder and magnetically removes steel belting promises to broaden the range of recycled products. –[3]– The end product, a mixture of rubber and plastic, can be molded into vehicle parts, and they look new. The first product, a brake-pedal pad, is being field tested on fleets of police cars, rental cars, and taxicabs. –[4]– Each recycled tire can produce 250 brake-pedal pads.

1. What is the best title for this article?

   (A) "Making Tires from Recycled Materials"

   (B) "A New Use for Old Tires"

   (C) "Process Makes Old Cars Look New"

   (D) "New Brakes Make Cars Safer"

2. The word "discarded" in paragraph 1, line 2 is closest in meaning to

   (A) thrown away

   (B) produced

   (C) looked over

   (D) replaced

3. Which of the following best describes the order of steps in the new process?

   (A) Magnetize steel, mix rubber and plastic, make parts

   (B) Powder tires, belt with steel, melt parts

   (C) Grind tires, remove steel, mold into parts

   (D) Melt tires, broaden belt, install parts

4. What advantage of parts made by this process is mentioned by the author?

   (A) They are extremely safe.

   (B) They last a long time.

   (C) They are inexpensive.

   (D) They don't look used.

5. In which of the positions marked [1], [2], [3], and [4] does the following sentence best belong?

   "By next year, it could end up on production vehicles."

   (A) [1]

   (B) [2]

   (C) [3]

   (D) [4]

Questions 6–7 refer to the following passage:

According to a survey taken this year, some 260, or 52%, of the Fortune 500 companies in the United States had at least one woman on their corporate board of directors. That's up from 243, or 49%, last year. Last year's survey was the first such study done since the original one in 1997. At that time, only 46 women held seats on the boards of top U.S. corporations.

6. How many companies had one or more women on their boards of directors this year?

(A) 46

(B) 52

(C) 243

(D) 260

7. How many surveys regarding women as members of boards of directors have been done BEFORE this year?

(A) None

(B) One

(C) Two

(D) Three

Questions 8–12 refer to the following article:

The British Crown Jewels were given a new home in March 1994. The collection includes some 20,000 gems, among which is the world's largest diamond. It had been housed in an underground bunker at the Tower of London which could not accommodate the 2 million visitors a year who wanted to view the jewels. The Crown Jeweller himself, the only person allowed to handle the jewels, packed up the collection for the move to the 10-million-pound Jewel House in Waterloo Block, just above the old bunker.

The Crown Jewels have been at the Tower since 1327; they have been moved only twice since 1867, the last time to the bunker in 1967. The current premises feature a moving walkway which carries visitors past the displays more quickly, preventing the congestion that so often occurred at the previous site.

8. What claim is NOT made in the article about the Crown Jewel collection?

(A) It is the largest jewelry collection in history.

(B) Two million people want to see it each year.

(C) It contains the world's largest diamond.

(D) It consists of around 20,000 jewels.

9. When was the collection moved to the underground bunker?

(A) In 1327

(B) In 1867

(C) In 1967

(D) In 1994

10. What was the Crown Jeweller's responsibility during the move?

(A) To assess the value of the collection

(B) To locate a new site for the display

(C) To examine the jewelry for defects

(D) To pack up the jewelry by himself

11. Which of the following is closest in meaning to the word "congestion" in paragraph 2, line 6?

(A) crowding

(B) noise

(C) confusion

(D) accidents

12. According to the article, which of the following is one of the advantages of the current site?

(A) It is in a more convenient location.

(B) More jewels will be on display.

(C) The security system is improved.

(D) Visitors can move through it more quickly.

Questions 13–14 refer to the following passage:

> Critics of communities that pass smoke-free restaurant laws warn that business will suffer. But a seven-year study of 30 California communities showed that smoke-free restaurants do not lose business. The study, done by researchers from the University of California at San Francisco, involved fifteen towns that passed smoke-free laws and fifteen towns that did not. Smoke-free laws had no effect on restaurant sales, said researchers.

13. What is the main conclusion of the study?

(A) Businesses suffer if they restrict smoking.

(B) Smoke-free restaurants had higher sales than restaurants that permitted smoking.

(C) Criticism of smoke-free restaurant laws is increasing.

(D) Restaurant sales were unaffected by smoke-free laws.

14. How long did the study last?

(A) 1 year

(B) 7 years

(C) 15 years

(D) 30 years

Questions 15–19 are based on the following Internet article:

Golf has become increasingly popular in Thailand over the past few decades with Thai golfers and tourists alike. In fact, Thailand is now known as the golf capital of Asia. The number of Thai golfers has nearly tripled in the last five years, and the number of international visitors coming to Thailand to play golf increased to 750,000, up 50% in the past three years. –[1]–

The country boasts over 280 courses. Over half are located in the vicinity of Bangkok, but there are other golf resorts scattered around the country, from the highlands of the north to the seaside of the south. Some are even located on Thailand's stunning islands, such as Phuket and Koh Samui. The dramatic natural settings are a key factor in attracting large numbers of golfers, and because of its climate, golf can be played all year long. –[2]– Experienced golfers appreciate the challenge of numerous water features and strategically positioned bunkers. A number of Thailand's courses were designed by some of golf's biggest names, such as Jack Nicklaus, Gary Player, and Nick Faldo. –[3]–

According to a spokesperson for the Thailand Golf Association, Thailand's golfing heritage dates back to 1923, during the reign of King Vajiravudh, who was himself a golfing fan. He gave permission for Thailand's first 18-hole course, the Royal Hua Hin, to be constructed. Upgraded in 1980, this course continues to be popular. The Thai Golf Association was formed in 1963, and the following year, the first major golf tournament—the Thailand Open tournament—was held. –[4]–

For information on golf vacations for individuals or groups, visit www.globalgolf/thailand.

15. Where are most of Thailand's golf courses located?

(A) On islands

(B) At mountain resorts

(C) In suburban Bangkok

(D) At the seaside

16. Which of the following is NOT one of the factors that makes Thailand's golf course attractive?

(A) The scenery

(B) The weather

(C) The low cost

(D) The level of difficulty

17. When was the first Thailand Open tournament played?

(A) In 1923

(B) In 1963

(C) In 1964

(D) In 1980

18. Which of the following is closest in meaning to the word "heritage" in paragraph 3, line 2?

(A) history

(B) enthusiasm

(C) organization

(D) profession

19. In which of the positions marked [1], [2], [3], and [4] does the following sentence best belong?

"This is now one of the premier golfing events in Asia."

(A) [1]

(B) [2]

(C) [3]

(D) [4]

How much money do fliers leave behind on airlines? One international carrier took in $75,000 last year, which it donated to charities. That's an average of $0.18 per passenger. If that figure holds true for all 320 million people who fly on the hundreds of international airlines, it amounts to $58 million per year.

Much less is found on domestic U.S. flights. A cleaning crew in Chicago reported finding less than $0.10 per flight. An executive of one international airline suggested that on international flights, passengers disposed of surplus coins from the countries they were departing by leaving the coins in their seats or in the seat pockets in front of them.

20. Which is the best headline for this article?

(A) "Saving Money on International Travel"

(B) "The Changing Face of Air Travel"

(C) "How to Hold on to Your Money"

(D) "Loose Change Found on Planes"

21. What is the figure of $58 million mentioned in the first paragraph based on?

(A) Data from hundreds of airlines

(B) Interviews with numerous cleaning crews

(C) Information provided by one airline

(D) Estimates made by airline executives

22. What explanation is offered for the greater amount of money left on international flights than on U.S. domestic flights?

(A) International passengers discard unwanted coins.

(B) U.S. cleaning crews are keeping the money.

(C) International airlines gave more to charity.

(D) U.S. passengers carry less change.

23. Which of these questions CANNOT be answered from information in the article?

(A) How many passengers flew on international airlines last year?

(B) Where did most passengers put the coins that they did not want?

(C) What was the average amount of money left by a U.S. domestic passenger?

(D) Who reported finding less than $0.10 per flight?

24. Which of the following is closest in meaning to the word "surplus" in paragraph 2, line 6?

(A) invaluable

(B) inconvenient

(C) illegal

(D) unnecessary

B. Business Correspondence

This type of reading involves any type of communication sent to or from a business. In Part 7, you will usually see one to three business communications per test. They may be business letters, emails, or faxes. You may also see interoffice memos, which are business communications between two or more employees at the same company. These also have many purposes: to schedule a meeting, to ask for a report, to discuss a problem, to thank someone for a job well done, or to request help or information. The tone and language of memos, faxes, and emails tend to be less formal than those of letters.

Overview questions about business correspondence usually ask about the purpose of the communication. This is generally stated in the first paragraph — usually the first few lines — of the body of the communication.

Answers to detail questions are usually found in the body of the communication but may also be found in the heading or opening.

The Richmond Hotel
Chicago, Illinois

Warren Purcell, Convention Chair
American Association of Photoengravers
North Central District
Suite 28
621 Plum Street
Detroit, Michigan 48201

Dear Mr. Purcell:

Mr. Scarlotti, our general manager, passed on your letter requesting information regarding our convention facilities and asked me to respond. I am happy to comply.

As you can see from our brochure, we offer large meeting rooms for plenary sessions and display areas, and an ample number of small "breakout" rooms for workshops and concurrent meetings. Banquet facilities are also available. Our centralized location is convenient to other hotels, fine restaurants, and all the sights of downtown Chicago, as you can see from the map I've sent. I'm also enclosing a list of special room rates for convention attendees.

I think you will find the Richmond Hotel the perfect host for your convention. Our experienced and courteous staff really knows what it takes to make a convention run smoothly.

Please let me know if there is any other information or help I can provide.

Sincerely,

Diana Lockhurst

Diana Lockhurst, Convention and Banquet Manager

Encl: (3)

---

1. What is the main purpose of this letter?

    (A) To ask for further information

    ● To respond to a request

    (C) To confirm a reservation

    (D) To explain the general manager's opinion

2. Which of the following is NOT enclosed?

    ● A schedule of events

    (B) A publicity brochure

    (C) A map of downtown Chicago

    (D) A list of room rates

The purpose of the letter is given in the first paragraph of the communication. The writer states that she was asked by the general manager to respond to a previous request for information, and that she is doing so in this letter.

Three enclosures are mentioned: the brochure, the map, and the list of rates for rooms. There is no mention of a schedule of events.

Focus: Understanding and answering questions about business correspondence.

Directions: Read the passages, and then mark the best answers to the questions.

Questions 1–4 are based on the following letter:

Drake Industries

Lucy Rickenbach, Director
Office of Financial Planning
SouthBank
3520 Rawlins Drive
Dallas, Texas 75219

Dear Ms. Rickenbach:

Bonnie Whitmer has requested that I write to recommend her for a position in your office. Ms. Whitmer worked in my department for two years. –[1]– Ms. Whitmer is well-organized and has excellent workplace communication skills. She is honest and energetic. –[2]– With her degree in economics and her experience in accounting, I am sure she will contribute positively to your organization. Her only fault, as far as I know, is that, because she is such a perfectionist, she sometimes spends too much time on details. –[3]–

We at Drake Industries are anxious to find positions for our employees whose jobs will be eliminated in the reorganization that will follow our upcoming merger with the Hammond Group. –[4]– I'd appreciate your considering her for this position.

Please feel free to contact me for further particulars.

Sincerely,

Quentin Howe, Chief Financial Officer/Comptroller
Drake Industries

900 McCollough Ave., Charlotte, North Carolina 28262

1. Who asked that this letter be sent?

   (A) Lucy Rickenbach

   (B) Bonnie Whitmer

   (C) A representative of the Hammond Group

   (D) Ms. Whitmer's supervisor

2. For which of the following does the writer NOT praise Ms. Whitmer?

   (A) Her communication skills

   (B) Her honesty

   (C) Her energy

   (D) Her attention to detail

3. Why is Ms. Whitmer looking for another job?

   (A) Because her position will soon be eliminated

   (B) Because she disagreed with her supervisor

   (C) Because the company where she works has gone bankrupt

   (D) Because she wants to earn a higher salary

4. In which of the positions marked [1], [2], [3], and [4] does the following sentence best belong?

   "During her time here, she became a vital part of the Finance Department and was well-liked by her co-workers and by her supervisor."

   (A) [1]

   (B) [2]

   (C) [3]

   (D) [4]

Questions 5–6 are based on the following note:

WHILE YOU WERE OUT

To: _James_

Date: _2-17_ Time: _11.40 A.M._

Mr./Mrs./Ms. _Bingham_

of _Product Promotions Team_

Phone: ( ) _____ ext. _6972_

☐ TELEPHONED   ☑ CALLED TO SEE YOU

☐ PLEASE CALL   ☐ WILL CALL AGAIN

☐ RETURNED YOUR CALL   ☐ URGENT

☐ WANTS TO SEE YOU   ☐ OTHERS _____

Message _Came by to discuss your meeting in Rio with Dr. Garofalo on Monday. Call her after lunch._

Sally

5. Who took the message?

   (A) James

   (B) Dr. Garofalo

   (C) Ms. Bingham

   (D) Sally

6. What is James asked to do?

   (A) Join the Product Promotions Team

   (B) Call Dr. Garofalo

   (C) Go out to lunch

   (D) Contact Ms. Bingham

Interoffice Memo

Northfield Pharmaceuticals International

To: All department heads
From: Peter Manning, Director
Subject: United Charity Fund
Date: September 26

Next week marks the opening of United Charity Fund's fall campaign drive. As you probably know, UCF is the umbrella organization for about 35 local and regional charity organizations. It solicits funds from businesses and individuals, then divides them up among the member charities.

This is a chance for all of us here at Northfield to repay the community where we work and live. I'd like to have another record year.

Therefore, I'm asking all of you at your departmental meetings this week to remind everyone of Northfield's policy of contributing $0.50 for every dollar contributed by employees. And ask everyone in your department to dig deeply into their pockets and purses.

Thanks for your cooperation.

7. What are the department heads asked to do?

(A) Encourage employees to work harder

(B) Inform employees of a company policy

(C) Volunteer their time for charitable work

(D) Meet with Peter Manning

8. Which of the following is NOT one of United Charity Fund's roles?

(A) Asking businesses for contributions

(B) Distributing funds to charitable groups

(C) Helping individuals who have problems

(D) Asking individuals for contributions

Talon Peripherals

TO: e.sujano@westjavacompco.co.id
ATTN: Ms. Endang Sujano
SUBJECT: Inquiry
DATE: Dec. 1, 20--
FROM: Mary Lymon <marylymon@talon.co.ca>

Dear Ms. Sujano:

An old friend, Tony Drummond, just returned from Jakarta, and he mentioned to me that you and your firm might find our new line of products, particularly our new Talon Portable Color Laser Printer, of interest. With your marketing expertise, you could turn this into one of the best-selling printers in Indonesia, I believe.

One of our marketing representatives will be in Indonesia next month. If it is at all possible, I would like him to meet with you to demonstrate our products' capabilities. If you are interested, I would like you to become sole marketing agent for Talon Peripherals in Indonesia.

I'll ask our representative to contact you in order to arrange a meeting. Please call or email if you have any questions regarding our company or our products.

Best wishes,
Mary Lymon, Marketing Director

Talon Peripherals, Inc.
800-1444 W. Hasting Street, Vancouver, B.C. V6E 2K3

---

9. What is the purpose of this email?

   (A) To persuade Ms. Sujano to buy a printer

   (B) To request some advice from Ms. Sujano

   (C) To ask Ms. Sujano to market a product

   (D) To arrange a meeting in Vancouver

10. Who is Tony Drummond?

   (A) A friend of Ms. Sujano

   (B) A marketing representative

   (C) A friend of Ms. Lymon

   (D) An employee of Talon Peripherals

Questions 11–15 are based on the following communication:

| Aug. 5 | FRI | 4:05PM | Redfern Realty |

Fax No. 6038462-884

Dear Mr. Yamaguchi,

Ms. Foster of Ventura Enterprises has asked us here at Redfern Realty to look for a temporary housing situation for you and your family in order to make your process of relocation as smooth as possible. I have located a 3-bedroom condominium close to Ventura Enterprises. It is in a lovely condominium complex called Foxwood Gardens. It has a deck, a fireplace, and a garage. The rent is $2250 per month plus heat (oil) and electricity. Rubbish collection, snow removal, and water/sewer are paid by the condominium association.

If you want to reserve this unit, please send me a check by express mail for the first month's rent, and I will fax you a lease to sign. Make the check out to Atwater Properties, which is leasing the condominium for the owners. We cannot guarantee the lease until your check arrives. Call tomorrow if you have questions.

Best,

Charles Fincastle

Charles Fincastle, Jr.

11. What is Mr. Yamaguchi doing?

  (A) Moving to a new community

  (B) Renting out his house

  (C) Selling his condominium

  (D) Looking for a new job

12. Where does the writer of this communication work?

  (A) At Atwater Properties

  (B) At Redfern Realty

  (C) At Ventura Enterprises

  (D) At Foxwood Gardens

13. Which of the following is NOT paid by the condominium association?

  (A) The bill for snow removal

  (B) The water/sewer bill

  (C) The heating bill

  (D) The bill for rubbish collection

14. What must Mr. Yamaguchi do to guarantee the lease?

  (A) Bring in a signed copy of the lease

  (B) Call Mr. Fincastle immediately

  (C) Send a check for $2250 by express mail

  (D) Fax a copy of an agreement to Redfern Realty

15. The word "guarantee" in paragraph 2, line 3 is closest in meaning to

(A) release

(B) ensure

(C) explain

(D) rewrite

Questions 16–20 are based on the following email:

TelComCan

Subject: Payment Plans
Date: Mar. 9, 20-- 10:41 (EST)
From: Dennis_Todd@telcomcan.co.ca
To: BaldwinA@zbtservices.com

Ms. Baldwin,

You asked in your email of Mar. 7 about our payment plan for telecommunication equipment orders totalling more than $100,000. Because of company policy, we are unable to provide credit for more than 30 days. Therefore, we have arranged with Maritime Bank to issue loans to our customers. Their rates and payment schedules are competitive and our customers have been pleased with their services.

The person in charge of our account is Marcia Lepage. You can email her at lepage.m@maritimebank.co.ca or call her at 800-555-4670 to get current interest rates and credit reference requirements.

Our arrangement with Maritime Bank has allowed us to keep our prices fair and still offer our valued customers the convenience of paying on credit.

Kind regards,
Denny Todd
TelComCan, Inc.

---

16. What did Ms. Baldwin ask Dennis Todd in her email of March 7?

(A) How her company could pay for a large order

(B) What products were available

(C) How she could contact Marcia Lepage

(D) What the current interest rates are

17. Under what circumstances could Dennis Todd's company extend credit to Ms. Baldwin's company?

(A) If the order was for more than $100,000

(B) If the order could be paid for in less than 30 days

(C) If the interest rates were higher

(D) If her company had better credit references

18. What can be inferred about Maritime Bank?

(A) It charges much higher interest rates than most other banks.

(B) It has provided credit to TelComCan's customers in the past.

(C) It does not require credit references to provide loans.

(D) It does business only on the Internet.

19. What is Marcia Lepage's probable position?

(A) President of TelComCan

(B) Ms. Baldwin's assistant

(C) Government economist

(D) Credit manager of Maritime Bank

20. Which of the following is closest in meaning to the word "fair" in paragraph 3, line 1?

(A) stable

(B) reasonable

(C) clear

(D) unmanageable

C. Advertisements

These readings are similar to the commercial advertisements you see in newspapers and magazines and on the Internet. They may also include classified ads, especially from "Help Wanted," "Positions Wanted," and "Business Available" sections.

Overview questions about advertisements generally ask what the purpose of the ad is or what is being offered. They may also ask what type of reader would be interested in this ad or where this ad probably appeared.

Detail questions often ask about the price of an item that is offered or about the time or place goods or services are available.

Sample Items: Advertisements

Owning a **franchise** can be magical!

The expanding children's service market offers an excellent return on your investment — and puts a little magic into your summer. Summer Magic Day Camps franchises provide door-to-door pick-up services for children (ages 6–13) and a wide variety of activities in parks and other locations. No need to invest in expensive camp facilities, as all activities are held off-premises. You can operate the business part-time and from home. We provide all the know-how and direction needed for start-up and day-to-day operations. Very reasonable franchise fees.

1. For whom is this advertisement intended?

   ● People who want to operate their own business

   (B) Parents of young children

   (C) People who own summer camps

   (D) People who want to work as camp counselors

   > This is an advertisement meant to attract people interested in owning a summer camp franchise as a business.

2. The company placing this advertisement would probably NOT provide information on which of the following?

   (A) Where to hold activities

   (B) What kind of activities to provide

   (C) How to attract campers

   ● How to purchase a site for the camp

   > The summer camps described in this advertisement do not have permanent camp facilities — "all activities are held off-premises." There would be no need for franchise owners to buy a site.

Focus: Understanding and answering questions about advertisements.

Directions: Read the passages, and then mark the best answers to the questions.

Questions 1–5 are based on the following advertisement:

ACCESS YOUR FUTURE!

Today's software is wonderful, but the average software package takes about 100 hours to learn properly by yourself. Professional instruction can cut this to 20 hours — 12 hours in the computer lab and 8 hours of personal effort.

CompuClass offers instruction from top teachers in leading-edge, hands-on computer labs. Courses in all areas available, from basics to advanced applications. Mention this ad and get 25% off on any course priced less than $200.

Day sessions — Tues. and Thurs. 9–12, 1–4 (one-hour lunch break)
Evening sessions — Mon., Wed., and Fri. 5:30–9:30

Introduction to computers	$129	**Database**	$189
Word processing	$169	**Desktop publishing**	$229
Spreadsheets	$189	**Internet seminar**	$149
Graphics programs	$209		
Presentation software	$169		

Call for a complete information bulletin.

1. What is being offered?

   (A) Training

   (B) Computers

   (C) Software

   (D) Jobs

2. At what time do the Tuesday and Thursday sessions end?

   (A) At noon

   (B) At 1 p.m.

   (C) At 4 p.m.

   (D) At 9:30 p.m.

3. According to the advertisement, how many hours of lab work are recommended to learn a typical software package?

   (A) 8 hours

   (B) 12 hours

   (C) 20 hours

   (D) 100 hours

4. The word "areas" in paragraph 2, line 2 is closest in meaning to

   (A) brands

   (B) courses

   (C) fields

   (D) places

5. Which of the following is NOT available at a 25% discount?

   (A) "Introduction to computers"

   (B) "Word processing"

   (C) "Internet seminar"

   (D) "Desktop publishing"

Sonic Brush

This is the **Sonic Brush** — a remarkable new toothbrush that uses imperceptible ultrasonic vibrations to painlessly massage the tissues of your gums and interrupt the growth of bacteria. Tests show the Sonic Brush significantly reduces bacterial plaque and gum bleeding. Use as you would a regular toothbrush. No harsh vibrations, no messy water sprays. Dentist-recommended. Usual price $149, now only **$119** — a discount of almost 20%!

6. What claim is NOT made for this toothbrush?

(A) It is easier to use than ordinary toothbrushes.

(B) It reduces gum infections and plaque.

(C) It is recommended by dentists.

(D) It does not cause pain.

7. What is the current price of this toothbrush?

(A) $20

(B) $30

(C) $119

(D) $149

TWO AMBITIOUS PEOPLE NEEDED FOR INTERNATIONAL SALES TEAM

International publishing company requires diligent, articulate personnel to sell advertising for our worldwide family of magazines.

Successful candidates will receive comprehensive training in London. Posting to Singapore, Dubai, or Toronto follows. Generous base salary plus one of the highest commissions in the industry. Some top agents have earned up to **£45,000** in their first year.

Experience in international sales very desirable. Initially do not send CV but call the Personnel Office (mornings only).

8. In which of the following cities is a successful candidate NOT likely to work on a permanent basis?

(A) Toronto

(B) London

(C) Dubai

(D) Singapore

9. How should the figure of £45,000 mentioned in the advertisement be regarded?

(A) As a base salary

(B) As an average first-year commission

(C) As a maximum salary

(D) As an excellent first-year income

10. What should someone who is interested in one of these positions do first?

(A) Mail a CV to the company

(B) Call the Personnel Office in the morning

(C) Come to the office for an interview

(D) Attend the training session

Questions 11–12 refer to the following advertisement:

World Fares Travel
Great Rates to Europe!

	One way	Round trip
London	$520	——
Paris	$540	——
Frankfurt	——	$800
Rome	——	$840
Athens	$490	——

- Minimum two-day stay required.
- All fares require a two-week advance purchase.
- Non-refundable, no changes.
- Call for other cities.

(No Saturday overnight stay required.)
Offer good only on flights before **May 31.**

11. A trip to and from which of the following cities would be LEAST expensive?

(A) London

(B) Paris

(C) Frankfurt

(D) Rome

12. Which of the following is NOT a requirement for purchasers of these tickets?

(A) Departing before May 31

(B) Staying at least two days in these cities

(C) Buying tickets at least two weeks before flying

(D) Spending the weekend in the destination city

Questions 13–14 refer to the following advertisement:

MINDFOLD BLINDFOLD

IF YOU'RE A JET-LAGGED TRAVELER OR SOMEONE WHO NEEDS TO SLEEP DURING THE DAYTIME, THIS BLINDFOLD LETS YOU NAP ANYWHERE ANYTIME IN TOTAL DARKNESS. MADE OF LIGHTWEIGHT PLASTIC AND SOFT COMFORTABLE FOAM PADDING, IT COMPLETELY BLOCKS OUT EVEN THE BRIGHTEST LIGHT.

ITEM 16472   PRICE: $22.50 A PAIR OR TWO PAIRS FOR $40.00

13. Who would be most likely to buy this product?

(A) Opticians

(B) Moviegoers

(C) Airline pilots

(D) Night workers

14. Which of the following is true about this product?

(A) Two pairs cost $40.00.

(B) It is made completely of lightweight plastic.

(C) It can be ordered only on airline flights.

(D) It blocks out all but the brightest light.

D. Announcements

Announcements (and notices) are brief readings meant to inform the public. Typically, they concern the hours of a new business, the introduction of a new product or service, the availability of a business opportunity, the statement of a government or business policy, the opening of a cultural attraction, or other similar situations.

Overview questions about announcements often ask about the purpose of the announcement or the audience for it. Detail questions often ask about time, place, and price.

Sample Items: Announcements

AMERICAN IMPRESSIONISM AND REALISM
A Landmark Exhibition from the Met

20 JAN 20-- TO 22 APR 20--
WAMA | TICKETED

Exclusive to the Western Australia Museum of Art in Perth is the exhibition "American Impressionism and Realism: A Landmark Exhibition from the Met." This exhibition presents 71 paintings by 34 artists from New York's Metropolitan Museum of Art. –[1]– Among them are some of the Met's best examples of paintings in the American Impressionist and Realist traditions, many of which have never before been displayed outside their home in New York.

Leading figures — such as Impressionists John Singer Sargent, Mary Cassatt, Childe Hassam, and William Merritt Chase, and Realists Robert Henri, John Sloan, and William Blackins — are represented by several works. –[2]– The exhibition considers how proponents of two styles that flourished around 1900 responded artistically to modern life in very different fashions.

More than 30 iconic Australian paintings from those two schools that also flourished in Australia during the early twentieth century are also to be included in the exhibition. –[3]– They include works by artists such as Tom Roberts, Charles Conder, and Frederick McCubbin.

"American Impressionism and Realism" includes light-filled landscapes and seascapes, magnificent portraits of women and children, and images that reflect many aspects of modern life. –[4]–

1. What is the main theme of this display?

   (A) The range of contemporary painting in the U.S.

   (B) The contrast between today's art and art in 1900

   (C) A comparison between U.S. artists and Australian artists

   ● Differences between two important styles of art

> The announcement states that the paintings in the display show "how proponents of two styles that flourished around 1900 responded artistically to modern life in very different fashions."

2. What does the announcement suggest about some of the artists whose work is in this exhibition?

   (A) They have only one piece of art that is being displayed.

   (B) They are neither Realists nor Impressionists.

   (C) They are neither Australian nor from the U.S.

   ● They have never had their paintings exhibited outside the U.S. before.

> The announcement states that the exhibition includes "some of the Met's best examples of paintings . . . , many of which have never before been displayed outside their home in New York."

3. Which of the following artists is NOT considered a Realist?

   (A) John Sloan

   ● Mary Cassatt

   (C) William Blackins

   (D) Robert Henri

> The announcement identifies Mary Cassatt as an Impressionist and the other three artists as Realists.

4. In which of the positions marked [1], [2], [3], and [4] does the following sentence best belong?

   "These works highlight how artists from our country responded to key artistic developments of the period."

   (A) [1]

   (B) [2]

   ● [3]

   (D) [4]

> In the third paragraph, the announcement states that the exhibition will include Australian paintings. Since the show takes place in Perth, Australia, the reference to "artists from our country" must mean Australian artists. Therefore, the missing sentence belongs in position [3].

Focus: Understanding and answering questions about announcements.

Directions: Read the passages, and then mark the best answers to the questions.

Questions 1–5 refer to the following notice:

— IMPORTANT NOTICE —

- All passengers who are nationals of countries other than the United States or Canada must complete an Immigration Form before arrival in the U.S. Fill out one for each family member. Do not write on the back. Write in English in all capital letters. Keep the form until your departure from the United States. Use the white I-94 form if you have a valid U.S. visa. Use the green I-94W form if you hold a passport from one of the 38 countries participating in the visa-waiver program and do not have a valid U.S. visa. Use the blue I-94T form if you are only making an in-transit stop en route to another country.

- All passengers (or one passenger per family) are required to complete a Customs Declaration Form prior to arrival. Complete it in English and in capital letters. Be sure to sign your name on the back of the form. Travelers with passports from the U.S., Canada, or visa-waiver countries may also use Automated Passport Control (APC) self-service kiosks to submit their Customs Declaration Form and biographic information. APC is a free service and does not require pre-registration or membership. Travelers are prompted to scan their passport, take a photograph using the kiosk, and answer a series of questions verifying biographic and flight information. Once passengers have completed the series of questions and submitted their Customs Declaration Form, a receipt will be issued. Travelers then bring their passport and receipt to a Customs Officer to finalize their inspection. The kiosks allow people residing at the same address to be processed together.

---

1. How many Immigration Forms must be filled out by a family of two adults and one child who are not U.S. or Canadian nationals?

   (A) None

   (B) One

   (C) Two

   (D) Three

2. What should a traveler do with the Immigration Form?

   (A) Give it to an immigrations agent right after landing

   (B) Keep it until leaving the U.S.

   (C) Fill it out after arrival

   (D) Give it to a U.S. Customs Officer

3. If a passenger is changing planes in Miami on a flight from Madrid, Spain to Mexico City, which form should he or she fill out?

   (A) A white one

   (B) A green one

   (C) A blue one

   (D) No form is required.

4. What should passengers write on the back of the Customs Declaration Forms?

(A) Nothing

(B) Their signatures

(C) Their flight number

(D) The date

5. What can be inferred about the APC service?

(A) Travelers who use it must register in advance.

(B) Only one person per family is required to use it.

(C) It replaces the Customs Declaration Form.

(D) Only U.S. and Canadian nationals may use it.

Questions 6–8 refer to the following notice:

By signing this airbill, sender agrees that Nova Express is not responsible for any claim in excess of $100 due to loss, damage, nondelivery, or misdelivery, unless the sender declares a higher value and pays additional charges based on that higher value. Declared value of the package cannot exceed $500. In the event of untimely delivery, Nova Express will at sender's request refund delivery charges. See back of airbill for further information.

6. What is the purpose of this notice?

(A) To discuss how Nova Express can improve its service

(B) To inform customers of Nova Express's limits of liabilities

(C) To convince potential customers to choose Nova Express

(D) To explain how government regulations affect Nova Express

7. If a package is delivered late, how much money will Nova Express give to the sender?

(A) None

(B) $100

(C) $500

(D) The amount paid for delivery

8. To obtain more information, what should the sender do?

(A) Look at the other side of the airbill

(B) Ask for a special form

(C) Sign the back of the airbill

(D) Call a Nova Express office

Farm visits leave one with a renewed appreciation and awe of the miracle of growing food. Below is a list of local farms that will be welcoming visitors this summer.

Sunflower Farm offers free farm tours every Friday and Saturday during the summer at 3 PM. They also have a fall festival planned for the weekend of September 23rd and 24th. Click <u>here</u> for more information about this event. And you won't want to miss their end-of-season picking days. This Friday, farm owner Annie O'Reilly will be conducting a workshop on canning fruits and jam.

Appleby Dairy Farm invites visitors to an open house on the first Saturday and Sunday of every month during the summer. Come see what life on a dairy farm is really like. Be sure to bring the kids to visit the baby cows, sheep, and goats, and to enjoy tractor rides and pony rides. Visit the cheese house and watch master cheese-maker Will Appleby at work. Sample traditional farmhouse cheeses, all made with milk from their own herds.

On August 25th, the Farm-to-Table Association will host its fifth annual tour. The 8-mile bike tour features visits to local gardening projects, presentations from organic farmers at Black Oak Acres, and ends with a healthy lunch at the Springdale Food Co-op. Meet at the parking lot of the Co-op at 8 AM. Click <u>here</u> to register and pre-pay.

Sugarbush Farm offers farm visits by appointment. Owner Mark Tezuka supplies produce for the Sugarbush Café as well as several other farm-to-table restaurants. Sugarbush Farm has a calendar of local food events all year round, including their popular winter markets. Click <u>here</u> for more info.

9. What information is made available by clicking on the link in paragraph 2?

(A) Information about free farm visits

(B) Information on canning fruits and making jam

(C) Information on picking days

(D) Information on an event in the autumn

10. Which of the following farms specifically offers activities for children?

(A) Sunflower Farm

(B) Appleby Dairy Farm

(C) Black Oak Acres

(D) Sugarbush Farm

11. What is suggested about the bicycle tour mentioned in paragraph 4?

(A) It ends at the same place where it begins.

(B) It is longer this year than in previous years.

(C) It involves visits to more than one farm.

(D) It is offered free to participants.

12. In the notice, the word "produce" in paragraph 5 is closest in meaning to

(A) meats

(B) fruits and vegetables

(C) financial support

(D) dairy products

13. Which of the following is NOT held only during the summer?

(A) Open houses at Appleby Dairy Farm

(B) Farm tours at Sunflower Farm

(C) Markets at Sugarbush Farm

(D) Lunches at Springdale Food Co-op

E. Non-Prose Readings

These readings are not written in standard paragraph style and may not employ complete sentences. This category of readings includes forms (especially those used by businesses), lists, charts, graphs, schedules, and maps. There are usually one or two non-prose readings per test.

Unlike other types of readings, you should not read non-prose readings word for word. Glance at the reading to see what it concerns; then start working on the questions. Refer back to the reading to find specific information.

Sample Items: Non-Prose Reading

METRO LODGING REPORT: JULY

Location	Room Nights Occupied	Room Nights Available	Occupancy Percentage	Average Room Cost
AIRPORT	89,649	104,847	85.5%	$128.28
NORTH SUBURBAN	29,686	35,065	84.7%	$93.75
WEST SUBURBAN	46,279	50,950	90.8%	$97.78
MIDTOWN	29,681	37,851	78.4%	$89.70
DOWNTOWN	62,620	77,271	81.0%	$179.61

1. What does this report concern?

    (A) Apartment buildings

    ● Hotels

    (C) Parking lots

    (D) Office buildings

> The word *lodging* indicates that the report deals with hotel rooms.

2. Which area had the highest rate of occupancy in July?

    (A) North Suburban

    (B) Airport

    ● West Suburban

    (D) Downtown

> At 90.8%, the West Suburban area had the highest occupancy rate. (The airport location had 85.5%, North Suburban had 84.7%, Midtown had 78.4%, and Downtown had 81%.)

3. What does the chart indicate about Downtown?

    ● On average, it had the most expensive rooms.

    (B) It had fewer empty rooms in July than Midtown did.

    (C) It had more rooms than any other area.

    (D) There were more rooms per building than in other areas.

> At an average price of $179.61, Downtown hotel rooms were the most expensive.

Focus: Understanding and answering questions about non-prose readings.

Directions: Read the passages, and then mark the best answers to the questions.

Questions 1–4 refer to the following itinerary:

NORTHERN ODYSSEY TOUR
DEPARTING SEPT. 9

For your convenience, we recommend that you check your luggage through to Helsinki, Finland. Please wear your NORTHERN ODYSSEY TOUR badge during transfers to facilitate identification by our representatives.

SAT. SEPT. 9 — **DEPART U.S.A.** via air
(Please refer to your personal air itineraries for departure/arrival times.)

SUN. SEPT. 10 — **ARRIVE HELSINKI, FINLAND**
Accommodations: Presidenti Hotel

TUE. SEPT. 12 — **DEPART HELSINKI** motorcoach to dock
Accommodations: SS Northern Lights

FRI. SEPT. 15 — **ARRIVE STOCKHOLM, SWEDEN** via ship
Accommodations: Royal Viking Hotel

MON. SEPT. 18 — **DEPART STOCKHOLM** via Air Scandinavia
ARRIVE COPENHAGEN, DENMARK
Accommodations: Air Scandinavia Hotel

SAT. SEPT. 23 — **DEPART COPENHAGEN** via Air Scandinavia
ARRIVE OSLO, NORWAY
Accommodations: Princess Christiana Hotel

WED. SEPT. 27 — **DEPART OSLO** via railroad
ARRIVE BERGEN, NORWAY
Accommodations: Hotel Bryggen

SUN. OCT. 1 — **DEPART BERGEN** by air
ARRIVE U.S.A.
(Please refer to your personal air itineraries. All passengers are required to clear U.S. Customs.)

1. Why are the members of the tour asked to wear badges?

    (A) To get seats on the plane

    (B) To be recognized by tour representatives

    (C) To get through customs quickly

    (D) To recognize each other easily

2. How will members of the tour go from Helsinki to Stockholm?

    (A) By car

    (B) By air

    (C) By train

    (D) By ship

3. In which of these cities will members of the tour spend the most time?

    (A) Copenhagen

    (B) Stockholm

    (C) Bergen

    (D) Helsinki

4. How long will the entire tour take?

    (A) 1 week

    (B) 2 weeks

    (C) 3 weeks

    (D) 4 weeks

Type of lighting	Advantages	Drawbacks
Tungsten (incandescent)	Widely available; warm, yellowish light; inexpensive to purchase.	Needs frequent replacement; generates excessive heat; uses energy inefficiently.
Halogen	Cool, crisp light; brighter than tungsten, with a sparkling quality; excellent for display areas and decorative lighting.	Expensive; sometimes requires a transformer; generates heat.
Fluorescent	Uses the least amount of energy; inexpensive.	Distorts the appearance of colors and makes surroundings seem dull; sometimes flickers and often makes a humming noise.
Sodium	Useful in foggy or steamy conditions.	Distorts the appearance of colors; expensive; when disposed of may release toxic chemicals.
Xenon	Bright, white light that appears slightly blue; most closely simulates sunlight; very long lasting; no harmful chemicals released when disposed of; compact size.	Expensive; light may be blindingly bright.

5. What type of lighting would the author probably recommend for illuminating a display window of a jewelry store?

   (A) Sodium

   (B) Fluorescent

   (C) Tungsten

   (D) Halogen

6. What is one problem with fluorescent lights that is mentioned in the chart?

   (A) They sometimes make noise.

   (B) They must frequently be replaced.

   (C) They create too much heat.

   (D) They use too much energy.

7. What is one characteristic that xenon and halogen lights have in common?

   (A) They are both useful in the fog.

   (B) They both distort the appearance of colors.

   (C) They both cost a lot.

   (D) They can both be disposed of safely.

Questions 8–12 refer to the following instructions:

Dialing Instructions

Room to room	Floors 1 through 9	(6) + room number
	Floors 10 through 17	(7) + room number
Local calls	8 + phone number *($0.75 access charge)*	
Long distance direct dial	8 + 1 + area code + phone number *($1.00 access charge)*	
International direct dial	8 + 1 + 011 + country code + city code + phone number *($1.25 access charge)*	
Credit card calls	8 + 0 + area code + phone number, then follow instructions on card *($1.00 access charge)*	
Local information	8 + 411 *($0.75 access fee)*	
Long distance information	8 + 1 + area code + 555-1212	

A blinking red light on your phone signals that you have a message. Call the Message Center to receive your messsage.

Bell captain	57	Housekeeping/laundry	56	Messages	2
Business center	50	Concierge	3	Fitness club	59
Front desk	0	Room service	59	Coffee shop	51

8. Where would these instructions probably be found?

   (A) In an office building

   (B) In a phone booth

   (C) In a hotel room

   (D) In a hotel lobby

9. What number would someone call to speak to a person in Room 921?

   (A) 921

   (B) 6 + 921

   (C) 7 + 921

   (D) 0 + 921

10. According to the instructions, how is a person informed of messages?

    (A) By a phone call

    (B) By visiting the Message Center

    (C) By a written note

    (D) By a blinking light

11. How much is the access fee to obtain the phone number of someone who lives in this city?

    (A) Nothing

    (B) $0.75

    (C) $1.00

    (D) $1.25

12. What number would someone dial to have a room cleaned?

    (A) 2

    (B) 3

    (C) 56

    (D) 59

Questions 13–14 refer to the following chart:

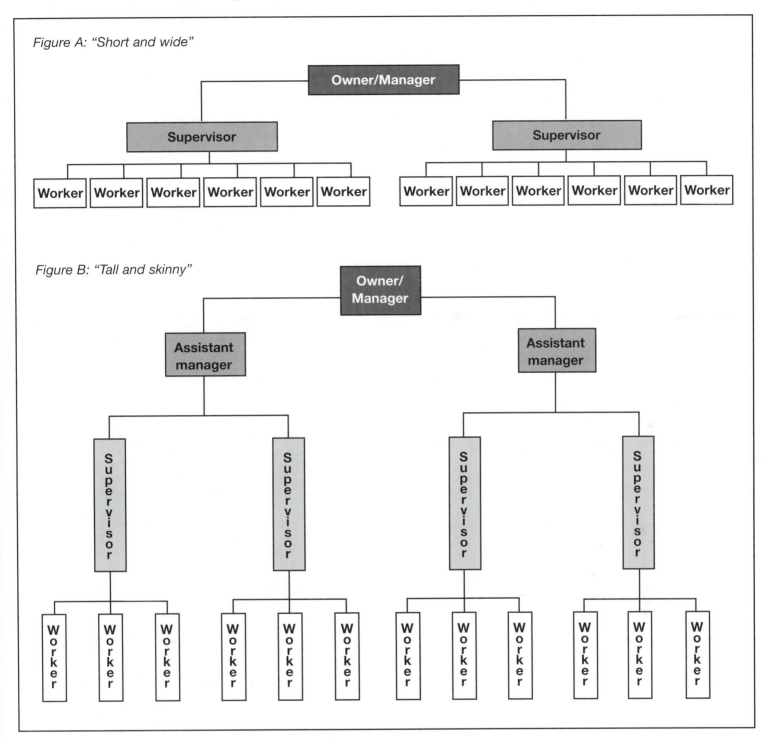

Figure A: "Short and wide"

Owner/Manager

Supervisor | Supervisor

Worker Worker Worker Worker Worker Worker | Worker Worker Worker Worker Worker Worker

Figure B: "Tall and skinny"

Owner/Manager

Assistant manager | Assistant manager

Supervisor Supervisor | Supervisor Supervisor

Worker Worker Worker | Worker Worker Worker | Worker Worker Worker | Worker Worker Worker

13. What would be the best title for this chart?

   (A) "Two Methods for Organizing Small Businesses"

   (B) "The Changing Structure of Management"

   (C) "The Role of the Assistant Manager"

   (D) "Workers' Responsibility: Before and After"

14. Based on the information in the chart, which of the following statements is true?

   (A) "Short and wide" involves fewer workers.

   (B) "Tall and skinny" involves another level of management.

   (C) "Short and wide" provides more jobs for more people.

   (D) "Tall and skinny" puts the owner/manager in closer contact with the workers.

F. Message Chains

Message Chain readings first appeared when the TOEIC was revised in 2016. They consist of an exchange of short text messages between two people such as those that can be sent from or read on smartphones. They may also involve an Internet chat with three or more people. Message chains may be fairly short — only 5 or 6 exchanges — and may be followed by only two or three questions. Other message chains, especially those involving an Internet discussion, may be longer and have more questions about them. Message chains are less formal and more conversational than most other readings.

Overview questions about message chains often ask about the business or profession one of the writers is in.

Sample Items: Message Chains

Moon, Ji-young [10:34]
Good morning, Rich, I hope you are having a good trip. Hey, I wonder if you can help us out—we're having a little problem here.

Palmer, Richard [10:35]
Morning, Ji-young. Sure, what's up?

Moon, Ji-young [10:35]
Ms. Poe needs to get into that old filing cabinet next to your desk. Do you know where the key is?

Palmer, Richard [10:37]
Well, I have one on my key ring here. I think there's another in the lock ... if not, look in the top drawer of my desk.

Moon, Ji-young [10:42]
No, it's not in the lock, and I don't see it in your drawer.

Palmer, Richard [10:42]
After my meeting with Mr. Delgado today, I could send it by express courier. It could be there by tomorrow.

Moon, Ji-young [10:42]
I'll ask Ms. Poe if that's what she wants you to do.

Poe, Diana [10:49]
Hi, Rich. It turns out that it wasn't actually locked. The filing cabinet drawers were just stuck. I gave the bottom drawer a good kick and it popped open. Thanks anyway.

Palmer, Richard [10:50]
Well, glad the problem is solved.

Poe, Diana [10:51]
See you next week. Hope you have a good meeting with Mr. Delgado. He's a tough negotiator.

1. Where is one of the keys to the filing cabinet?

    (A) It's inside the filing cabinet lock.

    ● Mr. Palmer has it.

    (C) It's in Mr. Palmer's desk drawer.

    (D) Ms. Poe has it.

> Richard Palmer says at 10:37, "I have one on my key ring here."

2. At 10:49, what does Ms. Poe mean when she writes, "Thanks anyway"?

    ● Mr. Palmer does not need to send her the key by express courier.

    (B) She appreciates the fact that Mr. Palmer is meeting Mr. Delgado.

    (C) She is happy that Mr. Palmer was able to help her locate the key.

    (D) Mr. Palmer should leave the key in the office when he goes out of town.

> When Ms. Poe writes, "Thanks anyway," she means that she appreciates Mr. Palmer's offer to send the key to her by express courier, but that this is not necessary since the cabinet was not actually locked, only stuck.

Intention Questions

One of the questions about Message Chains will be an intention question. This type of question first appeared in the 2016 revision of the TOEIC. You will probably see intention questions only after Message Chains in the Reading section, but they are similar to questions that you will hear in Parts 3 and 4 of the Listening test.

Intention questions ask what a phrase or a short sentence used by one of the writers means. (Question 2 above is an intention question.) The phrase or sentence may be somewhat idiomatic or colloquial (informal). If you are not familiar with the expression, you should be able to guess what it means by context — by looking at the sentences just before and after the expression being asked about. You can also use the process of elimination to rule out unlikely answer choices.

Exercise 7.6

Focus: Understanding and answering intention questions.

Directions: The following are short selections taken from Message Chains. Look at the underlined expression and then decide which of the two answer choices is closest in meaning to the underlined expression.

1. 4:10 pm: **Eduardo Perez:** Steve, can you work for me on Tue, and I'll take your shift on Wed?

    4:11 pm: **Steve Palmer:** Sure, why not?

    4:13 pm: **Eduardo Perez:** You have the evening shift on Wed, right?

    (A) Steve wants to know why Eduardo can't work on Tuesday.

    (B) Steve doesn't mind exchanging shifts with Eduardo.

2. Isaac Oshei — 9:21 AM

Jill, you'll need a visitor's badge when you go see Mr. Harding.

Jill Brooks — 9:23 AM

OK, how do I go about getting one?

Isaac Oshei — 9:23 AM

When you arrive at the facility, tell the security guard who you are and he'll call Mr. Harding. Then he'll give you a badge.

Jill Brooks — 9:24 AM

<u>Got it!</u> Thanks.

(A) Jill has a visitor's badge now.

(B) Jill understands what to do.

3. Chris Mattson [6:02]   Hey, everyone, I just heard that Ms. Trigo has resigned as head of department.

Robin Lee [6:04]   Wow, I wasn't expecting that. Who's going to be taking her place?

Jenn O'Brien [6:05]   <u>I don't know, but I could make a good guess.</u>

(A) Jenn thinks she knows who will be the new head of department.

(B) Jenn has no idea who Ms. Trigo's replacement will be.

4. [Wed Mar 4 11:44] **Luana Vale:**   Any idea where I should take the visiting party from the Kiyoshi Company to dinner tonight?

[Wed Mar 4 11:47] **Jack Schultz:**   <u>How about Goldini's?</u>

(A) Jack wants to know if Goldini's would be a good choice.

(B) Jack suggests taking the visitors to Goldini's.

5. 10:24   **Michael Healy:**   How are you going to move those boxes from the warehouse?

10:25   **Keiko Izawa:**   I thought I'd ask Mr. Roberts if we could use his van.

10:25   **Michael Healy:**   <u>Don't waste your time.</u>

(A) Mr. Roberts will not be very helpful.

(B) Moving the boxes will not be useful.

6.

Raj Batra: Ms. Phillips from the head office is coming by our staff meeting today to give a little talk about ergonomics.

Denise Kurtz: Ergonomics? Really? Before or after my presentation?

Raj Batra: <u>I don't have a clue.</u>

(A) Raj is not sure when Ms. Phillips will come to the meeting.

(B) Raj doesn't know what is meant by the term "ergonomics."

Exercise 7.7

Focus: Understanding and answering questions about message chains.

Directions: Read the passages, and then mark the best answers to the questions.

Questions 1–3 refer to the following text message chain:

Mon. Apr. 29 1:03 p.m.　　**Royce Kingsley**
Tony, I just got a call from Marie-Luz at Bustamante Construction. She seems to think that you quoted her the wrong prices for lumber and some other supplies she ordered this morning.

Mon. Apr. 29 1:06 p.m.　　**Royce Kingsley**
Her accountant told her that you were charging too little for the lumber and the paint, and too much for the window glass.

Mon. Apr. 29 1:13 p.m.　　**Antonio Scarpelli**
I don't see how that could have happened, Mr. Kingsley. I read the prices right off the price list.

Mon. Apr. 29 1:15 p.m.　　**Royce Kingsley**
What are the dates on the price list, and what color is the paper?

Mon. Apr. 29 1:19 p.m.　　**Antonio Scarpelli**
I'm embarrassed to say ... it's green, and it's from Jan to Dec of last year.

Mon. Apr. 29 1:19 p.m.　　**Royce Kingsley**
How long have you been quoting last year's prices to our customers?

Mon. Apr. 29 1:21 p.m.　　**Antonio Scarpelli**
Just today, I'm sure. Now that I think about it, I remember having the blue list on my desk last Friday. Don't worry, I'll contact every customer I spoke to this morning and tell them about the mistake.

Mon. Apr. 29 1:23 p.m.　　**Royce Kingsley**
You'd better let me handle that. Email me a list of whom you spoke to. And get rid of that old list right away.

---

1. What type of business do Royce Kingsley and Antonio Scarpelli probably work for?

   (A) An office supply store

   (B) A construction company

   (C) An accounting firm

   (D) A building supply company

2. What does Royce Kingsley indicate about the price list?

   (A) It is printed on a different color paper every year.

   (B) A new version of it comes out every month.

   (C) The prices on it always go up from year to year.

   (D) The current version of it is not up-to-date.

3. At 1:23 P.M., what does Royce Kingsley mean when he writes, "You'd better let me handle that"?

   (A) He is the only person who knows how to contact these customers.

   (B) He doesn't want Antonio Scarpelli to ever contact these customers again.

   (C) He thinks Antonio Scarpelli should email these customers immediately.

   (D) He will take responsibility for informing the customers of the mistake.

Questions 4–6 refer to the following online chat discussion:

Yu, Keith {7:31 PM}
Bike to Work Day is the day after tomorrow. I guess it's just us taking part this year.

Ariaga, Luciana {7:35 PM}
Well, we are the only ones registered, anyway. Too bad—last year there were about a dozen of us from Elsworth, Inc.

Maxwell, Amy {7:41 PM}
I registered last year but something came up. This will be a first for me.

Ariaga, Luciana {7:42 PM}
That's right—you always take the bus to work.

Maxwell, Amy {7:43 PM}
In fact, I have to borrow a bike from my sister. Not that she uses it very much.

Ariaga, Luciana {7:44 PM}
I think Keith is the only regular bike commuter.

Yu, Keith {7:45 PM}
There are around 40 breakfast stations that are open from 6:30 to 9. That's one of the best things about Bike to Work Day—free breakfasts.

Ariaga, Luciana {7:46 PM}
I remember last year, pancakes and coffee at the Riverside Café. Let's stop there again.

Maxwell, Amy {7:49 PM}
That doesn't work for me. I'm coming from the north.

Yu, Keith {7:50 PM}
Then let's meet on Cooper Street in the parking lot of the middle school. We'll bike up to Zeal Market on Hancock Street and get breakfast there. It's not that far from work.

Maxwell, Amy {7:52 PM}
Sounds good. I'm going to talk it up tomorrow, see if I can get some more people from Marketing to join us. Do you think you can get anyone from Engineering?

Yu, Keith {7:52 PM}
Beats me. It might be too late to register, but people can still ride anyway.

Ariaga, Luciana {7:54 PM}
Maybe they'll come along once they find out about the free breakfast.

---

4. Which of the following people rides a bike to work most often?

(A) Keith Yu

(B) Amy Maxwell

(C) Luciana Ariaga

(D) Amy Maxwell's sister

5. Where will they meet on Bike to Work Day?

(A) At work

(B) At Zeal Market

(C) Near a middle school

(D) At the Riverside Café

6. At 7:52 p.m., what does Keith Yu mean when he writes, "Beats me"?

(A) He doesn't think Amy should ask anyone else to join them.

(B) He isn't sure if anyone will be interested in riding to work.

(C) He doesn't know if anyone else will register for Bike to Work Day.

(D) He isn't planning to talk to anyone in the Engineering department.

Questions 7–9 refer to the following text message chain:

Thur July 25   09:55   Karen Chen
When we met Monday, you said you needed some time to consider Prestige Corporate Catering's proposal to provide a coffee & tea service for your offices. Can we get together next week? I can answer any questions and respond to any issues that you've thought of since our last meeting.

Thur July 25   11:23   James Maguire
Karen, sorry it took me a while to respond to your text. I was at a meeting and we were just talking about your proposal. I'm afraid we're going to stick with our current coffee service, Cuppa Joe.

Thur July 25   11:25   Karen Chen
Jim, I remember when we met earlier, you were concerned because your current vendor didn't always show up on time, and that they weren't exactly eco-friendly. Those are two concerns that you won't have to worry about with us. Not only that ... we can offer more than basic coffee services and basic coffee makers. We can supply you with cappuccinos, lattes, mochaccinos, flavored coffees, teas, and hot chocolate. And more.

Thur July 25   11:28   James Maguire
That sounds good, but here's the bottom line: The price difference between your service and theirs is just too significant.

Thur July 25   11:30   Karen Chen
Our accountants have been working on that. They've put together a new—and I believe substantially better—discount. If you're willing to sign a year-long contract, we can offer you a competitive price and I can guarantee first-class service.

Thur July 25   11:32   James Maguire
Well, if that's the case ... then let's talk.

Thur July 25   11:32   Karen Chen
Great. Maybe Monday?

Thur July 25   11:33   James Maguire
I'm out of town until Tuesday morning.

Thur July 25   11:34   Karen Chen
How about Tuesday noon? We can meet over lunch at the Oaken Bucket. My treat.

Thur July 25   11:34   James Maguire
Sounds good. See you then.

---

7. What advantages of using her coffee service does Karen Chen NOT point out?

(A) Her service is more environmentally friendly than Cuppa Joe's.

(B) Her company offers a variety of products.

(C) Her service is significantly less expensive than Cuppa Joe's.

(D) Her deliveries will arrive promptly when scheduled.

8. When will James Maguire and Karen Chen meet to discuss a possible contract?

(A) On Monday afternoon

(B) On Tuesday morning

(C) During lunch on Tuesday

(D) When lunch is over on Tuesday

9. At 11:34, what does James Maguire mean when he writes, "Sounds good"?

(A) He will accept her new proposal if the cost is low enough.

(B) He agrees to meet with Karen Chen for lunch on Tuesday.

(C) He has heard that the Oaken Bucket is a good place for lunch.

(D) He will confirm his appointment with Karen Chen when he comes back to town.

Questions 10–12 refer to the following online chat discussion:

02:23 **Kuriko Kito** Is anyone going to the Made in Italy exhibition in London in February?

02:27 **Simone Dufour** Unfortunately, I'm not. Too busy. I wish I could go. I went to the last one, which was in Paris. I loved the fashion shows.

02:29 **Michael Macdonald** Well, I can't go either—I'll be in California meeting with our advertising firm. But we have to have some people there representing us. It's such a great chance to meet designers and to see the latest products coming out of Italy.

02:29 **Simone Dufour** No question about it. Some of our best-selling shoes and boots last season were Italian imports.

02:30 **Kuriko Kito** And accessories— scarves and purses especially.

02:35 **Michael Macdonald** Well, I assume our purchasing manager will be there, and her assistant.

02:38 **Simone Dufour** She definitely needs to be there.

10. What kind of business do these people probably work for?

(A) A graphic design firm

(B) A fashion business

(C) An advertising firm

(D) An import-export company

11. Where was the most recent Made in Italy exhibition held?

(A) In London

(B) In Paris

(C) In California

(D) In Italy

12. At 02:29, what does Simone Dufour mean when she writes, "No question about it"?

(A) It is important to hire designers at the Made in Italy exhibition.

(B) Clearly, shoes and boots are their company's best-selling products.

(C) Their firm should certainly send people to the exhibition.

(D) Michael Macdonald must meet with the advertising companies.

The last five reading passages in Part 7 are Multiple Readings: Paired Readings and Three-Part Readings. Paired Readings consist of two related passages. The first might be a letter, a fax, a memo, an advertisement, a schedule, a chart, a business form, etc. The second passage is usually some form of correspondence: an email, a memo, a fax, a letter, a personal note, etc. The second passage responds in some way to the first passage. For example, if the first passage is a schedule, the second passage may be an email requesting changes in the schedule.

Three-Part Readings consist of three related readings: a newspaper review, an article, and an email, for example. The review might be a critical look at a new movie, the article might discuss how popular the movie has been in its first week, and the email might be a comment to the newspaper about how the writer found the movie uninteresting.

There are five questions after each of the five passages. Therefore, the last 25 questions in Part 7 are based on Multiple Readings.

Overview questions about Paired Readings usually ask about the purpose of one of the passages.

Detail questions ask about specific points in any one of the two or three readings.

At least one question in each Multiple Reading, and often two or three, requires you to look at more than one reading in order to answer the question.

You will see a vocabulary question about one or more of the Paired Readings or Three-Part Readings.

Sample Items: Questions About Paired Readings

Global Office Recruitment Services, Ltd.

Japanese + English Fluency   New!
£30,000 + good benefits! Challenging role as office manager with varied duties. Responsible person with accounting experience. University graduate preferred. File #1231.

Russian-speaking personal assistant
£32,500 + top benefits in the business! Executive assistant for director of investment firm. Must be fluent in English. Knowledge of Czech, Polish, or Hungarian useful. You will look after director's schedule and organize appointments and meetings. File #942.

Bilingual French-English customer relations manager
£42,000 + benefits package. International trading company with offices in London, Paris, New York, and San Francisco seeks supervisor for customer relations department. Must have management experience and good interpersonal skills. Advanced computer skills needed. Relocation from the UK not required but must be available for frequent travel. File #1194.

German/French-speaking project manager
£45,000 + benefits. Project manager with minimum two years' experience needed. Make best use of your interpersonal, professional, and linguistic skills. Varied tasks. Mother-tongue fluency in German, French, and English necessary. Must be available to begin work immediately. File #1083.

Spanish/English Fluency   New!
£23,000. Management trainee at lovely British-owned resort on the Costa Brava, Spain. No experience required. File #1321.

Contact Justina Birchmore at GORS, Ltd.
Russell House 60 Bedford Street London WC2E 9HP
Tel. 0147 372 8167 Fax 0147 372 9193 Email JTB@GORS.co.uk
Telephone 9–11 AM or 1–4 PM *or* Fax, mail, or email CV and cover letter
Include file number in all correspondence.

From: "Elizabeth Goodly" <elizgoodly@asu.edu>
To: "Justina Birchmore" <JTB@GORS.co.uk>
Subject: Employment position
Date: May 14, 20--
Attachment(s): 1

Ms. Birchmore,
I tried to call you yesterday morning about 10 your time but was unable to reach you. I wanted to let you know that I am quite interested in the position of Project Manager that you recently advertised.

My father is from the U.K. and my mother is French. My father worked in Germany and I spent three years there when I was in high school. Therefore, I am quite fluent in English, French, and German. As you can see from my résumé (attached), I have had two years' experience as a project manager in a government office and about a year as the manager of a large London bookstore. I want to work in an international environment and I believe I am well qualified for this position.

One problem: I am currently finishing my graduate business degree (MBA). I will not be available for employment until almost the end of this month.

I would very much like to further discuss this position with you. I will be in London by May 27 and will be available for an interview then. Please contact me by email or phone (1-480-555-6642).

Thanks,

Elizabeth Goodly

1. What do all the positions in the advertisement require?

   (A) At least two years of experience

   (B) The ability to relocate outside of the U.K.

   (C) A university degree

   ● The ability to speak more than one language

Choice (D) is best because all five of the positions require an applicant to speak at least two languages. Choice (A) is not correct because the management trainee job does not require any experience. Choice (B) is not correct because the customer relations manager job does not require the person who is hired to relocate. Choice (C) is not correct because only the office manager job mentions that a university degree is preferred, and none of the job listings say that a degree is required.

2. What can be said about the position that Ms. Goodly is interested in?

   (A) It has the best benefits.

   (B) It is a new listing.

   ● It has the highest pay.

   (D) It has already been filled.

Choice (C) is best because the project manager job that Ms. Goodly is interested in pays £45,000, which is more than any of the other positions listed in the advertisement. There is no "flag" next to the project manager position, so (B) is not correct. (The flag indicates a new listing.) The Russian-speaking personal assistant job claims to have "top benefits in the business," so (A) is incorrect. There is no reason to think that the position has already been filled, so (D) is not correct.

3. What problem does Ms. Goodly mention in her email?

   ● She is unable to start work immediately.

   (B) She is not free to come to an interview.

   (C) She does not have fluency in one of the three required languages.

   (D) She does not have enough experience as a project manager.

Choice (A) is best. Ms. Goodly writes: "One problem: I am currently finishing my graduate business degree (MBA). I will not be available for employment until almost the end of this month."

4. What instruction did Ms. Goodly fail to follow when contacting Justina Birchmore?

   (A) She did not attach a copy of her résumé.

   (B) She did not call GORS at the proper time.

   ● She did not include the file number in her email.

   (D) She did not say which languages she can speak.

The best answer is (C). At the bottom of the ad is the instruction "Include file number in all correspondence." Ms. Goodly does not mention the file number of the position she is interested in (File #1083). This is a good example of a question that requires you to look at both readings in order to find the answer.

5. What other job listed in the advertisement might Ms. Goodly be qualified for?

   (A) Office manager (File #1231)

   (B) Personal assistant (File #942)

   ● Customer relations manager (File #1194)

   (D) Management trainee (File #1321)

Ms. Goodly may be qualified for the customer relations manager job (File #1194) because she has management experience and she speaks French. The other three jobs require languages other than those Ms. Goodly speaks. Again, this is an example of a question that requires you to look at both readings in order to provide an answer.

EAGLE RIVER SCHOOL DISTRICT
DEPT. OF LIFELONG LEARNING
REGISTRATION FORM: SUMMER I TERM, JUNE 11 TO JULY 16

NAME: _Jenny Bryant_   ADDRESS: _4277 Grant Avenue_

PHONE: _541-555-7447_   _Eagleton, Oregon 97623_

EMAIL: _jennB123@pxmail.com_   DATE: _May 23, 20--_

Register early! Classes fill up fast. And if you register before May 11, you are eligible for a 10% "early bird" discount.

Class Number	Class	Cost
A239	Portrait Photography	$200
A131	Grow Your Own Vegetables	$100
T023	Driver's Ed*	$150
T122	Fencing 2*	$150

Subtotal _$600_
Discount _____
Total payment due _$600_

*Please register my son Peter Bryant for these two classes.

Payment: ___ Credit Card   ✔ Check
Credit Card Type: _____ Credit Card Number: _____ Expiration Date: _____

Receipt? ✔ Yes   ____ No (Receipts can be sent only if you provide an email
                              address or a self-addressed, stamped envelope.)

If a class is full or is cancelled due to low enrollment, you will be notified by phone or email. If you need to cancel a class registration, you must do so by May 11 to receive a full refund (minus $10 processing fee). If a class is full or is cancelled by Lifelong Learning, a full refund will be issued.

EAGLE RIVER SCHOOL DISTRICT
DEPT. OF LIFELONG LEARNING

May 27, 20—

Dear Ms. Bryant,

We are pleased to inform you that you and your son have been registered for the following classes for the fall term:

Confirmed Registration	Class Number	Time	Location	Instructor
	A239	Mon. & Wed. 7–9 p.m.	West Ridge High School Art Room	Asuka Kunihara
✔	A131	Sat. 11 a.m. –1 p.m.	Eagleton High School Room 119	Donna Bartel
✔	T023	Sat. 1–3 p.m.	Meet in Eagleton High School Cafeteria	Mike Holland
✔	T122	Mon. & Wed. 7–9 p.m.	Mountain Shadows Middle School Gymnasium	Carlos Escobar

Sorry, we could not confirm your registration for the Portrait Photography course because that class is already full. Your refund is being processed and will be sent to you within a week.

Sincerely,

Monica Rajeesh

Monica Rajeesh
Asst. Director, Dept. of Lifelong Learning
Eagle River School District
(541)-555-6578
MRajeesh@ERSD.edu

May 28, 20—
To: MRajeesh@ERSD.edu
From: jennB123@pxmail.com

Dear Ms. Rajeesh,

Thank you for confirming classes for myself and Peter. I am disappointed that the Portrait Photography class is unavailable, as I am a long-time admirer of Ms. Kunihara's work and was looking forward to taking her class. For that reason, I am going to ask you not to return the check for tuition for that class, as I would like to enroll in her Tuesday and Thursday Nature Photography class. I know the tuition for the nature photography class is $25 higher than for the class I had originally signed up for, so on Monday I will call in and give you my credit card information to cover the extra cost of that class.

Thank you,
Jenny Bryant

---

1. Why did Jenny Bryant not receive a discount?

    Ⓐ She did not register for enough classes.

    Ⓑ She registered after June 11.

    Ⓒ She received her confirmation late.

    ⬤ She did not register before May 11.

    > To get an "early bird" discount, Jenny Bryant had to sign up for classes before May 11, but she did not send her registration until May 23.

2. What is probably enclosed with Jenny Bryant's registration form?

    Ⓐ A schedule

    Ⓑ A self-addressed, stamped envelope

    ⬤ A check

    Ⓓ A registration form for her son

    > Jenny Bryant indicates on the form that she is paying by check. She does request a receipt, but since she has provided her email address at the top of the form, there is no reason she has to enclose a self-addressed, stamped envelope.

3. How many classes is Jenny Bryant confirmed for as of May 27?

    Ⓐ None

    ⬤ One

    Ⓒ Two

    Ⓓ Four

    > On the schedule Monica Rajeesh sent to Jenny Bryant on May 27, she indicates that the portrait photography class was full, so at that time, Jenny Bryant was registered only for the vegetable-growing class.

4. What will Peter Bryant learn to do on Saturdays?

    (A) To fence

    (B) To take photographs

    ● To drive

    (D) To grow vegetables

    > On Saturdays, Peter Bryant will be taking the Driver's Ed class. To answer this, you must look at both the first and second readings.

5. What do the portrait photography class and the nature photography class have in common?

    (A) They meet on the same evenings.

    (B) They cost the same.

    ● They are taught by the same teacher.

    (D) They are both unavailable.

    > They are both taught by Asuka Kunihara. Notice that to answer this question, you need information from both the second and third readings.

Focus: Understanding and answering questions about Paired and Three-Part Readings.

Directions: Read the passages, and then mark the best answers to the questions.

Questions 1–5 refer to the following two email messages:

E-cube

To: Walter Quan, Engineering Dept. <walterq@e-cube.com>
From: Judy Zimmer, Public Relations Dept. <judyz@e-cube.com>
Date: Tue 18 November, 20--
Subject: Questionnaire, etc.
Attachments: 2

Hi Walt, Could you do me a favor? I've attached a questionnaire to this email. Would you please take a minute to fill it in electronically and send it back to me? We need to update the information we have on the heads of departments for the new company brochures we are preparing for release in February. Please include non-confidential personal information such as awards, community service, and family news as well as work-related information. And do you want me to arrange to have a new photo taken of you for the brochure? The one that we have on file (also attached) seems to be from when you first started with the firm four or five years ago.

One other thing: part of my new job is to edit the company newsletter, so I'd appreciate hearing from you if there have been any exciting new developments or any interesting gossip from the engineering department. If so, please let me know right away because the deadline for submissions to the newsletter for next month is Friday, November 21.

Thanks so much,

Judy

To: Judy Zimmer, Public Relations Dept. <judyz@e-cube.com>
From: Walter Quan, Engineering Dept. <walterq@e-cube.com>
Date: Wed 19 November, 20--
Subject: Re. Questionnaire, etc.
Attachment(s): 1

Hey Judy,
I'll fill out the questionnaire and get it to you by the end of the week. I'm afraid I don't have all that much new to report since the last time I filled out one of these!

As far as information for the newsletter: I'd hoped to announce the release date of our newest product, the E-Cube Mark IV, in next month's newsletter, but there have been a few problems and the release date has been put off for a couple of weeks. However, you can report that the Mark IV will be released soon, and that it is the most advanced version of the E-Cube ever.

Gossip from the engineering department: My personal assistant Deborah Baines is getting married next Saturday. One of our engineers, Jae Sim, has organized an after-work video game tournament. Max Taggert, my old boss, is retiring in January.

About the photo: it's really not *that* old. I think it was taken about two years ago. Guess I just looked young that day! However, I'm attaching a more recent one.

Oh, by the way, congratulations on being named head of the Public Relations Department!

Best wishes,

Walter Q.

---

1. What is the main purpose of Judy Zimmer's email?
   - (A) To explain the purpose of the company brochure
   - (B) To inform Walter Quan of her new position
   - (C) To find out when a photograph was taken
   - (D) To ask Walter Quan to provide some information

2. What can be inferred about Walter Quan?
   - (A) He is head of the Engineering Department.
   - (B) He just began working for this company.
   - (C) He has recently been promoted.
   - (D) He is Judy Zimmer's supervisor.

3. What is attached to the email that Walter Quan sent?
   - (A) The answers to some questions
   - (B) A recent photo
   - (C) The most recent company brochure
   - (D) An article from a newsletter

4. Which of the following has been delayed?
   - (A) The release of a new product
   - (B) The start of a video game tournament
   - (C) The wedding of Walter Quan's assistant
   - (D) The deadline for submitting articles to the newsletter

5. What is Judy Zimmer mistaken about?
   - (A) When Walter Quan began working at this company
   - (B) How soon the corporate brochure will be published
   - (C) When Walter Quan's photograph was taken
   - (D) How old Walter Quan is

ValleyviewLabs

740 Potero Avenue, Sunnyvale, California 94086

May 17, 20--

Carlos Reyes
3205 Craycroft Road
Tucson, AZ 85729

Dear Mr. Reyes:

I read with interest your curriculum vitae and letter dated April 30. Your education and prior experience in both research and management were impressive. However, I'm afraid I cannot offer you the position of research technician that you applied for. This is an entry-level position and would not offer the challenge or, frankly, the salary someone with your qualifications should have. I'm afraid you may have been misled by the advertisement, which was not clearly worded, and for that I apologize.

However, due to expansion here at Valleyview, there is a possibility that the position of deputy coordinator of the research and development team may be created. Given your background, you would be a strong candidate for the position.

I plan to be in Tucson on business along with my assistant director, Leigh Elliott, from May 30 to June 2. If you are still interested in a position with Valleyview Labs, please contact my administrative assistant, Ms. Rachel Stone, within the next few days to arrange an appointment.

I look forward to meeting you.

Sincerely,

Philip H. Kappler

Philip H. Kappler, Executive Director
Valleyview Labs, Inc.

PHK/rs

```
┌─────────────────────────────────────────────────┐
│               Phone Message Sheet               │
│                                                 │
│  To: Mr. Kappler                                │
│  Date: May 19, 20--          Time: 2:30 P.M.    │
│                                                 │
│  From: Mr. Carlos Reyes                         │
│                                                 │
│  Message: Carlos Reyes called and said he would be happy to meet │
│  with you to discuss the deputy coordinator position. I know     │
│  you wanted to see him on the 30th but he is not free then.      │
│  I checked your schedule and it looks like you and Ms. Elliott are │
│  available the morning of your last day in Tucson, so I scheduled your │
│  meeting with Mr. Reyes at 9 A.M. that day.                       │
│                                                 │
│  Message taken by: rs                           │
│                                                 │
└─────────────────────────────────────────────────┘
```

6. What position did Mr. Reyes originally apply for?

   (A) Assistant director of Valleyview Labs

   (B) Deputy coordinator of a research team

   (C) Administrative assistant to Mr. Kappler

   (D) Research technician

7. Why was Mr. Reyes NOT offered the position for which he applied?

   (A) He lacked the proper experience for it.

   (B) He was overqualified for it.

   (C) It had already been filled.

   (D) The company decided not to fill it.

8. Why does Mr. Kappler apologize in his letter?

   (A) Because the advertisement was unclear

   (B) Because the salary is so low

   (C) Because he took so long to respond

   (D) Because his letter is so short

9. When will Mr. Kappler probably meet with Mr. Reyes?

   (A) May 30

   (B) May 31

   (C) June 1

   (D) June 2

10. Who probably filled out the phone message sheet?

   (A) Carlos Reyes

   (B) Philip H. Kappler

   (C) Rachel Stone

   (D) Leigh Elliott

Questions 11–15 are based on the following itinerary, email, and text message:

Hollyfield Travel

Travel plan for Paula Scott, Ion Software, Inc.

Date: September 23, 20--

Airline	Flight	Date	From	To	Depart	Arrive	Class
Northeastern Airlines	310	30 Sep	Washington, D.C.	New York City	3:50 PM	5:05 PM	Bus
TransAtlantic Air	403	30 Sep	New York City	Frankfurt, Germany	7:00 PM	7:35 AM	Bus
			(Note: TransAtlantic Air 403 arrives Saturday 1 Oct)				
Air Europa	3250	3 Oct	Frankfurt, Germany	Kiev, Ukraine	9:35 AM	1:10 PM	1st
Istanbul Air	610	6 Oct	Kiev, Ukraine	Istanbul, Turkey	2:20 PM	4:20 PM	Bus
Istanbul Air	2018	10 Oct	Istanbul, Turkey	Frankfurt, Germany	6:20 AM	8:45 AM	Bus
TransAtlantic Air	402	12 Oct	Frankfurt, Germany	New York City	10:40 AM	12:50 PM	Bus
Northeastern Airlines	341	12 Oct	New York City	Washington, D.C.	2:25 PM	3:40 PM	Bus

Reservations made by travel consultant   *James Schroeder*

Ion Software

To: James Schroeder <JS@hollyfield.com>
From: Paula Scott <Paula_Scott@IS.com>
Subject: Change in travel plans
Date: September 23, 20--

Hello James,

The itinerary and documents for my trip to Frankfurt, Kiev, etc. next week were just delivered by courier. Thanks for arranging everything. Unfortunately, I just found out that I need to make some last-minute changes.

I have to stay in Frankfurt a few extra days for a series of important meetings, so now I would like to fly from Frankfurt to Kiev on October 9th. I'm going to have to cancel the trip to Turkey, I'm afraid. I'll fly right back to Frankfurt from Kiev on the 11th on Air Europa, and then return to Washington as planned on TransAtlantic Air on the 12th.

Also, I noticed that I am booked in first class for the flight from Frankfurt to Kiev. I assume this means that business class was not available. While I would love to fly first class, company travel policy doesn't permit it and so you'll need to book me into the economy section.

Again, sorry!

Paula Scott

Schroeder, James   23 Sep, 4:20 p.m.

Hi Paula. Hey, don't apologize—that's what we're here for! I have made all the changes that you asked for. About the flight from Frankfurt to Kiev—that shouldn't be a problem. I checked with Air Europa and that is a two-class flight, so, as I understand it, that should not be a violation of your company's policy. One other, unrelated change: Your TransAtlantic Air flight on 12 Oct. is now scheduled to leave Frankfurt at 11:20 A.M. Have a great trip!

---

11. For which of these companies does James Schroeder work?

   (A) Air Europa

   (B) Ion Software

   (C) Northeastern Airlines

   (D) Hollyfield Travel

12. After her travel plan is changed, Paula Scott will spend the most time at which of these destinations?

   (A) New York

   (B) Frankfurt

   (C) Kiev

   (D) Istanbul

13. After her travel plan is changed, Paula Scott will NOT fly on which of these airlines?

   (A) Northeastern Airlines

   (B) Air Europa

   (C) Istanbul Air

   (D) TransAtlantic Air

14. What does James Schroeder tell Paula Scott about the flight from Frankfurt to Kiev?

(A) She must change from first class to business class.

(B) She must fly economy class.

(C) She may fly first class.

(D) She should get permission to fly first class.

15. What change must Paula Scott make in the schedule that James Schroeder sent her?

(A) She will be leaving Washington, D.C., on September 30 later than expected.

(B) She will be leaving New York City on September 30 sooner than expected.

(C) She will be arriving in Washington, D.C., on October 12 later than expected.

(D) She will be arriving in New York City on October 12 later than expected.

Questions 16–20 are based on the following email, business form, and memo:

From: S. H. Pham <Sang.Pham@IBI.com>
To: Dunn.Jason@IBI.com
Subject: Leave
Date: Dec. 1, 20—

Mr. Dunn,

I would like to request some time off in early January to attend a wedding in Vietnam and to take care of some pressing family business while I am there.

I only have 30 hours of vacation time left but I will miss 40 hours of work.

If you agree, the other members of my team said that they can cover for me because that is always a pretty slow time of year.

Thank you,

S. H. Pham
Production Team C

International Brands, Inc.

Leave Request / Absence Report Form

Name   _Ms. S. H. Pham_   Date   _4 Dec., 20--_

Dept.   _Production_

This form is to be submitted in advance by supervisors for any employee who wishes to take leave or who will be away for any other reason.

Period requested: _Jan. 7, 20-- to Jan. 12, 20--_

Leave to be recorded as

Vacation	_30_	hours
Medical leave*	_____	hours
Maternity/paternity leave	_____	hours
Compensatory time off	_10_	hours
Assignment away from office	_____	hours
Leave of absence without pay (special cases only)	_____	hours
Total	_40_	hours

*This form is not to be used to record sick leave if it involves fewer than three consecutive days.

Comments: Brief description of how assignments are to be covered during employee's absence.

_____

_____

_____

_____

Approval

_____

(supervisor)

Approval for administrative staff

_Jason Dunn: Supervisor, Production Team C_____

(appropriate department head / vice-president)

Approval for executive personnel (department heads / vice-presidents)

_____

(President)

Circulate approved copies to appropriate departments and return to the Human Resources Office, Room 1190.

Interoffice Memo

From the desk of Sarah Ingram
Human Resources Officer   Room 1190
International Brands, Inc.

TO: *Jason Dunn*   DATE: *6 Dec. 20--*

Hi Jason,

*I'm returning Ms. Pham's request for time off.
Please fill in the "Comments" section. Also, could
you sign her form on the proper line? Please return
to me afterwards.*

Sarah Ingram

---

16. Which of the following is closest in meaning to the word "pressing" in line 2 of Ms. Pham's email?

(A) Unfinished

(B) Official

(C) Urgent

(D) Unspecified

17. Which of the following is Mr. Dunn most likely to write in the "Comments" section of the form?

(A) "Ms. Pham will be attending a wedding in Vietnam during her vacation."

(B) "Ms. Pham has been doing a great job and deserves a promotion."

(C) "Ms. Pham's co-workers can cover for her because this is a slow time of year."

(D) "Ms. Pham will miss several days of work for medical reasons."

18. What mistake did Mr. Dunn make when filling out this form?

(A) He signed his name on the wrong line.

(B) He didn't add up the number of hours correctly.

(C) He didn't send this form to the appropriate department.

(D) He spelled the employee's name incorrectly.

19. Why did the president of International Brands not sign this form?

(A) Because he is on vacation

(B) Because Ms. Pham is asking for only five days off

(C) Because Ms. Pham is not an executive

(D) Because a vice-president has already signed it

20. Where will this form eventually be filed?

(A) In the president's office

(B) In Mr. Dunn's office

(C) In Ms. Pham's office

(D) In Ms. Ingram's office

Recipe Revelations by Joan Travis

Today is the first day of the Chinese New Year. Penny Zhang, proprietor of the Bamboo Forest, tells us that the traditional meal she serves at her restaurant on Chinese New Year ends with a sweet cake called nin go. *It is believed that those who eat this delicacy will have good luck in the year ahead.*

Nin Go Cake

2 cups water
1 cup sugar
2 1/2 cups glutinous rice flour

1/2 cup raisins
1/2 cup dried dates, apricots, or cherries (if desired)

Put sugar in a large mixing bowl and add water. Stir in flour 1/2 cup at a time, until a smooth mixture forms. Add fruit. Coat 10-inch pan with cooking spray, then pour in the mixture. Place cake in steamer basket and set over boiling water. Steam for 40–50 minutes, or until the *nin go* has risen and become translucent. Allow cake to cool, slice into wedges, and serve.

Nutritional information (per slice):
271 calories, 64.7 grams carbohydrates, 0 mg cholesterol, 0.6 grams fat, 2.2 grams protein, 3 mg sodium.

"Recipe Revelations" is a weekly feature that publishes recipes from a different local restaurant. If there is a recipe you would like to see, contact the *Daily Bugle* food editor by email (**Jtravis@dailybugle.com**) or call **272-555-0216**.

Editors:
I enjoy reading Joan Travis's column every week. I especially enjoyed her Jan. 28th column on Chinese New Year (CNY) and lucky cakes.

I love *nin go* (or as it is usually spelled, *nian gao*). I remember my grandmother making huge batches of this sweet, chewy cake every year for CNY, and she would share it with her extended family.

The reason that *nian gao* is part of the CNY festivities is because of the way these words sound in Chinese. *Nian* means "sticky" (it's sticky because of the glutinous rice flour), but it sounds like a word that means "year." And the word *gao* means "cake," but it sounds like the word that means "tall" or "high." So, symbolically, eating *nian gao* for CNY means that we pull ourselves higher every year.

After steaming the cakes, my grandmother would always dip slices of *nian gao* in an egg batter and deep fry it in oil in her wok.

Evelyn Sun
Springdale, CA

From: Joan Travis <Jtravis@dailybugle.com>
To: Evelyn Sun <e.sun444@vesta.com>
February 4, 20--

Dear Ms. Sun,

Thank you for your response to last week's column. I was delighted to find out why *nin go* (or *nian gao*) is thought to be a lucky food. I'm sure our readers will be glad to learn more about the significance of these cakes, especially since the Chinese New Year is just around the corner.

I had a chat with Penny Zhang, owner of the Bamboo Forest, who supplied the recipe that was printed in "Recipe Revelations." She agreed that *nian gao* is often deep fried. She prefers to simply slice the *nian gao* and dust it with coconut. Healthier that way, she said. Sometimes, she mentioned, *nian gao* is baked or fried without batter.

Penny said that there are many different recipes for *nian gao* — ones from North China, from South China, from Beijing, from Hong Kong.

Anyway, thanks for reading "Recipe Revelations"!

Joan Travis
Daily Bugle

---

21. Which of the following is given as an optional ingredient in Penny Zhang's recipe for *nin go*?

(A) Cherries

(B) Salt

(C) Raisins

(D) Flour

22. In Penny Zhang's recipe, the word "translucent" in paragraph 2, line 4, is closest in meaning to

(A) nearly clear

(B) slightly warm

(C) completely solid

(D) extremely hot

23. What will probably appear in Joan Travis's column next week?

(A) Another recipe for *nian gao*

(B) Some information about *nian gao* that was supplied by Evelyn Sun

(C) Another way to have good luck in the New Year

(D) A recipe for another dish served at the Bamboo Forest

24. Why is it considered lucky to eat *nian gao* on Chinese New Year?

(A) Because of the pronunciation of the words *nian* and *gao*

(B) Because some of the ingredients are traditionally considered lucky

(C) Because it is one food that is eaten by people all over China

(D) Because the phrase *nian gao* sounds like the phrase "good luck" in Chinese

25. What is one thing that Penny Zhang's and Evelyn Sun's grandmother's recipes have in common?

(A) The cakes are both dusted in coconut.

(B) The cakes are both deep fried.

(C) The cakes are both made with the same type of flour.

(D) The cakes are both baked.

Directions: Read the passages, and then mark the best answers to the questions.

Questions 1–3 are based on the following notice:

City Golf Course

City Golf Course encourages reservations.

Only one reservation per call. For weekdays, call one full day in advance. Call Wednesday between 5 and 8 p.m. for Saturday, and Thursday between 5 and 8 p.m. for Sunday. **Anyone making reservations is expected to check in with the pro shop a quarter hour prior to tee time.**

1. Which of these is the best heading for this notice?

   (A) "Tips for Improving Your Golf Game"

   (B) "Procedures for Making Golf Reservations"

   (C) "City Golf Course: Hours of Operation"

   (D) "Special Activities This Week at the Golf Course"

2. If golfers want to play golf on Sunday, when should they call?

   (A) Wednesday

   (B) Thursday

   (C) Saturday

   (D) Sunday

3. What should golfers do on the day of their game?

   (A) Confirm their reservations by phone

   (B) Practice their golf strokes

   (C) Stop by the pro shop 15 minutes before playing

   (D) Purchase necessary equipment in the pro shop

Getting the right octane level in gasoline—a key to engine performance—is costly because of current evaluation methods. -[1]- To ensure compliance with government regulations, refineries add more octane than necessary. Now an oil company based in Ashland, Kentucky, has developed a more accurate testing technique.

-[2]- The new procedure, which is called InfraTane, instead uses infrared light to assess octane levels. Different molecules absorb light at specific frequencies, so by measuring the amount of absorbed light, refiners can evaluate octane levels and adjust them online to achieve the proper mix.

-[3]- InfraTane has been installed in the company's St. Paul, Minnesota, refinery and will save more than $1 million a year. -[4]- InfraTane has been licensed to a firm in Merrick, New York, that is expected to offer it to other refineries around the world for around $300,000.

4. Why do refineries add more octane than is necessary?

(A) To save money on insurance

(B) To follow government rules

(C) To simplify the refining process

(D) To satisfy customer demand

5. Which of the following is NOT true about the InfraTane procedure?

(A) It is used during the refining process.

(B) It is more expensive than the current method.

(C) It is more accurate than the current method.

(D) It uses infrared light.

6. In the article, the word "assess" in paragraph 2, line 1, is closest in meaning to

(A) increase

(B) reroute

(C) measure

(D) delay

7. Where is the InfraTane procedure currently being used?

(A) All over the world

(B) In Ashland, Kentucky

(C) In Merrick, New York

(D) In St. Paul, Minnesota

8. In which of the positions marked [1], [2], [3], and [4] does the following sentence best belong?

"Currently, octane levels are measured by determining how much a special test engine 'knocks' during combustion."

(A) [1]

(B) [2]

(C) [3]

(D) [4]

WRITE THAT CONTRACT YOURSELF workbooks contain examples of the contracts most commonly used today. The purpose of this series of workbooks is not to replace attorneys. Rather, it is to remove the mystery and expense from contractual work by making these simple contract forms accessible to everyone.

- Each workbook has a wide range of contract forms related to the area designated by the workbook title. The contracts are simplified in language to make them easier to understand.
- Each workbook has a glossary at the back, defining terms found in the book.

Many forms are so straightforward that they can be taken from the books and used right away. There will be times when readers will decide to get legal advice. In those cases, readers who have already familiarized themselves with terminology and typical contractual agreements will realize a savings in time and expense.

9. Who are the workbooks meant for?

(A) The general public

(B) Contract attorneys

(C) Business executives

(D) Authors

10. How is the material in the series organized?

(A) According to subject matter

(B) According to alphabetical order

(C) According to level of difficulty

(D) According to chronological order

11. How do actual contracts differ from the ones in these workbooks?

(A) They are shorter.

(B) They are less expensive.

(C) They are more complex.

(D) They are less specific.

12. The word "straightforward" in paragraph 3, line 1 is closest in meaning to

(A) important

(B) complete

(C) short

(D) uncomplicated

13. What would the author probably suggest to someone who wanted legal assistance with writing a contract?

(A) To use these books instead

(B) To consult with more than one attorney

(C) To refer to these workbooks first

(D) To give the lawyer copies of these books

Cathy Donahue   **8:13**
So, once I land, how should I get into the central city? Should I just take a taxi?

Tingai Pan   **8:15**
You can, but it's really expensive—the airport is a long way from the downtown area.

Cathy Donahue   **8:15**
OK, then, is there a shuttle?

Tingai Pan   **8:17**
Some of the hotels have shuttles, but I don't think yours does. What I'd suggest is, once you arrive and get your bags, go to the light rail station—it's right there at the airport. Take the train to the central train station.

Cathy Donahue   **8:17**
Is that walking distance to my hotel?

Tingai Pan   **8:18**
You could walk there, but you'll have your luggage with you. If I were you, I'd catch a taxi at the station—it won't cost much.

Cathy Donahue   **8:20**
OK, so I'll need to exchange money at the airport so that I'll have cash for the train ticket and to pay the taxi driver.

Tingai Pan   **8:23**
You can use your credit card to get your train ticket. Then you can get cash from an ATM at the central station. You'll probably get a better rate there than at your hotel or at the airport.

Tingai Pan   **8:25**
By the way, do you know when your meeting with Mr. Lee is? The same day you arrive?

Cathy Donahue   **8:27**
No idea. I'm waiting for a text from him.

Tingai Pan   **8:28**
Well, good luck with the meeting.

Cathy Donahue   **8:30**
OK, thanks, and thanks for the advice.

14. How will Ms. Donahue probably get to her hotel?

(A) She'll take a train and a taxi.

(B) She'll take a shuttle bus.

(C) She'll take a taxi all the way there.

(D) She'll take a train and then walk.

15. What does Mr. Pan suggest about Ms. Donahue's hotel?

(A) It is connected to the airport.

(B) It is not very far from the train station.

(C) It is not easy to find.

(D) It is connected to the train station.

16. According to Mr. Pan, where should Ms. Donahue get cash?

(A) At her hotel

(B) At the central train station

(C) At the airport train station

(D) At the airport

17. At 8:27, what does Ms. Donahue mean when she writes, "No idea"?

(A) She isn't sure if Mr. Lee will send her a text.

(B) She hasn't met Mr. Lee before this.

(C) She doesn't know when she will see Mr. Lee.

(D) She doesn't know how to contact Mr. Lee.

Questions 18–20 are based on the following article:

Australian archaeologists have found a huge Stone Age "factory" where, 2,000 years ago, aboriginal people crafted stone blades and cutting tools for barter. -[1]- The site at Tiboobura is so large that archaeologists believe it formed the basis for an export business. -[2]- The ancient toolmakers probably traded for *pituri*, a drug used to counteract hunger pangs during long treks between hunting grounds. -[3]- The find follows the recent discovery of a 60,000-year-old human bone in central Australia. -[4]-

18. Why did the aboriginal people make tools at Tiboobura?

(A) For hunting

(B) To trade them

(C) For self-defense

(D) To make other tools

19. How did the aboriginal people use the drug *pituri*?

(A) To relieve feelings of hunger

(B) To make themselves more alert

(C) To treat injuries

(D) To relax

20. In which of the positions marked [1], [2], [3], and [4] does the following sentence best belong?

"That discovery pushed back the date of human habitation in Australia by 20,000 years."

(A) [1]

(B) [2]

(C) [3]

(D) [4]

Questions 21–23 refer to the following document:

21. What does the reading probably represent?

(A) The index of a business textbook

(B) The outline of a business plan

(C) The table of contents for a company's policy manual

(D) The schedule for a corporate training program

22. A person who wanted information about taking a business trip would look on what page?

(A) Page 2

(B) Page 19

(C) Page 22

(D) Page 36

23. The most information is probably available regarding which of the following?

(A) Insurance

(B) Overtime

(C) Profit sharing plan

(D) Educational assistance

Questions 24–26 refer to the following article:

If you are driving in the snow and need to stop, "pump the brakes." This technique allows you to stop your car on the iciest street. Depress the brake pedal firmly with a single stroke, then release the pressure immediately. Repeat until you come to a stop. (Do not use this technique if your car is equipped with anti-lock brakes!) When turning on icy streets, if your car starts to spin, steer into the turn. In other words, if your car's rear end slides to the right, gently steer to the right. If it slides to the left, gently steer to the left. Once the car has begun to straighten, steer straight ahead. When at a dead stop, use gentle acceleration to move forward in order to avoid spinning the tires so rapidly that they fail to grip the snow.

24. Which of these techniques is NOT discussed in the reading?

(A) Turning the car on icy streets

(B) Getting the engine started on cold days

(C) Stopping the car on icy streets

(D) Getting the car into motion on snowy streets

25. According to the article, drivers should not "pump their brakes" in which of these situations?

(A) If their cars have a certain type of brake

(B) If it is actually snowing at the time

(C) If they are making a turn

(D) If the streets are icy rather than snowy

26. Which of the following should you do if your car's rear end starts to slide to the right on an icy street?

(A) Gently steer to the right.

(B) Hit the brakes hard, then release.

(C) Quickly turn the steering wheel to the left.

(D) Accelerate, then steer straight ahead.

Angela Iachini	(9:21)	Hello everyone. Anyone know anything about that seminar on Thursday? Have any of you signed up for it yet?
Richard Jarboe	(9:25)	Sorry, I'm out of the loop. I've been out of the office for the last week.
Elba Mueller	(9:27)	Angela, do you mean the one on workplace communication? That's on Friday.
Angela Iachini	(9:27)	Is it? That's too bad. I have a meeting with clients on Friday.
Elba Mueller	(9:28)	I don't think I'll go. It's the second part of a seminar—the first part was a couple of weeks ago.
Richard Jarboe	(9:29)	Those business seminars—boring, boring, boring.
Jillian Zhao	(9:33)	I took the first part—I thought it was pretty good. I got a lot of hints for improving my writing skills. How to write better letters and reports. This one focuses on giving presentations, talking to clients, that sort of thing.
Elba Mueller	(9:35)	And I think part 3 is about handling personality clashes and negativity at work.
Jillian Zhao	(9:38)	Now *that's* something I could definitely use.
Richard Jarboe	(9:40)	At least I'll get out of the office for a day if I decide to go.
Elba Mueller	(9:42)	Not exactly. They're holding this one in-house, in Conference Room B.
Richard Jarboe	(9:43)	Oh, well, forget it then.

27. Which of the following people is most likely to attend the seminar this Friday?

(A) Angela Iachini

(B) Elba Mueller

(C) Richard Jarboe

(D) Jillian Zhao

28. Which of the following topics will most likely be discussed at the seminar this Friday?

(A) Dealing with negative people at work

(B) Improving public speaking skills

(C) Writing clearer emails

(D) Handling disagreements in the office

29. At 9:42, what does Elba Mueller mean when she writes, "Not exactly"?

(A) She thinks it is too late to sign up for the seminar.

(B) Richard Jarboe won't be able to leave the office on the day of the seminar.

(C) She doesn't think Jillian Zhao needs to take part 3.

(D) Only part of the seminar will be held at the office.

THE BARONG GRILL

Service **	**Value** ***	**Weekday evenings** $$$
Atmosphere ***	**Food** *****	**Weekend evenings** $$$$

120 Stanhope Street
Open 6–10 Tues–Thurs
6–11 Fri–Sun
Tel: 236-4274

This new Indonesian restaurant, located in a building that has housed a Mexican and an Indian restaurant in recent times, seems headed for success. The restaurant has been completely remodeled and decorated with fascinating Javanese and Balinese artifacts. Indonesian gamelan music plays in the background. Indonesian food favorites, such as *satay* (grilled meat on a skewer), *gado gado* (spinach salad with peanut dressing), and *nasi goreng* (fried rice) are specialties here. On Friday, Saturday, and Sunday nights, *rijstafel* (a Dutch word meaning "rice table") is served. This is a magnificent feast involving dozens of exotic Indonesian dishes. My only complaint was the service, which was a bit slow the night I dined there.

Ratings guide:		Price per person	
Poor	*	Less than $10	$
Fair	**	$10 to $20	$$
Good	***	$21 to $35	$$$
Excellent	****	$36 to $50	$$$$
Best in town	*****	Over $50	$$$$$

Editors:

I enjoyed reading the review of the Barong Grill which appeared in last Friday's newspaper. The Barong Grill is one of my favorite restaurants in the area. I worked in Jakarta for several years and I had been missing Indonesian food.

I have to agree with the reviewer that the service at the Barong is slow, sometimes painfully slow. That may partly be because the restaurant is so busy these days. However, the food there is so good that it's worth the annoying wait!

I believe the reviewer must have visited the Barong Grill at least a month or more ago. Prices for the weekend *rijstafel* have gone up. My wife and I ate there last Saturday night and our bill for dinner came to over $100. However, they now offer some wonderful live Indonesian music on weekends. Personally, I'd now rate the Barong Grill as "Excellent" when it comes to atmosphere.

I'd recommend the Barong Grill to anyone who likes good food and an intriguing atmosphere!

Frank Van der Griff

30. What did the reviewer like best about the Barong Grill?

    (A) The service

    (B) The food

    (C) The value

    (D) The atmosphere

31. What kind of food is served in the Barong Grill?

    (A) Indonesian

    (B) Dutch

    (C) Indian

    (D) Mexican

32. According to the review, how much does an average dinner cost per person on weekday evenings?

    (A) Less than $10

    (B) Between $21 and $35

    (C) Between $36 and $50

    (D) Over $50

33. How would Frank Van der Griff rate the atmosphere at the Barong Grill?

    (A) **

    (B) ***

    (C) ****

    (D) *****

34. Which of the following is the best description of Frank Van der Griff's letter to the editors?

    (A) It is mostly critical of the Barong Grill but offers one positive point.

    (B) It disagrees with all the ideas in the restaurant review.

    (C) It offers some criticism of the restaurant, but it is generally positive.

    (D) Its view of the Barong Grill is completely positive.

You're Invited!

We welcome contributions for publication in the monthly journal *Workplace*. Submissions may be published in one of the following five sections:

"Innovative Practices" features articles about an organization engaged in practices, at least on a pilot basis, that are at the forefront of workplace change.

"From the Floor" provides a forum for those whose lives have been changed through innovative workplace practices. Articles of workplace transformation should include an analysis of why they have been successful or unsuccessful.

"Cross Currents" contains news and commentary highlighting the resistance to, or lack of understanding of, progressive workplace practices.

"Readers' Forum" contains short pieces of commentary, discussion, and exchange of information about the changing workplace.

"In the News" serves as a clearinghouse for published information on pathbreaking workplace practices worldwide. We encourage you to send clippings from newspapers, magazines, and other publications.

Address inquiries and submissions to

Lynn Venable, Senior Editor, *Workplace*
Box 2527   Auckland 1023, New Zealand

venable.editor@workplace.org.nz

From: Hoshi Kitano <hkitano@whitestar.net>
To: Lynn Venable <venable.editor@workplace.org.nz>
Subject: Submission
Date: Apr. 2, 20--
Attached file(s): wp.article.doc

Hello Ms. Venable,

I am submitting a long (10-page) article that a co-worker and I wrote about the situation at our factory. A group of workers tried to get our company to replace its unofficial policies regarding age and gender discrimination in hiring and promoting with a more enlightened written policy. The article we wrote talks about the strong opposition we faced from upper management and how we eventually got them to accept a modified version of our proposal.

Your invitation to publish did not mention payment for articles that are accepted. I am wondering if you pay for articles that you accept for publication and, if so, at what rate?

I look forward to hearing from you.

Hoshi Kitano

---

35. What does the journal *Workplace* probably deal with?

(A) Analytical discussions of successful businesses

(B) Changes in the way people work

(C) New ways to look for job opportunities

(D) The best locations for new businesses

36. Which of the following is closest in meaning to the word "pilot" in paragraph 2, line 2 of the announcement?

(A) Long-term

(B) Unorganized

(C) Leading

(D) Trial

37. Which of the following would most likely be found in the section of the journal called "In the News"?

(A) Materials published in other journals

(B) Letters from readers

(C) Book reviews

(D) Fictional stories about working

38. In which section would Hoshi Kitano's article most likely be published?

(A) "Readers' Forum"

(B) "From the Floor"

(C) "Cross Currents"

(D) "Innovative Practices"

39. Hoshi Kitano points out that there is no information in the announcement about which of the following?

(A) How much money writers receive

(B) How much a subscription costs

(C) What kind of articles are wanted

(D) How often the journal is published

PACIFIC MARKETING ASSOCIATES, INC.
448 Townsend Street, Suite D
San Francisco, CA 94107 USA
www.pacmark.com

Ms. Stephanie Bricault, Director
Les Pailettes, SA
17 Place de Roi
69000 Lyon, France

Feb. 11, 20--

Dear Ms. Bricault:

We have learned from business associates that you may be looking for an agency to help promote your charming line of children's clothing in North America. We feel that we may be of assistance to you. We are an established agency with our head office in San Francisco and with branch offices in Toronto, Chicago, Atlanta, and Boston. We have an excellent track record helping European and Asian firms boost sales in the United States and Canada, and are convinced that you too could benefit from our experience and expertise. Our European representative, Mr. Peter Greenwood, is currently in London and you may contact him by phone at 0171 745 7489 or at p.greenwood@pacmark.com. He will be in Lyon early next week (Feb. 18–20) and will certainly take the opportunity to call on your firm. If you are not at the clothing trade show in Amsterdam, I hope you can meet with him.

Sincerely,

John Bowles

John Bowles
CEO, Pacific Marketing Associates, Inc.

Pailettes

To: Peter Greenwood <p.greenwood@pacmark.com>
From: Stephanie Bricault <S.Bricault@pailettes.fr>
Subject: Meeting
Date: Feb. 13, 20--
Cc: John Bowles <j.bowles@pacmark.com>

Mr. Greenwood,

I received your contact information from Mr. John Bowles at your San Francisco office.

As Mr. Bowles surmised, we are interested in expanding our marketing efforts and sales in the United States and Canada and are actively looking for a partner to help with North American distribution.

Unfortunately, I will not be able to meet with you as I will be at the trade show on the days when you are in Lyon. However, my associate Jules Bellanger will be available to meet with you then. He has suggested that you come by our offices on Place de Roi at about 11 a.m. on Tuesday, February 19.

In the meantime, could you please supply us with a list of European firms that you have assisted, along with contact information for the person(s) whom you worked most closely with at those firms?

Thank you,

Stephanie Bricault

From: Charlotte Pilkington <charlotte.pilkington@quench.co.uk>
To: Stephanie Bricault <S.Bricault@pailettes.fr>
Date: Feb. 15, 20--
Subject: Query

Ms. Bricault,

In response to your query: All in all, we at Quench, Ltd. have been quite pleased with the services provided by Pacific Marketing Associates. Our firm—which deals in packaged herbal teas and bottled teas—has been working with PMA for around 3 years. During that time, sales in the US have gone up an average of 5%–10% a year. PMA has managed to get our product on the shelves of quite a few US supermarkets and chain stores, including some important ones such as Megamart. Internet sales to US customers have not grown at quite as high a rate as was initially predicted, but Mr. Greenwood has assured us that online sales should pick up this year.

If you would like further information, please feel free to give me a call at 0113 496 4759.

Charlotte Pilkington

Marketing Mgr., Quench, Ltd.

40. What business does Mr. Bowles's company engage in?

(A) Helping companies sell their products in North America

(B) Manufacturing various types of clothing

(C) Arranging financing for manufacturing companies

(D) Helping North American firms market products in Asia and Europe

41. The word "charming" in line 1 of Mr. Bowles's letter is closest in meaning to

(A) unusual

(B) expanded

(C) wonderful

(D) durable

42. Who will meet in Lyon?

(A) Mr. Greenwood and Ms. Bricault

(B) Mr. Bellanger and Mr. Greenwood

(C) Mr. Bellanger and Mr. Bowles

(D) Ms. Pilkington and Ms. Bricault

43. Where will Ms. Bricault be on February 19?

(A) London

(B) Amsterdam

(C) San Francisco

(D) Lyon

44. Why did Ms. Pilkington write to Ms. Bricault?

(A) To provide a reference for Pacific Marketing Associates

(B) To complain about a lack of online sales

(C) To respond to a request made by Mr. Greenwood

(D) To ask Ms. Bricault for some information

Casa del Sol

Conference Hotel and Golf Resort

Near Ensenada, Baja California, Mexico

Almost 3,000 square meters of flexible meeting space

with state-of-the-art media equipment.

2 large ballrooms, 10 meeting rooms

The beautiful Casa del Sol offers an ideal seaside setting for a business conference or just a golfing vacation. The Casa del Sol is a full-service hotel just 120 kilometers (75 miles) south of San Diego. The resort overlooks the blue Pacific Ocean and the port of Ensenada and features a lovely beach.

Among the amenities:

- A challenging nine-hole golf course
- One hundred guest suites with ocean views, seventy-five with views of the gardens and golf course
- Round-the-clock dining services
- Free wireless Internet service in the public areas (lobby, restaurant, lounge, etc.) of the hotel
- Indoor and outdoor swimming pools, a spa, and a fitness center
- Facilities for windsurfing and diving
- Free shuttle to and from the airport

○ Click here for more views of the hotel

○ Click here to see a typical guest suite

○ Click here for information about rates and reservations

Fire causes extensive damage at San Diego Hotel

By Deborah Flaherty

Staff writer

A fire swept through the conference center at the Wellington Inn last night. The hotel had just completed renovating the center. There was also damage to the structure housing the indoor tennis courts.

It was believed that the blaze began in a trash dumpster behind the conference center and quickly spread, destroying most of the structure and the nearby tennis facility. It did not spread to the residential section of the hotel.

No injuries were reported. Some 540 guests were evacuated from the hotel with the help of firefighters. They were allowed to return to their rooms after several hours.

To: <reservations@casadelsol.net>
From: Meg Sweeney <megsweeney@seawell.com>
Subject: Corporate Retreat
Date: Aug. 27, 20--

I am writing to see if your hotel could host a corporate retreat Sept. 7–9. I realize this is very short notice, but we are unable to hold our retreat at our usual venue, the Wellington Inn, and there is no other space available in San Diego. We would need to use all of your conference facilities and would like to book 92 guest suites.

I realize that you might not have 92 guest suites available. If your conference facilities are free on those dates but there are not enough available guest suites, we would be willing to book rooms for some of our employees at nearby hotels.

Some quick questions:
A few employees will not be coming from the San Diego area. How far is the nearest airport?
Is Internet access available in guest rooms?
What hours is the restaurant open?
If employees decide to stay for the weekend after the retreat, can they get group rates?

I look forward to hearing from you as soon as possible.

Meg Sweeney
Executive Secretary, Seawell Enterprises, Inc.

---

45. How many guest suites at Casa del Sol face the ocean?

(A) Seventy-five

(B) Ninety-two

(C) One hundred

(D) One hundred and seventy-five

46. The word "challenging" in paragraph 3, line 2 on the web page is closest in meaning to

(A) beautiful

(B) difficult

(C) expansive

(D) convenient

47. Casa del Sol's web page does NOT mention that the hotel has facilities for which of the following?

(A) Swimming

(B) Golfing

(C) Tennis

(D) Diving

48. Why is Seawell Enterprises NOT holding its retreat at the Wellington Inn?

(A) Because it was completely booked up

(B) Because the conference center was damaged

(C) Because Ms. Sweeney forgot to make a reservation there

(D) Because there were not enough guest suites available

49. Which one of Ms. Sweeney's questions is already answered on the web site?

(A) Her question about the closest airport

(B) Her question about Internet access in guest rooms

(C) Her question about group rates for the weekend

(D) Her question about the restaurant hours

Soares

From: Izabel Soares <m.i.soares@soaresprop.co.mo>
Subject: Singapore site
To: Paul Wu <paulwu@cre.sg>
Sent: 13 Mar. 20--

Hi Paul,

I have a client, Phillip Loi, who is interested in a light-industrial site located in Singapore. I know you usually handle condominium sales but I thought you might have some suggestions. Mr. Loi is the CEO of a Macau firm, and one of his employees has invented a new high-tech toy that he thinks will be the next big thing. My client is frantically trying to find a manufacturing facility in Singapore where he can start producing this toy right away. He needs a facility that is at least 5,000 square meters in size and that costs less than US$4.5 million. If you have any leads on this type of site, could you let me know? Of course, I'd be happy to pay a finder's fee if you should locate something useable.

Izabel

From: Paul Wu <paulwu@cre.sg>
To: Izabel Soares <m.i.soares@soaresprop.co.mo>
Date: 13 Mar. 20--
Subject: Re: Singapore site

Hello Izabel,

You're right, I don't have much information about industrial properties, but I came across this advertisement for a property that might be of interest to your client. Except for the location, it seems suitable.

If Mr. Loi or any of his staff are interested in finding housing in Singapore, please have them get in touch.

Best of luck,
Paul

For sale by owner

Prime 6,000 m^2 (64,500 sq. ft.)

Light manufacturing and warehouse facility near Singapore on 15,000 m^2 (3.7 acre) fenced lot within industrial park, with full infrastructure including water supply and electrical transformer. About one-third of the facility air-conditioned.

Located on good road.

Ample parking, bus station nearby.

Conveniently situated in Johor Bahru, Malaysia.

Currently vacant and available immediately.

Asking price $US 3.8 million.

Send inquiries to owner Ahmed R. Malek

(60) 523-97-44-3171

ARMalek@fajar.com.my

---

50. The word "frantically" in line 4 of Ms. Soares's email is closest in meaning to

(A) seriously

(B) currently

(C) anxiously

(D) casually

51. What problem with the property does Mr. Wu refer to?

(A) It cannot be used for manufacturing.

(B) It is not quite big enough.

(C) It is not available soon enough.

(D) It is not actually in Singapore.

52. What is suggested about Mr. Wu?

(A) He generally handles residential sales.

(B) He will definitely receive a finder's fee.

(C) He has worked with Mr. Loi in the past.

(D) He has properties for sale in Macau.

53. How is the property being used at present?

(A) It is the site of a factory.

(B) It is being developed into condominiums.

(C) It is being used for storage.

(D) It is empty.

54. Who currently owns the property for sale in Johor Bahru?

(A) Ahmed Malek

(B) Izabel Soares

(C) Paul Wu

(D) Phillip Loi

Two Practice TOEIC® Tests

How to Take the Practice Tests

These practice tests are designed to be as close as possible to those given by ETS in terms of length, format, and level of difficulty.

If you are taking these tests at home, be sure to follow these procedures:

- Take an entire test at one time. This will help you work on your overall timing and give you a feel for what it is like to take an actual test.
- Work at a desk or table, not in an easy chair or sofa. Work away from distractions such as televisions and phones.
- Mark your answers on the answer sheets provided rather than on the tests.
- Check your answers in the Audio Script and Answer Key and read the explanations provided for Parts 4, 6, and 7.
- Go back and look at items that you answered incorrectly. Make sure you understand why you answered that item incorrectly.
- If possible, take each test a second time, using another answer sheet. (You may want to copy the answer sheet before you take the test the first time.)

Scoring the Practice Tests

No practice test can provide you with a completely accurate prediction of what your score will be on an actual test. However, this chart will help you make a reasonable estimate of what your score on the TOEIC® test may be.

To use the chart, calculate your raw score from both Listening and Reading by counting the number of correct answers. Then use the chart to calculate your converted score for each section. Add these two scores for your comprehensive test score.

For example, if your raw score for Listening is 74, your converted score is 390. If your raw score for Reading is 88, your converted score is 440.

390 + 440 = 830
Your comprehensive score is 830.

Score Conversion Chart

Raw Scores	Converted Scores: Listening	Converted Scores: Reading	Raw Scores	Converted Scores: Listening	Converted Scores: Reading
100	495	495	50	260	205
99	495	495	49	255	200
98	495	495	48	250	195
97	495	490	47	245	190
96	495	485	46	240	185
95	495	480	45	230	180
94	495	475	44	225	175
93	490	470	43	220	170
92	490	465	42	210	165
91	490	460	41	205	160
90	485	455	40	200	155
89	485	450	39	195	150
88	480	440	38	190	145
87	475	430	37	185	140
86	470	425	36	180	135
85	465	420	35	175	125
84	455	415	34	165	120
83	450	410	33	160	115
82	445	400	32	155	110
81	440	395	31	145	105
80	435	385	30	140	100
79	430	380	29	135	95
78	425	375	28	130	90
77	420	370	27	120	85
76	410	365	26	115	80
75	400	360	25	110	75
74	390	350	24	105	65
73	385	345	23	100	60
72	380	335	22	95	55
71	375	330	21	90	50
70	365	320	20	85	45
69	360	315	19	80	40
68	350	310	18	75	35
67	355	300	17	65	30
66	350	295	16	60	25
65	345	290	15	55	20
64	340	285	14	50	15
63	335	280	13	45	10
62	330	270	12	40	5
61	325	265	11	35	5
60	320	260	10	30	5
59	315	255	9	25	5
58	310	250	8	20	5
57	305	245	7	15	5
56	300	240	6	10	5
55	295	230	5	5	5
54	290	225	4	5	5
53	280	220	3	5	5
52	275	215	2	5	5
51	265	210	1	5	5
			0	5	5

Practice Test 1 Answer Sheet

Listening Comprehension

1. Ⓐ Ⓑ Ⓒ Ⓓ	26. Ⓐ Ⓑ Ⓒ	51. Ⓐ Ⓑ Ⓒ Ⓓ	76. Ⓐ Ⓑ Ⓒ Ⓓ
2. Ⓐ Ⓑ Ⓒ Ⓓ	27. Ⓐ Ⓑ Ⓒ	52. Ⓐ Ⓑ Ⓒ Ⓓ	77. Ⓐ Ⓑ Ⓒ Ⓓ
3. Ⓐ Ⓑ Ⓒ Ⓓ	28. Ⓐ Ⓑ Ⓒ	53. Ⓐ Ⓑ Ⓒ Ⓓ	78. Ⓐ Ⓑ Ⓒ Ⓓ
4. Ⓐ Ⓑ Ⓒ Ⓓ	29. Ⓐ Ⓑ Ⓒ	54. Ⓐ Ⓑ Ⓒ Ⓓ	79. Ⓐ Ⓑ Ⓒ Ⓓ
5. Ⓐ Ⓑ Ⓒ Ⓓ	30. Ⓐ Ⓑ Ⓒ	55. Ⓐ Ⓑ Ⓒ Ⓓ	80. Ⓐ Ⓑ Ⓒ Ⓓ
6. Ⓐ Ⓑ Ⓒ Ⓓ	31. Ⓐ Ⓑ Ⓒ	56. Ⓐ Ⓑ Ⓒ Ⓓ	81. Ⓐ Ⓑ Ⓒ Ⓓ
7. Ⓐ Ⓑ Ⓒ	32. Ⓐ Ⓑ Ⓒ Ⓓ	57. Ⓐ Ⓑ Ⓒ Ⓓ	82. Ⓐ Ⓑ Ⓒ Ⓓ
8. Ⓐ Ⓑ Ⓒ	33. Ⓐ Ⓑ Ⓒ Ⓓ	58. Ⓐ Ⓑ Ⓒ Ⓓ	83. Ⓐ Ⓑ Ⓒ Ⓓ
9. Ⓐ Ⓑ Ⓒ	34. Ⓐ Ⓑ Ⓒ Ⓓ	59. Ⓐ Ⓑ Ⓒ Ⓓ	84. Ⓐ Ⓑ Ⓒ Ⓓ
10. Ⓐ Ⓑ Ⓒ	35. Ⓐ Ⓑ Ⓒ Ⓓ	60. Ⓐ Ⓑ Ⓒ Ⓓ	85. Ⓐ Ⓑ Ⓒ Ⓓ
11. Ⓐ Ⓑ Ⓒ	36. Ⓐ Ⓑ Ⓒ Ⓓ	61. Ⓐ Ⓑ Ⓒ Ⓓ	86. Ⓐ Ⓑ Ⓒ Ⓓ
12. Ⓐ Ⓑ Ⓒ	37. Ⓐ Ⓑ Ⓒ Ⓓ	62. Ⓐ Ⓑ Ⓒ Ⓓ	87. Ⓐ Ⓑ Ⓒ Ⓓ
13. Ⓐ Ⓑ Ⓒ	38. Ⓐ Ⓑ Ⓒ Ⓓ	63. Ⓐ Ⓑ Ⓒ Ⓓ	88. Ⓐ Ⓑ Ⓒ Ⓓ
14. Ⓐ Ⓑ Ⓒ	39. Ⓐ Ⓑ Ⓒ Ⓓ	64. Ⓐ Ⓑ Ⓒ Ⓓ	89. Ⓐ Ⓑ Ⓒ Ⓓ
15. Ⓐ Ⓑ Ⓒ	40. Ⓐ Ⓑ Ⓒ Ⓓ	65. Ⓐ Ⓑ Ⓒ Ⓓ	90. Ⓐ Ⓑ Ⓒ Ⓓ
16. Ⓐ Ⓑ Ⓒ	41. Ⓐ Ⓑ Ⓒ Ⓓ	66. Ⓐ Ⓑ Ⓒ Ⓓ	91. Ⓐ Ⓑ Ⓒ Ⓓ
17. Ⓐ Ⓑ Ⓒ	42. Ⓐ Ⓑ Ⓒ Ⓓ	67. Ⓐ Ⓑ Ⓒ Ⓓ	92. Ⓐ Ⓑ Ⓒ Ⓓ
18. Ⓐ Ⓑ Ⓒ	43. Ⓐ Ⓑ Ⓒ Ⓓ	68. Ⓐ Ⓑ Ⓒ Ⓓ	93. Ⓐ Ⓑ Ⓒ Ⓓ
19. Ⓐ Ⓑ Ⓒ	44. Ⓐ Ⓑ Ⓒ Ⓓ	69. Ⓐ Ⓑ Ⓒ Ⓓ	94. Ⓐ Ⓑ Ⓒ Ⓓ
20. Ⓐ Ⓑ Ⓒ	45. Ⓐ Ⓑ Ⓒ Ⓓ	70. Ⓐ Ⓑ Ⓒ Ⓓ	95. Ⓐ Ⓑ Ⓒ Ⓓ
21. Ⓐ Ⓑ Ⓒ	46. Ⓐ Ⓑ Ⓒ Ⓓ	71. Ⓐ Ⓑ Ⓒ Ⓓ	96. Ⓐ Ⓑ Ⓒ Ⓓ
22. Ⓐ Ⓑ Ⓒ	47. Ⓐ Ⓑ Ⓒ Ⓓ	72. Ⓐ Ⓑ Ⓒ Ⓓ	97. Ⓐ Ⓑ Ⓒ Ⓓ
23. Ⓐ Ⓑ Ⓒ	48. Ⓐ Ⓑ Ⓒ Ⓓ	73. Ⓐ Ⓑ Ⓒ Ⓓ	98. Ⓐ Ⓑ Ⓒ Ⓓ
24. Ⓐ Ⓑ Ⓒ	49. Ⓐ Ⓑ Ⓒ Ⓓ	74. Ⓐ Ⓑ Ⓒ Ⓓ	99. Ⓐ Ⓑ Ⓒ Ⓓ
25. Ⓐ Ⓑ Ⓒ	50. Ⓐ Ⓑ Ⓒ Ⓓ	75. Ⓐ Ⓑ Ⓒ Ⓓ	100. Ⓐ Ⓑ Ⓒ Ⓓ

Practice Test 1 Answer Sheet

Reading

101. (A) (B) (C) (D)	126. (A) (B) (C) (D)	151. (A) (B) (C) (D)	176. (A) (B) (C) (D)
102. (A) (B) (C) (D)	127. (A) (B) (C) (D)	152. (A) (B) (C) (D)	177. (A) (B) (C) (D)
103. (A) (B) (C) (D)	128. (A) (B) (C) (D)	153. (A) (B) (C) (D)	178. (A) (B) (C) (D)
104. (A) (B) (C) (D)	129. (A) (B) (C) (D)	154. (A) (B) (C) (D)	179. (A) (B) (C) (D)
105. (A) (B) (C) (D)	130. (A) (B) (C) (D)	155. (A) (B) (C) (D)	180. (A) (B) (C) (D)
106. (A) (B) (C) (D)	131. (A) (B) (C) (D)	156. (A) (B) (C) (D)	181. (A) (B) (C) (D)
107. (A) (B) (C) (D)	132. (A) (B) (C) (D)	157. (A) (B) (C) (D)	182. (A) (B) (C) (D)
108. (A) (B) (C) (D)	133. (A) (B) (C) (D)	158. (A) (B) (C) (D)	183. (A) (B) (C) (D)
109. (A) (B) (C) (D)	134. (A) (B) (C) (D)	159. (A) (B) (C) (D)	184. (A) (B) (C) (D)
110. (A) (B) (C) (D)	135. (A) (B) (C) (D)	160. (A) (B) (C) (D)	185. (A) (B) (C) (D)
111. (A) (B) (C) (D)	136. (A) (B) (C) (D)	161. (A) (B) (C) (D)	186. (A) (B) (C) (D)
112. (A) (B) (C) (D)	137. (A) (B) (C) (D)	162. (A) (B) (C) (D)	187. (A) (B) (C) (D)
113. (A) (B) (C) (D)	138. (A) (B) (C) (D)	163. (A) (B) (C) (D)	188. (A) (B) (C) (D)
114. (A) (B) (C) (D)	139. (A) (B) (C) (D)	164. (A) (B) (C) (D)	189. (A) (B) (C) (D)
115. (A) (B) (C) (D)	140. (A) (B) (C) (D)	165. (A) (B) (C) (D)	190. (A) (B) (C) (D)
116. (A) (B) (C) (D)	141. (A) (B) (C) (D)	166. (A) (B) (C) (D)	191. (A) (B) (C) (D)
117. (A) (B) (C) (D)	142. (A) (B) (C) (D)	167. (A) (B) (C) (D)	192. (A) (B) (C) (D)
118. (A) (B) (C) (D)	143. (A) (B) (C) (D)	168. (A) (B) (C) (D)	193. (A) (B) (C) (D)
119. (A) (B) (C) (D)	144. (A) (B) (C) (D)	169. (A) (B) (C) (D)	194. (A) (B) (C) (D)
120. (A) (B) (C) (D)	145. (A) (B) (C) (D)	170. (A) (B) (C) (D)	195. (A) (B) (C) (D)
121. (A) (B) (C) (D)	146. (A) (B) (C) (D)	171. (A) (B) (C) (D)	196. (A) (B) (C) (D)
122. (A) (B) (C) (D)	147. (A) (B) (C) (D)	172. (A) (B) (C) (D)	197. (A) (B) (C) (D)
123. (A) (B) (C) (D)	148. (A) (B) (C) (D)	173. (A) (B) (C) (D)	198. (A) (B) (C) (D)
124. (A) (B) (C) (D)	149. (A) (B) (C) (D)	174. (A) (B) (C) (D)	199. (A) (B) (C) (D)
125. (A) (B) (C) (D)	150. (A) (B) (C) (D)	175. (A) (B) (C) (D)	200. (A) (B) (C) (D)

Practice Test 2 Answer Sheet

Listening Comprehension

1. (A) (B) (C) (D)	26. (A) (B) (C)	51. (A) (B) (C) (D)	76. (A) (B) (C) (D)
2. (A) (B) (C) (D)	27. (A) (B) (C)	52. (A) (B) (C) (D)	77. (A) (B) (C) (D)
3. (A) (B) (C) (D)	28. (A) (B) (C)	53. (A) (B) (C) (D)	78. (A) (B) (C) (D)
4. (A) (B) (C) (D)	29. (A) (B) (C)	54. (A) (B) (C) (D)	79. (A) (B) (C) (D)
5. (A) (B) (C) (D)	30. (A) (B) (C)	55. (A) (B) (C) (D)	80. (A) (B) (C) (D)
6. (A) (B) (C) (D)	31. (A) (B) (C)	56. (A) (B) (C) (D)	81. (A) (B) (C) (D)
7. (A) (B) (C)	32. (A) (B) (C) (D)	57. (A) (B) (C) (D)	82. (A) (B) (C) (D)
8. (A) (B) (C)	33. (A) (B) (C) (D)	58. (A) (B) (C) (D)	83. (A) (B) (C) (D)
9. (A) (B) (C)	34. (A) (B) (C) (D)	59. (A) (B) (C) (D)	84. (A) (B) (C) (D)
10. (A) (B) (C)	35. (A) (B) (C) (D)	60. (A) (B) (C) (D)	85. (A) (B) (C) (D)
11. (A) (B) (C)	36. (A) (B) (C) (D)	61. (A) (B) (C) (D)	86. (A) (B) (C) (D)
12. (A) (B) (C)	37. (A) (B) (C) (D)	62. (A) (B) (C) (D)	87. (A) (B) (C) (D)
13. (A) (B) (C)	38. (A) (B) (C) (D)	63. (A) (B) (C) (D)	88. (A) (B) (C) (D)
14. (A) (B) (C)	39. (A) (B) (C) (D)	64. (A) (B) (C) (D)	89. (A) (B) (C) (D)
15. (A) (B) (C)	40. (A) (B) (C) (D)	65. (A) (B) (C) (D)	90. (A) (B) (C) (D)
16. (A) (B) (C)	41. (A) (B) (C) (D)	66. (A) (B) (C) (D)	91. (A) (B) (C) (D)
17. (A) (B) (C)	42. (A) (B) (C) (D)	67. (A) (B) (C) (D)	92. (A) (B) (C) (D)
18. (A) (B) (C)	43. (A) (B) (C) (D)	68. (A) (B) (C) (D)	93. (A) (B) (C) (D)
19. (A) (B) (C)	44. (A) (B) (C) (D)	69. (A) (B) (C) (D)	94. (A) (B) (C) (D)
20. (A) (B) (C)	45. (A) (B) (C) (D)	70. (A) (B) (C) (D)	95. (A) (B) (C) (D)
21. (A) (B) (C)	46. (A) (B) (C) (D)	71. (A) (B) (C) (D)	96. (A) (B) (C) (D)
22. (A) (B) (C)	47. (A) (B) (C) (D)	72. (A) (B) (C) (D)	97. (A) (B) (C) (D)
23. (A) (B) (C)	48. (A) (B) (C) (D)	73. (A) (B) (C) (D)	98. (A) (B) (C) (D)
24. (A) (B) (C)	49. (A) (B) (C) (D)	74. (A) (B) (C) (D)	99. (A) (B) (C) (D)
25. (A) (B) (C)	50. (A) (B) (C) (D)	75. (A) (B) (C) (D)	100. (A) (B) (C) (D)

Practice Test 2 Answer Sheet

Reading

101. Ⓐ B C D				126. Ⓐ B C D				151. Ⓐ B C D				176. Ⓐ B C D		
102. Ⓐ B C D				127. Ⓐ B C D				152. Ⓐ B C D				177. Ⓐ B C D		
103. Ⓐ B C D				128. Ⓐ B C D				153. Ⓐ B C D				178. Ⓐ B C D		
104. Ⓐ B C D				129. Ⓐ B C D				154. Ⓐ B C D				179. Ⓐ B C D		
105. Ⓐ B C D				130. Ⓐ B C D				155. Ⓐ B C D				180. Ⓐ B C D		
106. Ⓐ B C D				131. Ⓐ B C D				156. Ⓐ B C D				181. Ⓐ B C D		
107. Ⓐ B C D				132. Ⓐ B C D				157. Ⓐ B C D				182. Ⓐ B C D		
108. Ⓐ B C D				133. Ⓐ B C D				158. Ⓐ B C D				183. Ⓐ B C D		
109. Ⓐ B C D				134. Ⓐ B C D				159. Ⓐ B C D				184. Ⓐ B C D		
110. Ⓐ B C D				135. Ⓐ B C D				160. Ⓐ B C D				185. Ⓐ B C D		
111. Ⓐ B C D				136. Ⓐ B C D				161. Ⓐ B C D				186. Ⓐ B C D		
112. Ⓐ B C D				137. Ⓐ B C D				162. Ⓐ B C D				187. Ⓐ B C D		
113. Ⓐ B C D				138. Ⓐ B C D				163. Ⓐ B C D				188. Ⓐ B C D		
114. Ⓐ B C D				139. Ⓐ B C D				164. Ⓐ B C D				189. Ⓐ B C D		
115. Ⓐ B C D				140. Ⓐ B C D				165. Ⓐ B C D				190. Ⓐ B C D		
116. Ⓐ B C D				141. Ⓐ B C D				166. Ⓐ B C D				191. Ⓐ B C D		
117. Ⓐ B C D				142. Ⓐ B C D				167. Ⓐ B C D				192. Ⓐ B C D		
118. Ⓐ B C D				143. Ⓐ B C D				168. Ⓐ B C D				193. Ⓐ B C D		
119. Ⓐ B C D				144. Ⓐ B C D				169. Ⓐ B C D				194. Ⓐ B C D		
120. Ⓐ B C D				145. Ⓐ B C D				170. Ⓐ B C D				195. Ⓐ B C D		
121. Ⓐ B C D				146. Ⓐ B C D				171. Ⓐ B C D				196. Ⓐ B C D		
122. Ⓐ B C D				147. Ⓐ B C D				172. Ⓐ B C D				197. Ⓐ B C D		
123. Ⓐ B C D				148. Ⓐ B C D				173. Ⓐ B C D				198. Ⓐ B C D		
124. Ⓐ B C D				149. Ⓐ B C D				174. Ⓐ B C D				199. Ⓐ B C D		
125. Ⓐ B C D				150. Ⓐ B C D				175. Ⓐ B C D				200. Ⓐ B C D		

Practice Test 1

General Directions

This exam is designed to test how well you can understand and use the English language. The test takes approximately two hours to complete. It consists of seven separate parts, each with its own directions. Before you begin to work on a part, be certain that you understand the directions.

Some items will seem harder than other items. However, you should answer every one if possible. Remember, you are not penalized for guessing. If you are not able to answer every question, don't worry.

All your answers should be marked on the answer sheets found on pages 282–283. Remove or copy these sheets before the test begins. When you are marking an answer, fill in the circle corresponding to the letter that you have chosen. The space in the circle should be completely filled in so that the letter inside is not visible, as shown in the example below:

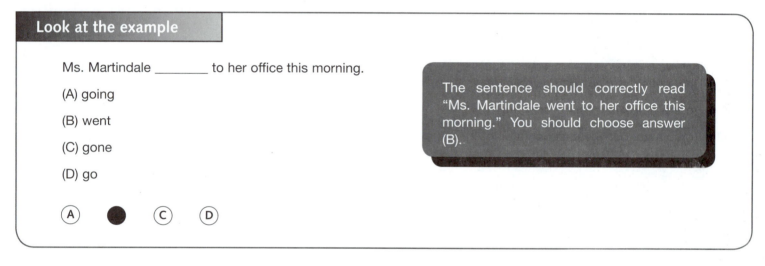

Look at the example

Ms. Martindale _____ to her office this morning.

(A) going

(B) went

(C) gone

(D) go

The sentence should correctly read "Ms. Martindale went to her office this morning." You should choose answer (B).

(A)   ●   (C)   (D)

For each question, you may mark only one answer. If you decide to change your answer, you should erase your original answer completely.

Listening Comprehension

In this first section of the exam, your ability to understand spoken English will be tested. This section consists of four separate parts, each having its own directions.

Part 1

Directions: For each item, there is a photograph in the book and four short sentences about it on the audio program. The sentences are NOT written out, so you must listen carefully.

You must choose the one sentence — (A), (B), (C), or (D) — that is the best description of what can be seen in the photograph. Then mark the letter that corresponds to the best answer on your answer sheet.

Look at the example

You see this photograph:

Listen to the four sentences:

(A) (B) (C) ●

Choice (D) — "The mechanic is repairing the engine." — is the best description of what can be seen in the photograph.

GO ON TO THE NEXT PAGE →

1.

2.

3.

4.

GO ON TO THE NEXT PAGE

5.

6.

Part 2

Directions: In this part of the test, you will hear a question or statement on the audio program. After that, you will hear three possible responses to the question or statement. Each question or statement and each response is given only once and is not written out in your book, so listen carefully. Mark the answer that corresponds to the best response to the question or statement on your answer sheet.

Listen to a sample

You hear:

You then hear:

Choice (A), "At the gymnasium," is the best response to the question "Where have you been, Steve?" You should mark (A) on your answer sheet.

---

7. Mark your answer on the answer sheet.

8. Mark your answer on the answer sheet.

9. Mark your answer on the answer sheet.

10. Mark your answer on the answer sheet.

11. Mark your answer on the answer sheet.

12. Mark your answer on the answer sheet.

13. Mark your answer on the answer sheet.

14. Mark your answer on the answer sheet.

15. Mark your answer on the answer sheet.

16. Mark your answer on the answer sheet.

17. Mark your answer on the answer sheet.

18. Mark your answer on the answer sheet.

19. Mark your answer on the answer sheet.

20. Mark your answer on the answer sheet.

21. Mark your answer on the answer sheet.

22. Mark your answer on the answer sheet.

23. Mark your answer on the answer sheet.

24. Mark your answer on the answer sheet.

25. Mark your answer on the answer sheet.

26. Mark your answer on the answer sheet.

27. Mark your answer on the answer sheet.

28. Mark your answer on the answer sheet.

29. Mark your answer on the answer sheet.

30. Mark your answer on the answer sheet.

31. Mark your answer on the answer sheet.

GO ON TO THE NEXT PAGE

Directions: In this part of the test, you will hear some short conversations involving two or three speakers. Each conversation is spoken only once and is not written in the book, so listen carefully.

In your book, you will read three questions about each conversation. Following each question are four answer choices — (A), (B), (C), or (D). Mark the letter that corresponds to the best answer on your answer sheet.

32. What problem do the men have?

(A) Their flight was cancelled.

(B) Their luggage was lost.

(C) They are late for a flight.

(D) They forgot their tickets.

33. What time did Stan want to check out of the hotel?

(A) At 8:00

(B) At 9:00

(C) At 10:00

(D) At 11:00

34. What will the woman probably do next?

(A) Reschedule a flight

(B) Board a plane

(C) Check in a suitcase

(D) Issue new tickets

---

35. The first speaker is looking for what kind of items?

(A) Gifts

(B) Food

(C) Carry-on luggage

(D) Clothing

36. Where does this conversation probably take place?

(A) At a fruit market

(B) On a farm

(C) At customs

(D) In a restaurant

37. What will probably happen to the gift the second man is carrying?

(A) It will be taken from him.

(B) It will be tasted by the first man.

(C) It will be returned to him.

(D) It will be sent to another country.

38. What is the problem?

    (A) The woman doesn't understand the orders.

    (B) The orders haven't come back yet.

    (C) There are too many orders to fill.

    (D) The man doesn't want to order any more inventory.

39. What is Mr. Heath's plan?

    (A) To increase the number of workers

    (B) To double the amount of orders

    (C) To make all employees part-time workers

    (D) To take an inventory

40. What does Mr. Heath say about his current employees?

    (A) They aren't working hard enough.

    (B) They should be working on a new project.

    (C) They should take a vacation.

    (D) They shouldn't work more than they are now.

---

41. What are they discussing?

    (A) A car

    (B) A movie

    (C) A sale

    (D) A book

42. What is the woman's opinion of Mark Westbrook?

    (A) She hasn't made up her mind yet.

    (B) She doesn't like his work.

    (C) She thinks he is very creative.

    (D) She thinks he is overrated.

43. When will the man take a vacation?

    (A) In March

    (B) In May

    (C) In June

    (D) In August

GO ON TO THE NEXT PAGE

44. How often does the man have this type of problem?

   (A) Frequently

   (B) Sometimes

   (C) Not often

   (D) Never

45. Why is Phil worried?

   (A) His company is having financial problems.

   (B) He might not be reimbursed.

   (C) He might not be able to take a trip.

   (D) He has lost his wallet.

46. Where does the woman suggest the man look for the receipt?

   (A) In his car

   (B) At his office

   (C) In his clothing

   (D) At the ticket counter

---

47. What type of accident are they discussing?

   (A) An accident at work

   (B) A skiing accident

   (C) An automobile accident

   (D) An accident at the hospital

48. When did the accident probably occur?

   (A) A month ago

   (B) A week ago

   (C) A day ago

   (D) A few hours ago

49. What does the man mean when he says, "It'll be at least a month before she's back in the office"?

   (A) Brenda needs time to recover.

   (B) Brenda has a newborn baby.

   (C) Brenda will stay in the hospital.

   (D) Brenda will take a business trip.

50. Why is Mr. Briggs calling?

    (A) To check on David's progress

    (B) To buy some electronics

    (C) To set a date for the meeting

    (D) To ask where David will be going

51. Where does David probably work?

    (A) At a radio station

    (B) At an advertising agency

    (C) At a recording studio

    (D) At a newspaper office

52. What can be inferred about the newspaper ads?

    (A) They will appear next week.

    (B) They have been canceled.

    (C) They aren't finished yet.

    (D) They aren't very interesting.

---

53. Where are they?

    (A) In a new apartment

    (B) In a post office

    (C) In a bookstore

    (D) In a card shop

54. Why does Rosa say, "As a matter of fact, I did"?

    (A) To confirm that she changed a plan

    (B) To say that she received something

    (C) To mention that she has made a purchase

    (D) To state that she arrived home

55. What will Rosa be doing on Saturday?

    (A) Working

    (B) Filling out forms

    (C) Going to a party

    (D) Getting married

GO ON TO THE NEXT PAGE

56. Why did Joshua call the woman?

    (A) To place an order with her company

    (B) To give her some information about Alison Swift

    (C) To inform her that her order had arrived

    (D) To tell her about Appleton's new hours

57. What kind of a business is Appleton's?

    (A) A publishing company

    (B) A delivery company

    (C) A florist shop

    (D) A bookstore

58. What time will the woman come to Appleton's?

    (A) Today at 5:30

    (B) Today at 6:00

    (C) Friday at 6:30

    (D) Friday at 8:00

---

59. How long would the man's proposal probably be in effect?

    (A) Two weeks

    (B) One month

    (C) Half a year

    (D) One year

60. Why does the woman think the staff will not like the proposal?

    (A) They are not motivated by bonuses.

    (B) They have already lost another benefit.

    (C) They will be afraid that they will lose their jobs.

    (D) They won't have the chance to make many sales.

61. What is the man's primary concern?

    (A) Motivating the staff

    (B) Bringing in new business

    (C) Creating a long-term policy

    (D) Saving the company money

Telephone Directory	
Name	**Extension**
Brian Shelton	346
Joan McGee	476
Glenda Keller	649
Hugh Duncan	764

62. What is the conversation mainly about?

(A) Business trips

(B) Charge accounts

(C) Retirement ceremonies

(D) Employment benefits

63. When did Hugh change his position?

(A) April

(B) May

(C) June

(D) July

64. Look at the graphic. Which extension will the woman most likely dial next?

(A) 346

(B) 476

(C) 649

(D) 764

Port City Shopping Center
SHOP OVER 50 STORES IN ONE LOCATION

40% OFF

GOOD FOR ONE
REGULARLY
PRICED ITEM

Coupon must be presented at time of purchase.
Not valid for online shopping.
Valid through May 10

65. Where are the speakers probably located?

(A) In a grocery store

(B) In a hardware store

(C) In a jewelry shop

(D) In a clothing store

GO ON TO THE NEXT PAGE

66. Look at the graphic. Why can't the woman use the coupon for her entire purchase?

    (A) The coupon has expired.

    (B) Her total is too low.

    (C) She has too many items.

    (D) She is shopping online.

67. How will the woman probably pay for her purchase?

    (A) With cash

    (B) With a check

    (C) With a credit card

    (D) With a debit card

Cleaning Schedule	
Name	**Date**
Theresa Lane	July 1
João Cunha	July 2
Pat Brown	July 3
Tracy Kim	July 4

68. Where do the speakers most likely work?

    (A) At a construction company

    (B) At a hotel

    (C) At a cleaning company

    (D) At a supply business

69. Look at the graphic. Who failed to clean the floor?

    (A) Theresa Lane

    (B) João Cunha

    (C) Pat Brown

    (D) Tracy Kim

70. What will the man most likely do next?

    (A) Speak to an employee

    (B) Phone a hotel

    (C) Clean a lobby

    (D) View a schedule

Part 4

Directions: During this part of the exam, there are ten brief talks. These talks are not written out and are spoken only once, so you must listen carefully.

There are three questions about each of the talks. Following each question are four possible answers — (A), (B), (C), and (D). You must decide which of these best answers the question and then mark the letter that corresponds to the best answer on your answer sheet.

71. What does the woman mean when she says, "this summer is no exception"?

    (A) The season's weather will be normal.

    (B) The same thing happens every year.

    (C) Citizens must follow temporary laws.

    (D) Roads are expected to be crowded.

72. Why is the blood supply low?

    (A) Because of a typical seasonal drop

    (B) Because donations have been lower than usual

    (C) Because of numerous accidents

    (D) Because the blood center has been closed

73. Which of these will a donor NOT receive?

    (A) Free blood for a year

    (B) A decorative pin

    (C) Special mention on the radio

    (D) A small snack

74. How did airline industry analysts react to the announcement?

    (A) They were disappointed.

    (B) They were angry.

    (C) They were pleased.

    (D) They were surprised.

75. Where is North American Airline's training facility presently located?

    (A) In Minneapolis

    (B) In Salt Lake City

    (C) In Saint Louis

    (D) In Atlanta

76. What benefit will the city of Minneapolis receive?

    (A) Cash payments

    (B) The prospect of jobs

    (C) Tax revenues

    (D) The status of hub city

GO ON TO THE NEXT PAGE

77. In what field are Clio Awards given?

   (A) Film

   (B) Music

   (C) Advertising

   (D) Television

78. According to the speaker, what happened in 1991?

   (A) The first Clio Award ceremony was held.

   (B) The Clio Award organization was reorganized.

   (C) The Clio Award organization collapsed.

   (D) The Clio Award ceremony was first televised.

79. How did the ceremony change after the reorganization?

   (A) Fewer prizes were awarded.

   (B) The international judges were dismissed.

   (C) More money was awarded.

   (D) New categories were created.

---

80. Who is Diana Hartwick?

   (A) An office worker

   (B) A physical therapist

   (C) A university professor

   (D) A medical doctor

81. What is the purpose of the seminar?

   (A) To help the workers feel better in their office environment

   (B) To discuss methods for organizing files efficiently

   (C) To encourage the workers to put more effort into their jobs

   (D) To teach employees to develop better working relationships

82. Which of these is Diana Hartwick LEAST likely to tell her seminar audience?

   (A) How to sit properly in a desk chair

   (B) How to arrange office equipment

   (C) How to exercise to recover from injury

   (D) How to position one's hands while working at a computer

83. What is the main purpose of this talk?

    (A) To forecast a change in the weather

    (B) To advertise a new brand of juice

    (C) To explain the coming citrus fruit shortage

    (D) To describe a flood in California

84. When is the change in prices expected to occur?

    (A) Tonight or tomorrow

    (B) In a month

    (C) In two or three months

    (D) In five years

85. What does the speaker suggest?

    (A) Instituting flood control

    (B) Eating more fruit

    (C) Stabilizing fruit prices

    (D) Buying low-cost juice

86. Where would someone going on the City Hall tour meet?

    (A) In front of the staircase

    (B) At the art museum

    (C) In front of the library

    (D) Next to the Mermaid Fountain

87. What would people learn about on the Art Deco tour?

    (A) The design of Italian staircases

    (B) The social history of the Hill District

    (C) A twentieth-century architectural style

    (D) The influence of modern art on fountain design

88. Why does the woman say, "It's spectacular"?

    (A) To advertise a sale

    (B) To summarize a plan

    (C) To describe a building

    (D) To show surprise

GO ON TO THE NEXT PAGE

89. Who is this talk probably being given to?

    (A) Hospital staff

    (B) Fire fighters

    (C) Patients in a nursing home

    (D) Teachers

90. What will happen if the alarm is turned on?

    (A) The windows and doors will automatically close.

    (B) Lights will flash throughout the building.

    (C) A white bar will be activated.

    (D) The emergency power system will turn on.

91. What will Bob Frist probably do next?

    (A) Ask the listeners to prepare for a fire drill

    (B) Discuss what each person should do in case of a fire

    (C) Allow time for a question and answer session

    (D) Visit another medical facility

> **FULLY COOKED
> SPICY CHICKEN THIGHS**
>
> *Chef's Cut Premium Chicken Thighs*
>
> Keep frozen
> Net Weight: 2.5 pounds
>
> Ingredients: chicken, salt, onion & garlic
> powder, black pepper, chili powder, vinegar,
> citric acid, molasses

92. What is the company preparing to do?

    (A) Open a supermarket

    (B) Start a restaurant chain

    (C) Introduce a new product

    (D) Supply restaurants

93. Look at the graphic. What does the man suggest excluding from the ingredients?

    (A) Black pepper

    (B) Onion powder

    (C) Citric acid

    (D) Molasses

94. What does the man say about people in the Product Development Division?

(A) They are positive.

(B) They are struggling.

(C) They are cheerful.

(D) They are slow.

Thank you for your contribution!
Please check the amount you wish to contribute.
☐ $10
☑ $20
☐ $30
☐ $40
☐   Other: $_____

95. Who does the speaker most likely work for?

(A) A charity

(B) A government

(C) A school

(D) A bank

96. Look at the graphic. Which box on the card should Marion Casey probably have checked?

(A) $10

(B) $30

(C) $40

(D) Other: $_____

97. What does the speaker say she will do?

(A) Make a call

(B) Mail a check

(C) Hold a meeting

(D) Donate some money

GO ON TO THE NEXT PAGE ➤

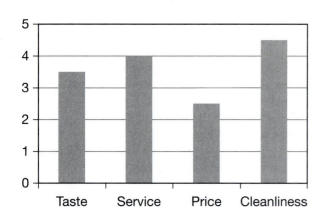

98. What most likely is the speaker's job?

(A) Chef

(B) Waiter

(C) Host

(D) Manager

99. What does the speaker say about the average rating for service?

(A) It is confusing.

(B) It is satisfying.

(C) It is average.

(D) It is disappointing.

100. Look at the graphic. What does the speaker want the listeners to research further?

(A) Taste

(B) Service

(C) Price

(D) Cleanliness

THIS IS THE END OF THE LISTENING COMPREHENSION SECTION OF THE TEST.
GO ON TO THE READING SECTION.

111. Shinji enjoys _____ on crossword puzzles while commuting to work on the train.

(A) work

(B) to work

(C) works

(D) working

112. The new bridge is not as picturesque _____ the old one, but it is much safer.

(A) as

(B) so

(C) like

(D) than

113. The scientific method is the _____ of all scientific research.

(A) basic

(B) basis

(C) basing

(D) base

114. I invited Marie-Claire to join us _____ work.

(A) afterwards

(B) later

(C) subsequent

(D) after

115. Only about three percent of the total money supply of most nations _____ coins.

(A) made up of

(B) made up

(C) is made up of

(D) is made up

116. This new policy must be _____ gradually to avoid confusion.

(A) implemented

(B) affected

(C) exercised

(D) resulted

117. The architects_____ up some preliminary plans for the new office building last month.

(A) draws

(B) drawing

(C) drawn

(D) drew

118. There are some very interesting _____ to see in New Zealand.

(A) sights

(B) looks

(C) viewings

(D) sightings

119. In her speech, Dr. Villano offered several _____ examples to support her ideas.

(A) instructing

(B) compelling

(C) opposing

(D) determining

120. Mr. Chopra cautioned _____ adopting the plan.

(A) along

(B) to

(C) at

(D) against

GO ON TO THE NEXT PAGE

121. The executive assistant uses a time-management chart _____ how much time she should spend on each project.

    (A) in determination

    (B) determines

    (C) to determine

    (D) determination of

122. Throwing litter from cars is _____ by law.

    (A) forbidding

    (B) prohibited

    (C) inadmissible

    (D) punishing

123. Nonprofit corporations are established for purposes of public service and _____ special privileges by the government.

    (A) are given

    (B) give

    (C) gave

    (D) are giving

124. Mr. and Ms. Wills have been planning to attend the home show, but they _____ have not had the opportunity.

    (A) already

    (B) still

    (C) anymore

    (D) yet

125. Let's _____ at the Harbor House for dinner tonight.

    (A) meet

    (B) meeting

    (C) to meet

    (D) met

126. The departmental meeting _____ next Tuesday.

    (A) to be held

    (B) is going to hold

    (C) will hold

    (D) will be held

127. _____ Mr. Addison was not feeling well, he went to work anyway.

    (A) Despite

    (B) However

    (C) Although

    (D) Even so

128. I asked Habib to _____ me of the meeting.

    (A) remember

    (B) comment

    (C) inquire

    (D) remind

129. We were certain _____ we could reach an agreement by the next day.

    (A) of

    (B) about

    (C) that

    (D) to

130. Mr. Sulochana was _____ as the firm's accountant after it was learned that he had not been involved in the scheme to embezzle funds.

    (A) reinstated

    (B) overstaffed

    (C) contradicted

    (D) reprimanded

GO ON TO THE NEXT PART.

Directions: Read the passages on the following pages. Four words, phrases, or sentences have been replaced by blanks. Four answer choices are given for each blank. Mark the answer choice — (A), (B), (C), or (D) — that best completes the text.

Questions 131–134 refer to the following article:

A memorandum of understanding (MOU) is a document, usually prepared by a buyer or investor, which _____

131.

in general terms a business agreement between two or more parties. _____ main purpose is to assure that

132.

the parties agree on the general terms of the deal. _____. However, it does share with contracts certain

133.

provisions, such as _____. Some business experts refer to the MOU as a "handshake in writing."

134.

---

131. (A) submits
    (B) outlines
    (C) specifies
    (D) enacts

132. (A) One's
    (B) Their
    (C) Another
    (D) Its

133. (A) Unlike a contract, it is generally not a legally binding commitment to buy, sell, invest, or cooperate.
    (B) Often, it is a first step towards a more formal, legally binding contract.
    (C) Generally, an MOU indicates that the parties agree to work together on some joint project.
    (D) Like a contract, MOUs generally include a timeline and a discussion of funding issues.

134. (A) confidential
    (B) confidentially
    (C) confidentiality
    (D) confiding

GO ON TO THE NEXT PAGE

Perfect Arrangements specializes in filling your company's need for unique floral gifts. Flowers create a positive atmosphere at meetings and corporate events and can _____ the attractiveness of your company's products during
135.
promotions. Flowers can be used as effective and beautiful incentives to motivate your staff. Another use of flowers that should be seriously _____ is as thoughtful gifts for your valuable customers. _____. One study showed that people
136.   **137.**
working in an office environment in which flowers were present generated more original ideas and created better solutions to problems than workers in a flower-free office. Our experienced floral designers and sales representatives are trained to provide you with the best personal service. _____ that, but they can also select floral gifts with a special
138.
significance.

135. (A) enhance
     (B) add
     (C) rise
     (D) expand

136. (A) consider
     (B) considering
     (C) considered
     (D) considers

137. (A) And there is evidence that flowers may actually lead to more creativity and productivity in the workplace.
     (B) Office workers feel more awake and energetic when they look at flowers first thing in the morning.
     (C) Some workers may spend time watering flowers or just staring at them rather than working.
     (D) A number of bosses have arranged "flower Fridays," scheduling a delivery of flowers the last day of every work week.

138. (A) Not only
     (B) In contrast to
     (C) Regarding
     (D) In spite of

Questions 139–142 refer to the following information:

Downtown check-in centers open to all air travelers have been popping _____ all over the world. For example, in June,
139.
Argentine Airways opened a site in downtown Buenos Aires _____ passengers can pick up boarding passes, check in
140.
luggage, get a snack or a full meal, and take ground transport to the airport. They can also shop at duty-free stores. That same month, the Central City Air Terminal in Montreal's business district opened. It offers passenger and luggage check-in shuttles to _____ Dorval and Mirabel airports. There is also a foreign exchange desk and a duty-free shop. At the COEX
141.
Mall City Terminal in downtown Seoul, passengers can check in for flights, drop off their bags, and get a shuttle directly to the Incheon Airport. Passengers can even go through Immigration there. _____. The downtown centers tend to be far
142.
less crowded and less confusing, and lines are short or non-existent. One passenger remarked that he felt like a first-class traveler even though he was flying economy.

139. (A) in
(B) up
(C) over
(D) out

140. (A) which
(B) there
(C) that
(D) where

141. (A) either
(B) not only
(C) both
(D) neither

142. (A) Guests at Disney resorts in Orlando, Florida may check in for return flights at their hotels.
(B) Some passengers, such as unaccompanied minors, must check in at the airport.
(C) What passengers like best about downtown centers is the convenience and speed of the check-in process.
(D) Even if passengers check in downtown, they are advised to arrive at the airport an hour and a half before international flights.

Questions 143–146 refer to the following article:

Following in the footsteps of other European cities, such as Stockholm, Vienna, Barcelona, and Copenhagen, Paris launched a large-scale public bicycle sharing system in 2007. The system is known as Vélib', a word made by _____ "velo" (bike) and "liberte" (freedom). The system encompasses around 21,000 distinctive gray bicycles and around
143.
1,450 bicycle stations in and around Paris, with an average daily ridership of over 100,000. Vélib' is the third most _____
144.
system of its kind in the world, surpassed in station numbers only by systems in Hangzhou and Wuhan in China. The great news for tourists is that City Hall has made sure the service is convenient for tourists, not just Parisians, by offering short-term passes and access in eight languages. You can grab a bike from any station around town—they can be found every 300 meters or so—and return it at any _____ station.
145.
Vélib' was part of Mayor Bertrand Delanoe's effort to make Paris greener and more bike-friendly. Beginning in 2001, the city began to rip up car lanes and install bike lanes. This antagonized many drivers, who complained that it created bottlenecks. Today, there are some 700 kilometers (440 miles) of cycling paths in Paris. _____. There's still a lot of car traffic
146.
and confusing one-way streets, and there have been accidents involving Vélib' riders—but a ride is no longer the dangerous obstacle course it once was.

143. (A) blending
(B) structuring
(C) translating
(D) correcting

144. (A) extended
(B) extending
(C) extension
(D) extensive

145. (A) another
(B) other
(C) the others
(D) of the other

146. (A) Although Vélib' is the oldest bike-for-hire program in Europe, it is not necessarily the safest.
(B) With more bike stations than are found in any other city in the world, Vélib' is the most convenient system in the world.
(C) Despite some tremendous progress since 2001, Paris is still not a paradise for bicyclists.
(D) Riders now have the right to travel both ways on some—but not all—one-way streets.

GO ON TO THE NEXT PART.

Part 7

Directions: Questions in this part of the test are based on a wide range of reading materials, including articles, letters, advertisements, and notices. After reading the passage, decide which of the four choices — (A), (B), (C), or (D) — best answers the question, and then mark the letter that corresponds to the best answer on your answer sheet. All answers should be based on what is stated in or on what can be inferred from the readings.

Look at the example

La Plata Dinner Theater announces the opening of *Life on the River*, a musical based on a book by Mark Twain. Dinner is served from 6:30 to 8:00, and the performance begins at 8:30 every evening.

What is opening?

(A) A bookstore

(B) An art exhibit

(C) A play

(D) A restaurant

(A)   (B)   ●   (D)

The reading states that *Life on the River* is a musical that is opening at La Plata Dinner Theater. You should choose (C).

While unusual restaurant decor is not a new concept, its popularity is growing for one good reason: increased competition. Five hundred billion dollars was spent in restaurants in the United States last year, an increase of about 5% from the previous year, and the number of restaurants increased by 3%. Restaurateurs can no longer focus entirely on food and service. Ambience — the synthesis of architecture, furniture, fixtures, lighting, and even staff attire — is now an important criterion when consumers choose a restaurant.

147. By how much did the amount of money spent in United States restaurants increase since last year?

(A) 3%

(B) 5%

(C) 50%

(D) 500%

148. Which of these is NOT given as a component of restaurant ambience?

(A) The architecture of a restaurant

(B) The quality of the food and service

(C) The tables and chairs

(D) The clothing worn by waiters and waitresses

GO ON TO THE NEXT PAGE

MEMO

TO: ALL PERMANENT EMPLOYEES
FROM: SOHEILA DARVISHALA, BENEFITS OFFICER
SUBJECT: NEW BENEFITS PLAN
DATE: AUG. 7, 20--

SYNCO TECHNOLOGIES IS INITIATING A NEW BENEFITS PLAN FOR ALL ELIGIBLE EMPLOYEES* BEGINNING SEPT. 1. IT IS IMPORTANT THAT THEY UNDERSTAND HOW THIS PLAN WORKS IN ORDER TO MAKE INFORMED DECISIONS. IT IS ALSO REQUIRED BY LAW THAT ALL ELIGIBLE EMPLOYEES ACCEPT OR DECLINE THIS NEW BENEFIT PLAN IN WRITING. (A FORM WILL BE PROVIDED AT THE MEETING.)

THERE WILL BE A MANDATORY MEETING ON FRIDAY, AUGUST 11 AT NOON IN ROOM 202 OF THE CENTER BUILDING. PLEASE MAKE A POINT OF ATTENDING. (THE MEETING OF AUGUST 4 WAS CALLED OFF BECAUSE OF POOR ATTENDANCE.)

A BROCHURE IS ATTACHED WHICH PROVIDES GENERAL INFORMATION ABOUT THE PLAN. EMPLOYEES SHOULD FAMILIARIZE THEMSELVES WITH THIS INFORMATION BEFORE THE MEETING AND BRING QUESTIONS.

*ELIGIBILITY FOR PARTICIPATION IS THE SAME AS ELIGIBILITY FOR HEALTH INSURANCE COVERAGE. IT IS LIMITED TO PERMANENT EMPLOYEES WHO WORK AT LEAST 30 HOURS A WEEK.

149. What is true about the August 11 meeting?

(A) Eligible employees must attend.

(B) It has to be canceled.

(C) Health insurance issues will be discussed.

(D) It will be held early in the morning.

150. Who is eligible for the benefits package?

(A) All Synco employees

(B) Permanent employees who work 30 hours or more weekly

(C) Employees who do not currently have health insurance

(D) Part-time employees only

151. What is attached to this memo?

(A) A form

(B) An agenda

(C) A brochure

(D) A check

Nancy Barringer (10:05) Bennet, I just talked to your assistant, and she said that you were on a bus on your way home.
Bennet Hill (10:10) Actually, I just got home.
Nancy Barringer (10:10) But the presentation on the Centauri Project for the clients from Hong Kong is today at 1.
Bennet Hill (10:14) Believe me, I know.
Nancy Barringer (10:15) So are you going to be back in the office in time to give the presentation?
Bennet Hill (10:17) No way. I have a terrible sore throat and I'm so hoarse I can barely speak. And I'm running a fever. Don't worry, though. I asked Ms. Bakos to give it for me.
Nancy Barringer (10:18) Ms. Bakos from the accounting department? I don't think she's all that familiar with the project.
Bennet Hill (10:21) Maybe not, but she's a good presenter.
Nancy Barringer (10:21) I'm going to skip lunch and come down and get your notes. Can you send me the PowerPoint presentation right away?

152. Who will probably give the presentation on the Centauri Project?

(A) Mr. Hill

(B) Ms. Bakos

(C) Ms. Barringer

(D) Clients from Hong Kong

153. At 10:17, what does Mr. Hill mean when he writes, "No way"?

(A) He isn't familiar with the Centauri Project.

(B) He didn't know the presentation was today.

(C) He's not sure what time he will return to the office.

(D) He can't possibly give the presentation today.

GO ON TO THE NEXT PAGE

Questions 154–157 refer to the following reading:

The Moroccan government encourages foreign investment, especially when it creates jobs and transfers technology. -[1]- Foreign-owned holdings are subject to the same regulations as locally owned businesses. Any regulations that do exist are principally related to financial service companies. There are also certain restrictions on businesses concerned with rail and air transport, water and energy supply, mining, and industries potentially harmful to public health or safety. -[2]-

The Industrial Investment Code provides tax relief and other incentives to non-service companies with investment programs exceeding DH100,000, certain service industries (including engineering and consulting), and small- and medium-sized businesses with investment programs not exceeding DH5 million. -[3]- Incentives include a 2.5 percent discounted tax rate for land acquisitions intended for housing developments; a 0.5 percent tax on any company contributing to capital formation or capital increase; and an exemption from registration fees when purchasing land intended for capital investment.

The Investment Charter Law also shields foreign investors from paying value added tax (VAT) on imported equipment, materials, and goods, and exempts start-up firms from license fees. -[4]- Furthermore, Morocco is improving its labor pool by investing in appropriate vocational training.

154. What is the purpose of this reading?

(A) To acquaint readers with Morocco's foreign investment policies

(B) To explain the best way to start a business in Morocco

(C) To discuss the current financial situation in Morocco

(D) To encourage Moroccans to take vocational classes

155. Which of the following types of foreign companies are NOT regulated in Morocco?

(A) Banks

(B) Mining companies

(C) Hotels

(D) Airlines

156. Which of the following would NOT receive incentives under the Industrial Investment Code?

(A) A non-service company investing more than DH100,000

(B) An engineering firm

(C) A medium-sized corporation investing less than DH5 million

(D) A large service company investing more than DH5 million

157. In which of the positions marked [1], [2], [3], and [4] does the following sentence best belong?

"As an additional incentive, the law simplified Morocco's customs regulations."

(A) [1]

(B) [2]

(C) [3]

(D) [4]

NEWSPAPER sales fell in most countries last year, especially in the developed world, according to an annual survey released by the International Federation of Newspaper Publishers.

Daily circulation fell in 23 of the 40 countries surveyed, slipping 1.2% in the United States, 1.87% in the European Union countries, and 0.17% in Japan.

But among less developed nations, Peru had a dramatic rise of 90% and India showed an increase of 28.5%.

The survey showed that Japan continued to lead the world in daily sales with 71.9 million, followed by the United States with 50.9 million and Germany with 25.7 million.

158. What is the author's main purpose in writing?

(A) To announce an increase in the number of newspapers worldwide

(B) To discuss the changing nature of journalism

(C) To contrast the way newspapers are operated in different nations

(D) To report on a survey regarding newspaper sales

159. In how many of the countries surveyed did sales NOT decline?

(A) 13

(B) 17

(C) 23

(D) 40

160. Which of the following is closest in meaning to the word "dramatic" in paragraph 3, line 2?

(A) slight

(B) unexplained

(C) spectacular

(D) estimated

161. In which of these countries was there the greatest increase in sales?

(A) Peru

(B) The United States

(C) India

(D) Germany

162. Which of these conclusions can be made about the sale of newspapers in Japan?

(A) Although there was a modest rise in sales, Japan still trails the United States and Germany.

(B) This year, sales continued their dramatic decline.

(C) Sales dropped slightly, but Japan continues to lead the world in daily sales.

(D) The sharp rise in sales was higher than that of any other country.

GO ON TO THE NEXT PAGE

Wildlife Protection League
Membership Renewal Reminder
March, 20--

Dear Member,

Your membership in the Wildlife Protection League is going to expire in a month. Please continue helping us in our work to conserve the Siberian tiger, the African elephant, the mountain gorilla, and all the other at-risk species around the globe. Your early renewal will continue your membership until April of next year.

And please, while you're at it, subscribe to *Wild!*, the WPL newsletter which details our wildlife-saving efforts and contains superb wildlife photography. For just $15, you'll receive six copies of this attractive bi-monthly journal. Thank you for your continuing support.

Karen McCauley

Karen McCauley, President

Enclosed please find:

Basic membership contribution	$25	____			
Subscription to *Wild!*	$15	____			
Additional contribution	$50	____	$100	____	Other $ ____

Total enclosed $ _____

---

163. How long will the recipient's membership continue if he or she renews now?

(A) Until March of this year

(B) Until April of this year

(C) Until March of next year

(D) Until April of next year

164. How often is the journal *Wild!* published?

(A) Every month

(B) Every two months

(C) Every six months

(D) Every year

165. How much is the basic membership fee?

(A) $15

(B) $25

(C) $50

(D) $100

The Pareto Principle, or Pareto Law (also known as the Law of the Vital Few), was first suggested by the Italian economist Vilfredo Pareto and was popularized by management expert Joseph M. Juran. (Because it was formulated by J. M. Juran, it probably should have been called the Juran Assumption.) -[1]- The principle states that for many phenomena, 80% of the effects are caused by 20% of the causes. For this reason, it is sometimes called the 80/20 Technique.

It is difficult to understand the Pareto Principle in completely abstract terms. -[2]- Suppose that a firm sells $100,000 worth of products to 100 clients. One would not expect that each customer would contribute equally to the total amount of sales. In fact, according to the Pareto Principle, about 80% of the variables (in this case, 80 clients) contribute only 20%, or $20,000, to the total sales. On the other hand, 20 clients contribute the remaining 80%. This statement is testable, and, for many companies, it has often been found to be approximately correct. -[3]-

Of course, the Pareto Principle should always be considered no more than a rule of thumb. -[4]- And while it may provide a quick way to analyze sales or other business situations, it is sometimes misapplied by managers to situations in which it is not meaningful.

166. In which of the positions marked [1], [2], [3], and [4] does the following sentence best belong?

"However, it is easy to understand it through the use of practical examples."

(A) [1]

(B) [2]

(C) [3]

(D) [4]

167. Which of these is NOT another common term for the Pareto Principle?

(A) The Pareto Law

(B) The Law of the Vital Few

(C) The Juran Assumption

(D) The 80/20 Technique

168. What can be inferred about the 20 clients mentioned in the example given in paragraph 2?

(A) They represent 80% of the variables.

(B) They account for 20% of total sales.

(C) They will bring the company 20% profits.

(D) They will contribute $80,000 to total sales.

169. Which of the following is closest in meaning to the phrase "a rule of thumb" in paragraph 3, line 1?

(A) A rule that is always true

(B) A principle that is helpful but not always accurate

(C) An interesting theory with little practical value

(D) A rule that is never true

170. According to the author, which of the following is a problem with the Pareto Principle?

(A) It is used in cases in which it should not be used.

(B) It does not supply answers quickly enough.

(C) It is not used by enough managers.

(D) It is used in business but not in other situations.

GO ON TO THE NEXT PAGE

Relocating Your Business?

For a smooth move across town or around the world, call **C & J Relocation Specialists** and take the worry and inconvenience out of your move.

Sure, you could
- research moving companies
- deal with phone and utility companies
- order new stationery
- prepare checklists
- take care of 1,001 other details

But don't you have a business to run?

Call for a free consultation!

Our business is to manage the details of the move so that you can STAY in business.

171. For whom is this advertisement intended?

(A) Businesses that want to expand their operations

(B) Executives being transferred to another city

(C) Employees who want to change careers

(D) Companies moving to another location

172. What does the advertiser offer potential clients?

(A) Lower prices

(B) Less inconvenience

(C) Greater speed

(D) More prestige

Questions 173–175 refer to the following online chat discussion:

| **Rick Waters** | *Jun 18* | *8:00 PM* |

Hello, everyone. I asked you all to come online this evening so we could chat about our company's anniversary. It's coming up on the 27th of next month.

| **Sarah Jefferson** | *Jun 18* | *8:02 PM* |

Right. It's been 10 years since Mr. Barelli founded the company.

| **Samuel Nyeni** | *Jun 18* | *8:02 PM* |

So, are we doing anything special to celebrate?

| **Sarah Jefferson** | *Jun 18* | *8:03 PM* |

Well, we're planning a company picnic.

| **Rick Waters** | *Jun 18* | *8:04 PM* |

Right, but I was thinking we should do something special for Mr. Barelli. We should think big.

| **Sarah Jefferson** | *Jun 18* | *8:05 PM* |

Maybe we could have his portrait painted. I think that would be a nice surprise.

| **Samuel Nyeni** | *Jun 18* | *8:05 PM* |

Nice idea. Anyone know any good artists?

| **Sarah Jefferson** | *Jun 18* | *8:06 PM* |

I was at an opening at the Centennial Gallery last week. It was an exhibit of Gladys Herrera's paintings and sculptures.

| **Rick Waters** | *Jun 18* | *8:07 PM* |

I've seen some of her paintings. She's very good. But she just paints landscapes.

Sarah Jefferson   *Jun 18   8:07 PM*

No, I saw still-lifes and portraits at her show.

Samuel Nyeni   *Jun 18   8:09 PM*

How are you going to get Mr. Barelli to pose for a portrait if it's going to be a surprise?

Sarah Jefferson   *Jun 18   8:09 PM*

I'll bet the painter could work from photographs. We could get his admin assistant, Ms. Cox, to take some pictures.

Rick Waters   *Jun 18   8:10 PM*

I don't know—she doesn't keep secrets very well.

Samuel Nyeni   *Jun 18   8:11 PM*

Or I could take some photos on my phone at the next staff meeting.

Rick Waters   *Jun 18   8:12 PM*

Let's just ask his wife. Ms. Barelli could probably get quite a few photos for us.

Sarah Jefferson   *Jun 18   8:12 PM*

Then I'll go by the gallery and see if I can get Gladys Herrera's contact information.

---

173. At 8:04 PM, what does Rick Waters mean when he writes, "We should think big"?

(A) They should do more to celebrate the anniversary of the company's founding.

(B) They should invite more people to come to the company picnic.

(C) They should ask other people to join their discussion.

(D) They should commission a very large painting of Mr. Barelli.

174. What was Rick Waters mistaken about?

(A) He didn't think anything had been planned to celebrate the anniversary.

(B) He thought Gladys Herrera did only one type of painting.

(C) He believed Ms. Cox could not get any photos of Mr. Barelli.

(D) He thought Gladys Herrera worked only on sculptures.

175. Who will probably be asked to provide photos of Mr. Barelli?

(A) Gladys Herrera

(B) Ms. Barelli

(C) Samuel Nyeni

(D) Ms. Cox

GO ON TO THE NEXT PAGE

Questions 176–180 are based on the following form and memo:

Internal Request for
Programming/Data Output

To: _Stuart Daniels, Director, Information Systems Department_

Description of desired program or data output
Postal addresses for all current and prospective customers

Reason for Request

To generate promotional mailings list for new product brochures

Target date _July 3_

Requested by	_Grace Heng_
Title	_Marketing Assistant_
Date	_June 19_
Department	_Marketing_
Approved by	_John Brusaw_
(Appropriate director or deputy director)	
Date	_June 20_
Department	_Marketing_

Date received by IS Dept _June 20_

Interdepartmental Memo

From: Stuart Daniels
To: Grace Heng
Date: June 21

Hi Grace,

I'm afraid I won't be able to deal with your request as quickly as you wanted. As you probably know, our department has been involved in creating a new program for the accounting office and we still have some bugs to work out. The CEO has stressed that getting this program up and running smoothly by July 1 is our number 1 priority. If we generate your list, it will be at least a week later than you requested it.

However, if you want to drop by our office, I'm sure someone can spare an hour or so to show you how you can get the addresses you need on your desktop computer and even print out address labels for your brochures. It's really pretty simple.

Stuart

176. What is the purpose of the form?

(A) To request a list of customer addresses

(B) To ask one department to distribute brochures for another

(C) To request Information Systems to repair her desktop computer

(D) To ask another company to supply information

177. Who is John Brusaw?

(A) Director of the Marketing Department

(B) Marketing Assistant

(C) Director of the Information Systems Department

(D) Deputy Director of the Marketing Department

178. In paragraph 1, line 3 of the memo, the phrase "some bugs to work out" is closest in meaning to

(A) some programs to write

(B) some problems to solve

(C) some tasks to begin

(D) some items to find

179. When is the earliest date that Information Systems can perform the service that Grace Heng has asked them to do?

(A) June 27

(B) July 3

(C) July 8

(D) July 10

180. What suggestion does Stuart Daniels give Grace Heng?

(A) That she call his office and speak to him

(B) That she contact him again in several months

(C) That she work on this project herself

(D) That she speak to the CEO

GO ON TO THE NEXT PAGE

FAX
InfoQuest Technology Projects, Inc.

To: Jane Deckard   **Fax number:** 303 555-1741
From: Terry Kim   **Fax number:** 231 555-4928
Total pages sent: 4   **Date:** 7 January, 20--

Printer Return Study
Your opinion matters!

Thank you in advance for participating in the **Printer Return Study.** A major Canadian printer manufacturer is interested in knowing why some customers who purchase an inkjet or laser printer return the printer for a refund to the place of purchase. If you are a recent inkjet/laser buyer (in the last three months), you qualify to answer this survey whether or not you returned that printer to its place of purchase. This survey takes five minutes or less to complete. To use your opinions, we must receive your answers by Friday, Feb. 2.

As our thanks for completing the survey form, you will receive a 10% discount on your next purchase from any of our client companies, which include some of the top high-tech companies in the world. For a list of these companies and information on how to obtain your discount, see pages 2 and 3 of this fax. When you have completed the survey, please fax only the survey page (do not send this cover sheet or pages 2 and 3) to 231-555-4928. Remember, your opinions are very important to us, so please answer all questions that apply to you and fill in all relevant blanks. Also, be sure to sign and date the form at the bottom.

Thanks,

Terry Kim

Terry Kim
IQTP, Inc.

Sent: Jan 12, 20--
Printer Return Survey Form

Type of printer purchased   Talon P6000 Inkjet Printer
Date of purchase   around Dec. 5
Approximate cost $225
Place of purchase   Computer Marketplace Superstore
Primary reason for purchase   Personal use _____   Business use _____
Other __X__ (Please explain)   Gift for daughter
How would you rate this printer? Excellent __X__ Very good _____ Good _____ Fair _____ Poor _____ Very poor _____

Did you return the printer after purchase? Yes _____   No __X__
Primary reason for return _____
Did you have any problems returning the printer? Yes _____   No __X__
If so, please describe _____

When you returned the printer, did you
_____ A) receive a cash refund?
_____ B) exchange the printer for another printer?
_____ C) exchange the printer for other merchandise?

Which of the following problems might lead you to return a printer?

Difficulty of installation	Yes __X__	No _____
Appearance of printer	Yes _____	No __X__
Damage to computer during shipping, etc.	Yes __X__	No _____
Problems with performance	Yes __X__	No _____
Problems getting technical support	Yes __X__	No _____
Problems with warranty	Yes __X__	No _____
Poor quality of copies (text)	Yes __X__	No _____
Poor quality of copies (photos)	Yes __X__	No _____

Comments   My daughter really loves the printer I bought her — it prints beautiful, professional looking photos.

Name   Jane Deckard   Date   Jan 12, 20--
Signature _____

181. How many pages of Ms. Kim's fax consist of a list of client companies and instructions on getting a discount?

(A) One

(B) Two

(C) Three

(D) Four

182. To fill out this survey, what must a person have done recently?

(A) Returned a printer to its place of purchase

(B) Bought a product from one of Ms. Kim's client companies

(C) Completed a previous survey

(D) Purchased an inkjet or laser printer

183. Which of the directions in Ms. Kim's fax did Ms. Deckard NOT follow?

(A) She did not sign the form.

(B) She did not fill in the form soon enough.

(C) She did not answer all the relevant questions.

(D) She did not date the form.

184. Ms. Deckard would NOT return a printer for which of these reasons?

(A) Because of the way it looks

(B) Because of the way it prints photos

(C) Because of difficulties getting customer support

(D) Because of damage that occurred during shipping

185. What will Ms. Deckard receive for filling out this form?

(A) A free printer

(B) A cash refund

(C) A discount on a purchase

(D) A fax machine

GO ON TO THE NEXT PAGE

Solange Corporation 21st Annual National Sales Conference

Thursday

9 AM–4 PM	Registration and badge pick-up
7–8 PM	Informal reception at West Ballroom, New Plaza Hotel
8–9 PM	Opening address by Ted Singer, Vice President for Sales

Friday

7:30 AM	Attendees bused to Carleton Ranch
8:30–9 AM	Coffee and rolls
9 AM–12 PM	Plenary Session
12–1 PM	Lunch
1–3:30 PM	Meetings led by regional sales managers
4–7 PM	Horseback ride and old-fashioned barbecue
7 PM	Attendees bused back to their hotels

Saturday

9 AM–12 PM	Sales seminars led by guest speakers, New Plaza Hotel
12–1:30 PM	Lunch, closing ceremony, and "Sales Manager and Sales Reps of the Year" awards

Your badge is your "ticket" to all events.

Dress: Business dress for Thursday and Saturday events. Casual western wear (blue jeans, boots, and cowboy hats!) for events at the Carleton Ranch.

All meals not listed on this schedule must be paid for by attendees. Room service bills are the responsibility of attendees. Attendees who stay over Saturday night must pay for accommodations for that night. Taxis, rental cars, and other ground transportation other than shuttle van to and from the airport and bus to the ranch will not be reimbursed. Keep receipts for hotel bills and airline tickets in order to be reimbursed.

Solange Corporation

Sent: 10:42 a.m. Wednesday 2 June 20--
From: Marilyn Brady <m.brady@solangecorp.com>
Subject: Mr. Yuan
To: Ted Singer <t.singer@solangecorp.com>

Mr. Singer,
I received the schedule for our Sales Conference. It looks great! All the sales reps in the Northwest Region are excited about it.

I want to let you know that, unfortunately, our regional manager Mr. Yuan won't be in attendance this year because of his recent hospitalization. Mr. Yuan is very sorry to miss this year's conference as he's attended the last 20 conferences! I'll be taking over his duties at the conference.

Look forward to seeing you in a couple of weeks.

Marilyn Brady
Assistant Regional Sales Manager, Northwest Region
Solange Corporation

Sent: 9:27 a.m. Thursday 3 June 20--
From: Ted Singer <t.singer@solangecorp.com>
Subject: Sales Conference
To: Liang Yuan <l.yuan@solangecorp.com>

Dear Liang,
I was just informed by Marilyn Brady that you were recently hospitalized. I am glad to hear that you are recovering and that you are home from the hospital.

I am sure that you must be disappointed not to be able to attend this year's sales conference—I know you look forward to it every year. I am disappointed too! I always enjoy getting caught up with you. And this year, we had a big surprise planned for you after lunch on Saturday!

Hope you get well soon. And don't worry; I am sure your assistant will do a very able job of taking over your duties for this one year.

Best wishes,
Ted

186. What must attendees bring to all events?

(A) Boots

(B) A ticket

(C) A badge

(D) Receipts

187. For which of the following will attendees be reimbursed?

(A) Airfares

(B) Room service charges

(C) Taxi fares

(D) Saturday night's hotel bill

188. What special task will Marilyn Brady have at the conference?

(A) Giving the opening address on Thursday evening

(B) Leading a meeting on Friday afternoon

(C) Directing the sales seminars on Saturday morning

(D) Presenting awards at the ceremony on Saturday afternoon

189. Before this year, how many sales conferences did Mr. Yuan miss?

(A) None

(B) One

(C) Ten

(D) Twenty

190. What does Mr. Singer imply in his email?

(A) Mr. Yuan will be named Sales Manager of the Year.

(B) Ms. Brady may be receiving a promotion soon.

(C) He knew about Mr. Yuan's illness before Ms. Brady did.

(D) He is worried that the conference will not go smoothly.

GO ON TO THE NEXT PAGE

FARWELL ENTERPRISES, INCORPORATED

Ms. Michelle Carrington
Director, Banquet and Catering Department
Vantage Hotel
Portland, Oregon 97205

Dec. 1, 20--

Dear Ms. Carrington,
I enjoyed meeting with you last week. Your enthusiasm for the menu for our Dec. 13 dinner meeting in the Redwood Room is contagious. My mouth is already watering!

According to my notes, you will be preparing the following for 87 people:

Main course
    Choice of chicken picata or vegetarian medley
Plus
    • Fresh spinach, mandarin orange, and almond salad
    • Angel hair pasta with white clam sauce
    • Raspberry and white chocolate tarts
    • Coffee or tea

Also, your staff of ten will arrive at 6 p.m. for set up, serve the food at 8 p.m. and handle the clean-up. The meeting will end no later than 10 p.m.

Does this sound right to you? Let me know if you have any questions.

Sincerely,

André Pettigrew
Chief Operating Officer
Farwell Enterprises, Inc.

From: Michelle Carrington <banquets@vantage.com>
Subject: Dinner meeting
To: André Pettigrew <a.pettigrew@farwell.com>
Sent: 2 Dec. 20--

Hello Mr. Pettigrew,

I enjoyed meeting you as well last week, and my staff and I are looking forward to serving you at your dinner meeting here at the Vantage Hotel later this month.

One thing to clear up: According to *my* notes, we decided to offer the choice of one more main dish, salmon with a honey-ginger glaze. Please let me know as soon as possible if you don't want to include this entrée.

Also, I told you that all ten members of my catering staff will be working on the evening of your dinner meeting. Unfortunately, one of my serving staff will be unavailable. This won't in any way affect our usual high standards of service, I promise!

Regards,

Michelle Carrington

From: André Pettigrew <a.pettigrew@farwell.com>
Subject: Re. Dinner meeting
To: Michelle Carrington
Sent: 14 Dec. 20--

Michelle,

I want to thank you again for your hard work and for putting together such a wonderful dinner last night. Everything was delicious. I had the salmon as a main dish and it was amazing. And those raspberry tarts . . . yum!

I must admit, I was at first a little nervous when it turned out that, not one but two of your serving staff were unable to work that evening, but I needn't have worried. The service was prompt and polite—those folks really hustled!

We've already decided to hold our next dinner meeting at the Redwood Room. And if I hear of anyone else who is looking for a venue for a banquet, I'll be happy to recommend you.

Best,

André Pettigrew

COO, Farwell Enterprises, Inc.

GO ON TO THE NEXT PAGE

191. What is the main purpose of André Pettigrew's letter?

(A) To confirm the arrangements for a dinner meeting

(B) To invite Michelle Carrington to attend a meeting

(C) To introduce himself to Michelle Carrington

(D) To reserve the Redwood Room at the Vantage Hotel

192. The word "contagious" in the letter is closest in meaning to

(A) overwhelming

(B) premature

(C) surprising

(D) catching

193. How many main dishes were people at the dinner meeting able to choose from?

(A) One

(B) Two

(C) Three

(D) Four

194. What promise does Michelle Carrington make?

(A) That she will find another server for the dinner

(B) That the service at the dinner will be fine

(C) That the salmon dish will be delicious

(D) That all the members of her staff will be at the dinner

195. How many people were on Michelle Carrington's staff at the dinner meeting?

(A) Seven

(B) Eight

(C) Nine

(D) Ten

Imprinted Audio Products from Impressions Unlimited

Everyone loves music! Your logo and these audio giveaways will make beautiful music together! Imprinted earbuds and headphones are always welcome promotional products. Earbuds in imprinted pouches or cases fit standard headphone jacks on most MP3 players and phones, and the included case or pouch helps keep them tangle-free. Your logo imprinted on the case or the pouch serves as a reminder to your customers every time they listen to music.

Earbuds with clear plastic traveler case imprinted with your logo
$0.98 each   Order as few as 250   Item #418609
Ships in 5 days

Earbuds with 3 pairs of interchangeable covers in 3 Colors
Available in clear plastic or blue plastic case imprinted with your logo
$1.79 each   Order as few as 250   Item #425716
Ships in 5 days

Earbuds with 3 pairs of interchangeable covers in 3 Colors
In a blue leather-like pouch imprinted with your logo
$2.19 each   Order as few as 250   Item #425717
Ships in 5 days

Cell phone cleaning kit in a pouch with earbuds
In a plush red leather-like pouch imprinted with your logo. Pouch holds both the kit and the earbuds.
$2.79 each   Order as few as 150   Item #417855
Ships in 5 days

Automatic cord winder for headphones and earbuds
Everyone hates tangled cords! This winder instantly and automatically retracts and rewinds the cord. Winder imprinted with your logo.
$3.99 each   Order as few as 100   Item #409918
Ships in 5 days

High fidelity headphones
These high-quality headphones make the perfect gift for your special clients or top employees. The audio quality of these headphones is as rich as that of headphones costing many times as much as these. On sale now for only $39.95.
Order as few as 10   Item #578031
Ships in 7 days

Free shipping on orders over $1,000.

If your logo is not on file with us, please send by email: add@impressionsunlmt.com

To see hundreds of other ideas for promoting your product, click here to return to our main catalogue.

GO ON TO THE NEXT PAGE

Impressions Unlimited, Inc.

| | | Order date: | Apr. 4 |
| | | Shipping date: | Apr. 8 |

Ship to: Rainier Lumber Company
411 Pinedale Street
Everett, WA 98201
attn. Robert Davies
Phone: (425) 555-1976

Item number	Description	Price	Quantity	Total
425717	Earbuds with inter-changeable covers (pouch)	$2.19	250	$547.50
425716	Earbuds with inter-changeable covers (case)	$1.79	250	$447.50
409918	Auto. cord winder	$3.99	150	$598.50
578031	Hi-Fi headphones	$39.95	10	$399.50
			Subtotal	$1,993.00
			Shipping	N/A
			Total	$1,993.00

Rainier Lumber Co.

Hello, Thanks for filling my order so promptly. Unfortunately, I have to return part of the order. The automatic cord winder worked well the first few times I tried it. After that, the retracting mechanism failed to rewind the cords. I tried this with 4 or 5 winders and the same thing happened every time. Also, the earbud covers keep coming off each time they are used or even handled.

When I placed a previous order (for computer flash drives), the logo for my company was printed so small that it was illegible, and I had to return those as well. I suggest you invest a little in quality control.

Rob Davies
Owner and CEO

196. What type of business is Impressions Unlimited most likely involved in?

(A) Making computer accessories

(B) Selling promotional products

(C) Manufacturing audio equipment

(D) Producing wood products

197. What is suggested about the pouches mentioned in the advertisement?

(A) They are available in only one color.

(B) They are made of leather.

(C) They are more expensive than the cases.

(D) They are available with only one type of product.

198. Why were there no shipping charges for Mr. Davies' order?

(A) Because the products were not shipped on time

(B) Because of the total cost of the products that he ordered

(C) Because of the poor quality of products he had previously ordered

(D) Because some of the products he ordered were not available

199. Which of the following products did Mr. Davies NOT order the minimum quantity of?

(A) #425717

(B) #425716

(C) #409918

(D) #578031

200. In the note, the word "illegible" in paragraph 2, line 2, is closest in meaning to

(A) unusable

(B) invisible

(C) unreadable

(D) impractical

THIS IS THE END OF THE READING SECTION. IF YOU FINISH BEFORE TIME IS UP, YOU MUST WORK ONLY ON PROBLEMS IN THIS SECTION.

Practice Test 2

General Directions

This exam is designed to test how well you can understand and use the English language. The test takes approximately two hours to complete. It consists of seven separate parts, each with its own directions. Before you begin to work on a part, be certain that you understand the directions.

Some items will seem harder than other items. However, you should answer every one if possible. Remember, you are not penalized for guessing. If you are not able to answer every question, don't worry.

All your answers should be marked on the answer sheets found on pages 284–285. Remove or copy these sheets before the test begins. When you are marking an answer, fill in the circle corresponding to the letter that you have chosen. The space in the circle should be completely filled in so that the letter inside is not visible, as shown in the example below:

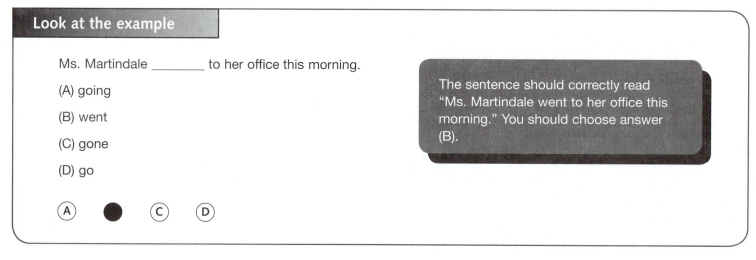

Look at the example

Ms. Martindale _____ to her office this morning.

(A) going

(B) went

(C) gone

(D) go

Ⓐ ● Ⓒ Ⓓ

The sentence should correctly read "Ms. Martindale went to her office this morning." You should choose answer (B).

For each question, you may mark only one answer. If you decide to change your answer, you should erase your original answer completely.

In this first section of the exam, your ability to understand spoken English will be tested. This section consists of four separate parts, each having its own directions.

Part 1

Directions: For each item, there is a photograph in the book and four short sentences about it on the audio program. The sentences are NOT written out, so you must listen carefully.

You must choose the one sentence — (A), (B), (C), or (D) — that is the best description of what can be seen in the photograph. Then mark the letter that corresponds to the best answer on your answer sheet.

Look at the example

You see this photograph:

Listen to the four sentences:

Ⓐ   Ⓑ   Ⓒ   ●

> Choice (D) — "The mechanic is repairing the engine." — is the best description of what can be seen in the photograph.

GO ON TO THE NEXT PAGE ➡

1.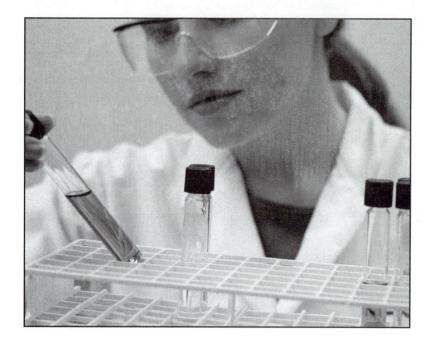

2.

3.

4.

GO ON TO THE NEXT PAGE ➡

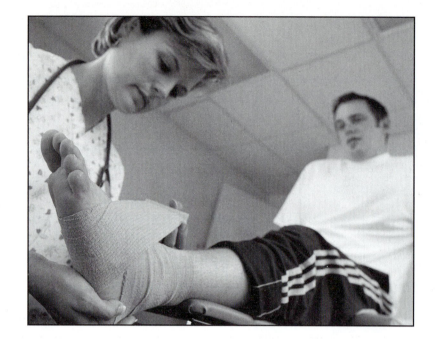

GO ON TO THE NEXT PART.

Part 2

Directions: In this part of the test, you will hear a question or statement on the audio program. After that, you will hear three possible responses to the question or statement. Each question or statement and each response is given only once and is not written out in your book, so listen carefully. Mark the answer that corresponds to the best response to the question or statement on your answer sheet.

Listen to a sample

You hear:

You then hear:

> Choice (A), "At the gymnasium," is the best response to the question "Where have you been, Steve?" You should mark (A) on your answer sheet.

---

7. Mark your answer on the answer sheet.

8. Mark your answer on the answer sheet.

9. Mark your answer on the answer sheet.

10. Mark your answer on the answer sheet.

11. Mark your answer on the answer sheet.

12. Mark your answer on the answer sheet.

13. Mark your answer on the answer sheet.

14. Mark your answer on the answer sheet.

15. Mark your answer on the answer sheet.

16. Mark your answer on the answer sheet.

17. Mark your answer on the answer sheet.

18. Mark your answer on the answer sheet.

19. Mark your answer on the answer sheet.

20. Mark your answer on the answer sheet.

21. Mark your answer on the answer sheet.

22. Mark your answer on the answer sheet.

23. Mark your answer on the answer sheet.

24. Mark your answer on the answer sheet.

25. Mark your answer on the answer sheet.

26. Mark your answer on the answer sheet.

27. Mark your answer on the answer sheet.

28. Mark your answer on the answer sheet.

29. Mark your answer on the answer sheet.

30. Mark your answer on the answer sheet.

31. Mark your answer on the answer sheet.

GO ON TO THE NEXT PART.

Part 3

Directions: In this part of the test, you will hear some short conversations involving two or three speakers. Each conversation is spoken only once and is not written in the book, so listen carefully.

In your book, you will read three questions about each conversation. Following each question are four answer choices — (A), (B), (C), or (D). Mark the letter that corresponds to the best answer on your answer sheet.

32. What kind of weather are they discussing?

(A) Snowy

(B) Windy

(C) Cold

(D) Sunny

33. What time is the plane now scheduled to leave?

(A) 12:30

(B) 1:30

(C) 2:00

(D) 3:00

34. What will the man probably do next?

(A) Call his client

(B) Get something to eat

(C) Write a report

(D) Catch the flight to Miami

---

35. Who is Mr. Weisberg?

(A) An audio technician

(B) A painter

(C) A public relations expert

(D) A journalist

36. How long has Mr. Weisberg worked for the firm?

(A) For several days

(B) For a week

(C) For a month

(D) For two months

37. What problem did they have at the last conference?

(A) The telephone reception wasn't clear.

(B) The sound equipment didn't operate properly.

(C) The traffic noise was too loud.

(D) The reporters asked difficult questions.

38. What does the woman mean when she says, "It's not quite on target"?

(A) A product is out-of-date.

(B) Sales goals were missed.

(C) Profit estimates are too low.

(D) A project is unacceptable.

39. Where do they probably work?

(A) At a modeling agency

(B) In a television studio

(C) At an electronics firm

(D) At a sporting goods store

40. What is the man planning to do next?

(A) Rewrite the brochure

(B) Write an advertisement

(C) Watch a movie on television

(D) Meet with the sales team

---

41. What are they discussing?

(A) A garden supply store

(B) A favorite restaurant

(C) A new magazine

(D) A new recipe

42. Why is The Sunflower not open now?

(A) It received a bad review.

(B) It is changing ownership.

(C) It suffered some damage in a fire.

(D) It is closed for a holiday.

43. What can be inferred about The Sunflower?

(A) It was a popular place.

(B) It was too crowded.

(C) It needed to be cleaned.

(D) It is having staffing problems.

GO ON TO THE NEXT PAGE

44. What is Tammy's primary reason for going to China?

 (A) She will be studying the Chinese language.

 (B) She will be working in her company's office there.

 (C) She will be teaching Chinese students there.

 (D) She will be taking a vacation there.

45. What is Tammy's biggest problem?

 (A) She doesn't have all her travel documents yet.

 (B) The airline has canceled the flight that she wants.

 (C) The company won't pay for her classes.

 (D) She doesn't have enough money for the trip.

46. What does the man suggest Tammy do?

 (A) Study Chinese on her own

 (B) Postpone her trip indefinitely

 (C) Ask the company to hire an interpreter for her

 (D) Ask the company to provide a private teacher

---

47. Who is the first speaker?

 (A) A banker

 (B) A construction worker

 (C) A mechanic

 (D) A dentist

48. What is Mr. Sutcliff's problem?

 (A) He had to wait a long time to get an appointment.

 (B) He was late for his appointment.

 (C) He has a toothache.

 (D) He lost his checkbook.

49. What advice does the first speaker give Mr. Sutcliff?

 (A) He should make appointments more regularly.

 (B) He shouldn't wait so long to deal with this kind of problem.

 (C) He should reschedule his appointment at a later time.

 (D) He should relax and not work so hard.

50. What are the speakers mainly discussing?

    (A) A sales meeting

    (B) An electronics conference

    (C) A business trip

    (D) A personal vacation

51. What problem do the speakers have?

    (A) Their booth is in a bad location.

    (B) A vehicle is too small.

    (C) Pamphlets were not delivered.

    (D) Their hotel is overbooked.

52. What will Janet most likely do next?

    (A) Contact her colleagues

    (B) Cancel a tour reservation

    (C) Phone a rental agency

    (D) Speak to a hotel clerk

53. What are they probably discussing?

    (A) A photograph

    (B) A recent exhibit

    (C) A painting

    (D) A new coffee shop

54. What can be inferred about Katie?

    (A) She finds the man's work very amusing.

    (B) She doesn't like this work as much as the man's earlier works.

    (C) She suggested that the man create more realistic works.

    (D) She doesn't think the man's works should be on display.

55. Why does the woman say, "The coffee's on me"?

    (A) She wants to suggest a new brand of coffee.

    (B) She wants to buy something for the man.

    (C) She has bought a large amount of coffee.

    (D) She has spilt a drink on herself.

GO ON TO THE NEXT PAGE

56. Why did the woman buy so much?

    (A) Her husband really likes soup.

    (B) There was no food in the house.

    (C) She saw some good deals.

    (D) They need it for their sailing trip.

57. How was the tuna fish priced?

    (A) Two for the price of one

    (B) A half dozen for ten dollars

    (C) Thirty cents per can

    (D) Ten for a dollar

58. What does the man imply?

    (A) They needed more toothpaste.

    (B) Buying the soup was a great idea.

    (C) The sale prices weren't so good.

    (D) Their storage space is limited.

---

59. What are the men talking about?

    (A) Watching a sports event

    (B) Going to an office party

    (C) Watching a comedy on television

    (D) Playing a game of catch

60. When is the earliest they can call the box office?

    (A) Nine o'clock

    (B) Eleven o'clock

    (C) One o'clock

    (D) Two o'clock

61. What does the second man imply?

    (A) The tickets are too expensive for him.

    (B) He'd rather go in person.

    (C) It's too late to get tickets.

    (D) He needs a big-screen television.

Mr. Adkins' Appointment Schedule

Time	Event
2:00	Presentation for Sales Director
3:00	Meeting with Personnel Director
3:30	Presentation for Mr. Ortega
4:30	Meeting with Loren Vega

62. What type of company most likely is Zenith, Inc.?

(A) A movie studio

(B) A restaurant chain

(C) An employment agency

(D) An advertising company

63. Look at the graphic. What time is the man's meeting scheduled for?

(A) 2:00

(B) 3:00

(C) 3:30

(D) 4:30

64. What would the man like to do next?

(A) Meet the Sales Director

(B) Phone Mr. Adkins

(C) Prepare a presentation

(D) Reschedule his appointment

Supplement Facts

Serving Size 1 Tablet

Amount Per Serving	% Daily Value
Vitamin A	100%
Vitamin B$_{12}$	80%
Vitamin C	75%
Vitamin D	100%

65. What most likely is the man's job?

(A) Pharmacist

(B) Radiologist

(C) Physician

(D) Laboratory Technician

GO ON TO THE NEXT PAGE

66. Look at the graphic. Which of the supplement's ingredients was NOT recommended by the doctor?

(A) Vitamin A

(B) Vitamin B$_{12}$

(C) Vitamin C

(D) Vitamin D

67. What will the man most likely do next?

(A) Send the woman to a clinic

(B) Go to the cash register

(C) Recommend a different product

(D) Write a prescription

Musical Performance Schedule	
3:00	Charlotte and Reuben
3:30	The Smokey Mountain Trio
4:00	Country Pride
4:30	The Banjo Brothers

68. What is the main topic of the conversation?

(A) Managing an event

(B) Finding accommodations

(C) Making a reservation

(D) Selecting performers

69. What does the man suggest?

(A) That other bands play earlier

(B) That they contact a replacement group

(C) That the event take place at another location

(D) That they ask another person what to do

70. Look at the graphic. At what time will a performance likely be cancelled?

(A) 3:00

(B) 3:30

(C) 4:00

(D) 4:30

GO ON TO THE NEXT PART.

Directions: During this part of the exam, there are ten brief talks. These talks are not written out and are spoken only once, so you must listen carefully.

There are three questions about each of the talks. Following each question are four possible answers — (A), (B), (C), and (D). You must decide which of these best answers the question and then mark the letter that corresponds to the best answer on your answer sheet.

71. For how long has the Robot Trade Fair been held in Japan?

(A) This is the first year.

(B) This is the third year.

(C) This is the twentieth year.

(D) This is the thirtieth year.

72. Which type of robot did the speaker NOT mention as being at the trade fair?

(A) Robots used to build cars

(B) Security-guard robots

(C) Robots used to clean teeth

(D) Toy animal robots

73. What does the speaker say about the robotic device that may be used by surgeons?

(A) It is capable of extremely precise work.

(B) It has been in use for several years.

(C) It is too expensive for most doctors to ever use.

(D) It requires many years of development before it can be used.

74. What characteristic of Quiet Springs Bottled Water does the speaker especially emphasize?

(A) Its low price

(B) Its large bottles

(C) Its fresh taste

(D) Its nutritional value

75. What does the speaker imply about most other brands of bottled water?

(A) They will soon contain vitamins too.

(B) They are not as pure.

(C) They are slightly less expensive.

(D) They are not available in two sizes.

76. What does the speaker suggest for people who want to save money?

(A) Buying four boxes of half-liter bottles

(B) Bottling water themselves

(C) Taking vitamin pills rather than drinking bottled water

(D) Buying four one-liter bottles in a pack

GO ON TO THE NEXT PAGE

77. Which of these San Francisco Denim Company plants will remain open?

    (A) The one in New Orleans, Louisiana

    (B) The one in Panama City, Panama

    (C) The one in Windsor, Ontario

    (D) The one in Guadalajara, Mexico

78. What does the speaker say about the South San Francisco plant?

    (A) It was closed down several years ago.

    (B) It produces clothing other than jeans.

    (C) It is no longer the company's main plant.

    (D) It has recently become more efficient.

79. What percentage of their income do consumers today spend on clothing?

    (A) One percent

    (B) Eight percent

    (C) Fourteen percent

    (D) Forty percent

---

80. What is the main purpose of this talk?

    (A) To discuss Indian handicrafts and jewelry

    (B) To announce the new appointment of an Indian diplomat

    (C) To provide information about an event at the MiraVista Hotel

    (D) To describe the cuisine of India

81. Who is Mr. Sohan Bhatt?

    (A) A chef from India

    (B) A spokesperson for the hotel

    (C) A representative of the Indian Embassy

    (D) A jewelry maker from India

82. Where will the opening ceremony of the food festival take place?

    (A) At the Indian Embassy

    (B) In the Wellington Restaurant

    (C) In the MiraVista Gallery

    (D) In the Somerset Banquet Hall

83. Which of the following does Warren Holt cancel in this message?

(A) His dinner with Robert Panella

(B) His trip to Miami

(C) His meeting with Ms. Watson

(D) His breakfast with Robert Panella

84. What does the man imply when he says, "I had some matters to attend to at home"?

(A) His home office was being remodeled.

(B) His hometown's airport was closed.

(C) He had to reschedule his flight.

(D) He had to take care of personal business.

85. Which of the following does Warren Holt ask Robert Panella to do?

(A) Meet him at the airport

(B) Confirm a meeting

(C) Reserve a rental car for him

(D) Return his phone call

---

86. How long were Kevin and Sean Doyle missing?

(A) Two days

(B) Three days

(C) Eight days

(D) Ten days

87. Where were Kevin and Sean found?

(A) In a campground

(B) In an abandoned gold mine

(C) In a small cabin

(D) In a hollow in the woods

88. The two boys were probably NOT suffering from which of the following?

(A) Hunger

(B) Thirst

(C) Exhaustion

(D) Cold

GO ON TO THE NEXT PAGE

89. Why does the woman say, "We couldn't have been so successful without you"?

   (A) To offer employment

   (B) To make a contract

   (C) To show appreciation

   (D) To ask for forgiveness

90. Where would an employee go to get a free subway pass?

   (A) To the new day-care center

   (B) To the Human Resource Department

   (C) To a supervisor's office

   (D) To the Engineering Department

91. What determines the percentage that the company will pay for classes?

   (A) Content and price

   (B) Approval by a supervisor

   (C) Time and distance

   (D) Application by the deadline

Purchase Invoice

Item	Quantity
1. corn flour	5
2. green chilies	40
3. coriander	2
4. cheddar cheese	4

92. What is the purpose of the phone call?

   (A) To order more items

   (B) To request an invoice

   (C) To schedule a delivery

   (D) To correct an order

93. Look at the graphic. Which item is the listener asked to change?

   (A) Item 1

   (B) Item 2

   (C) Item 3

   (D) Item 4

94. What does the speaker ask the listener to do?

(A) Give him a refund

(B) Send him an email

(C) Visit his location

(D) Hurry a shipment

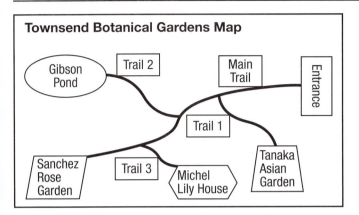

Townsend Botanical Gardens Map

Gibson Pond — Trail 2 — Main Trail — Entrance — Trail 1 — Sanchez Rose Garden — Trail 3 — Michel Lily House — Tanaka Asian Garden

95. Who most likely is the woman?

(A) A florist

(B) A clerk

(C) A gardener

(D) A guide

96. Look at the graphic. Which location will the listeners be unable to visit?

(A) Tanaka Asian Garden

(B) Gibson Pond

(C) Michel Lily House

(D) Sanchez Rose Garden

97. What does the speaker suggest the listeners do?

(A) Ask questions

(B) Wear a jacket

(C) Take flowers home

(D) Buy some food

GO ON TO THE NEXT PAGE

BOB'S WAREHOUSE

Show this coupon and enjoy an additional 20% off of your purchase during our Annual Summer Sale!!!

Good until August 30.
Not good with any other printed offer.

98. What is mainly being advertised?

(A) Furniture

(B) Electronics

(C) Utensils

(D) Decorations

99. What does the speaker imply about the sales staff?

(A) They are new.

(B) They are professional.

(C) They are friendly.

(D) They are punctual.

100. Look at the graphic. How much is the total discount for customers who bring in the coupon?

(A) 20%

(B) 30%

(C) 40%

(D) 50%

**THIS IS THE END OF THE LISTENING COMPREHENSION SECTION OF THE TEST.
GO ON TO THE READING COMPREHENSION SECTION.**

Reading Comprehension

In this second section of the exam, your ability to understand written English will be tested. This section consists of three separate parts, each with its own directions.

Part 5

Directions: This part of the test consists of incomplete sentences. Beneath each sentence, four words or phrases appear. Select the answer choice — (A), (B), (C), or (D) — that best completes the sentence. Then mark the letter that corresponds to the best answer on your answer sheet.

Look at the example

Mr. Morales read over the contract with great _____.

(A) interesting

(B) interest

(C) interested

(D) interestingly

This sentence should correctly read "Mr. Morales read over the contract with great interest." Therefore, the answer is (B).

 ●

GO ON TO THE NEXT PAGE

101. Dominique Lamarque, the firm's information technology officer, has developed a new computer program that should _____ the employees' workloads.

(A) lighter

(B) lighting

(C) lighten

(D) light

102. Liquid assets are _____ converted into cash.

(A) easy

(B) easily

(C) easier

(D) ease

103. The value of Crosswell Corporation's stock has _____ slightly since January.

(A) falling

(B) fell

(C) fall

(D) fallen

104. The board voted to raise prices in small _____.

(A) successions

(B) acquisitions

(C) increments

(D) additions

105. My brother invited me to attend the tennis matches with him on Saturday, but I would _____ stay home and watch them on television.

(A) prefer

(B) rather

(C) want

(D) like

106. Most employees respond with _____ when they are given the freedom to develop their own work methods.

(A) enthusiastic

(B) enthusiast

(C) enthusiastically

(D) enthusiasm

107. Even _____ the bid arrived after the deadline, it will still be considered.

(A) though

(B) when

(C) so

(D) although

108. The two most _____ systems of accounting in use today are the cash system and the accrual system.

(A) popular

(B) popularity

(C) popularly

(D) popularized

109. Paris is famous for the many sidewalk cafés that _____ its boulevards.

(A) line

(B) run

(C) arrange

(D) reside

110. The first buildings _____ air-conditioned were mainly factories.

(A) were

(B) that

(C) to be

(D) being

111. I hope that all of you will _____ Ms. Mateo your undivided attention for the next half hour.

   (A) take

   (B) pay

   (C) give

   (D) turn

112. The *Brunswick Explorer* is a submersible robotic vehicle designed to search for mineral deposits far _____ the surface of the sea.

   (A) between

   (B) below

   (C) behind

   (D) beyond

113. The economy has been sluggish for the last few quarters, but several signs _____ to a speedy recovery.

   (A) indicate

   (B) show

   (C) demonstrate

   (D) point

114. _____ business experts call the "point of sale" is the location in a retail establishment where customers actually make their purchases.

   (A) What

   (B) That

   (C) How

   (D) Some

115. Because his partner had to go to Sydney, Mr. Zazueta had to finish work on the advertising campaign by _____ .

   (A) him

   (B) himself

   (C) themselves

   (D) theirs

116. In the _____ 1940s, television first began to seriously compete with radio for audiences and advertising.

   (A) high

   (B) late

   (C) deep

   (D) last

117. Ms. Csupo said that she would return to work at least _____ Wednesday, but she didn't come back until Friday.

   (A) at

   (B) until

   (C) in

   (D) by

118. The council will contact you as _____ as they have made a decision.

   (A) long

   (B) soon

   (C) much

   (D) far

119. Many of the women in the office spent _____ lunch hour discussing the company's latest proposals.

   (A) her

   (B) their

   (C) hers

   (D) theirs

120. Rooms at the Aqua Bay Resort are considerably more expensive during the _____ season.

   (A) tip

   (B) summit

   (C) peak

   (D) higher

GO ON TO THE NEXT PAGE

121. The _____ of this investigation is to determine if anyone in this department was responsible for the accident that occurred.

(A) purpose

(B) explanation

(C) account

(D) reason

122. Although training programs for employees are quite expensive, in the long _____, they are good investments in human capital.

(A) terms

(B) run

(C) period

(D) time

123. Please sign the last page of the rental agreement and _____ all the other pages.

(A) initial

(B) initiate

(C) initialize

(D) initially

124. Last weekend, Barclay Department Stores reduced prices by _____ much that customers were practically breaking down the doors to get to the bargains.

(A) too

(B) very

(C) so

(D) enough

125. After her meetings in Geneva, Ms. Yee decided to _____ skiing in the Swiss Alps.

(A) play

(B) do

(C) go

(D) get

126. Michael Barnes and I have known _____ since we were in high school.

(A) one other

(B) another one

(C) the two of us

(D) each other

127. _____ of their final destination, Comet Express first ships all packages to St. Louis.

(A) Regardless

(B) Regarding

(C) In regards

(D) Disregarding

128. When the company raised prices, new price _____ had to be put on all the merchandise.

(A) charts

(B) tickets

(C) blanks

(D) tags

129. The maintenance crew soon had the high-pressure pump back in perfect _____ order.

(A) work

(B) worked

(C) working

(D) worker

130. After he won the award, Mr. Galves was grinning from _____.

(A) eye to eye

(B) mouth to mouth

(C) head to toe

(D) ear to ear

GO ON TO THE NEXT PART.

Part 6

Directions: Read the passages on the following pages. Four words, phrases, or sentences have been replaced by blanks. Four answer choices are given for each blank. Mark the answer choice — (A), (B), (C), or (D) — that best completes the text.

Questions 131–134 refer to the following information:

Many small business owners don't consider advertising on TV because they think it's _____ expensive. While this might
    131.

be true for advertising on primetime network television, there are other affordable alternatives and strategies to consider.
With the growth of cable, satellite, and streaming Internet TV, the number of channels has multiplied rapidly, _____ even
                                                                                                        132.

your small business can benefit from television advertising. All those channels need advertising revenue and are
competing fiercely for your advertising dollar, resulting in very affordable rates. Clearly, you need to think very carefully
about your TV advertising campaign. A poorly produced ad may result in lost customers. _____. TV advertising is
                                                                                       133.

powerful. Products, services, and businesses gain instant _____ if they advertise on television. The phrase "As seen on TV"
                                                           134.

magnifies your image in the eyes of many of your prospective customers.

---

131. (A) enough
   (B) over
   (C) too
   (D) such

132. (A) but
   (B) so
   (C) yet
   (D) as

133. (A) On the other hand, an ad with a clever script and a strong message can completely change the fortunes of your small business.
   (B) Of course, advertising on television can eat up your budget, because you must pay for producing the ad as well as for airtime.
   (C) While an ad on a popular show reaches a wide audience, ads on shows that appeal to a specific audience help you target the customers you want to reach.
   (D) Unlike advertisements in newspapers or on the radio, changing an ad made for television is difficult and often quite costly.

134. (A) credible
   (B) credibility
   (C) crediting
   (D) credibly

GO ON TO THE NEXT PAGE

An invention by Stuart and Cedar Anderson, a father-and-son beekeeper team in Australia, allows both honey bees and beekeepers around the world _____ a sigh of relief. Their Flow Hive invention lets beekeepers harvest honey from

135.

beehives without disturbing the bees inside. The Flow Hive works by providing the bees with a partially-completed wall of honeycomb cells that they then complete with their own wax. After they fill these cells with honey and cap _____ with

136.

wax, the beekeeper can open the other end, allowing the honey to flow out into a tap without ever disturbing the bees. The bees simply reopen the cells and fill them up again. There's no need for beekeepers to wear protective gear, smoke the bees in order to calm them, or take apart the hive to harvest the honey. It's all done by flipping a switch, which activates a mechanism inside the hive, and fresh honey pours out. There's more to bees than harvesting honey. Systems that make it easier for humans to look after bees are crucial. Since 2006, honey bees around the world have been plagued by Colony Collapse Disorder. When a hive suffers from this disorder, all the worker bees in the hive disappear. _____ the help of bees, our crops would suffer devastating consequences. The Andersons' invention of the Flow Hive may

137.

help improve this situation. _____.

138.

135. (A) breathing
(B) they will breathe
(C) a breath
(D) to breathe

136. (A) it
(B) theirs
(C) them
(D) itself

137. (A) Without
(B) A lack of
(C) With
(D) Unless

138. (A) It may give weakened colonies of bees a much-needed break from stressful, intrusive visits from beekeepers.
(B) This disorder is highly worrisome because over one-third of the food we eat is dependent on bees for pollination.
(C) Pesticides, microbes, pollution, and even cellphone emissions have all been blamed for causing this disorder.
(D) If a disease in a hive goes undetected, it doesn't affect just that colony — it can affect hives within about a five-kilometer radius.

Larimer Candle Factory, Inc.
Denver, Colorado

October 14, 20--

Dear Valued Customers,

As you are probably aware, the chief _____ of candles is paraffin wax, a petroleum product. When oil prices
139.
increase, so do our costs. Despite increases in costs over the last two years, we have not raised our prices for
our wholesale customers. Now, however, our materials' costs are 30% higher than they were two years ago.

_____.
140.
The new pricing goes into effect with orders shipped after Jan. 1, allowing you some time in which to purchase
stock at today's prices. Please call or email me if you _____ to increase quantities on orders already being
141.
processed. We assure you that even though our wholesale prices are increasing, our candles are _____ of the finest
142.
quality and continue to offer you and your customers the best value in the marketplace.

Sincerely,

Eugene Benson

Eugene Benson
President, Larimer Candle Factory

139. (A) recipe
(B) mixture
(C) item
(D) ingredient

140. (A) Regrettably, we will have to raise our prices just as we did last year.
(B) Although we will increase our retail prices, our wholesale prices will go down.
(C) Unfortunately, our only choice is to adjust our prices upward.
(D) Happily, as our other costs have dropped, we can avoid a price increase.

141. (A) would like
(B) like
(C) will like
(D) are liking

142. (A) yet
(B) already
(C) still
(D) utmost

GO ON TO THE NEXT PAGE

Scotland hopes to soon be able to obtain over half its energy from renewable sources. Eventually, the goal is 100 percent. In Glasgow, Scotland's largest city, part of the answer may be under the streets, down in caverns more than 200 years old that were excavated for coal. As coal mining became too expensive in Glasgow in the 20th century, the mines were abandoned. The pumps that kept water from trickling in were shut _____, leaving the tunnels to flood.
143.

Now, below the feet of Glaswegians, there are more than 4 million liters of water sitting in the caverns, heated by the Earth's own geothermal energy. No matter _____ cold it gets in chilly Glasgow during the winter, the water still
144.

stays fairly warm: 11 degrees C near the surface. _____. The water is dirty, but the heat it holds is valuable. It is
145.

_____ that the energy in the water could meet the heating needs of more than 40 percent of Glasgow's homes and
146.

businesses.

143. (A) up
(B) out
(C) off
(D) in

144. (A) what
(B) how
(C) so
(D) that

145. (A) The deeper you go, the warmer it gets.
(B) Miners continue to take coal from these mines.
(C) Much of the water in the caves is unusable.
(D) In the summer, the water could be used for cooling.

146. (A) estimation
(B) estimating
(C) estimated
(D) estimate

GO ON TO THE NEXT PART.

Directions: Questions in this part of the test are based on a wide range of reading materials, including articles, letters, advertisements, and notices. After reading the passage, decide which of the four choices — (A), (B), (C), or (D) — best answers the question, and then mark the letter that corresponds to the best answer on your answer sheet. All answers should be based on what is stated in or on what can be inferred from the readings.

Look at the example

La Plata Dinner Theater announces the opening of *Life on the River*, a musical based on a book by Mark Twain. Dinner is served from 6:30 to 8:00, and the performance begins at 8:30 every evening.

What is opening?

(A) A bookstore

(B) An art exhibit

(C) A play

(D) A restaurant

Ⓐ   Ⓑ   ●   Ⓓ

The reading states that *Life on the River* is a musical that is opening at La Plata Dinner Theater. You should choose (C).

GO ON TO THE NEXT PAGE

21st Annual Children's Book Fair

Vienna, Austria
City of Vienna Exhibition Center
May 19–23 10 a.m.–8 p.m. daily

The European Book Foundation will open the doors of the 21st annual children's book fair from Thursday May 19 through Monday May 23. More than 200 exhibitors will take part, including the most important bookstores and publishing houses devoted to children's literature and education. For the first two days, from 10 to 2, the fair is open exclusively to groups of pupils on official school excursions. After 2 on these days, and from the 21st to the 23rd, it is open to all interested members of the public. There will be workshops on literature, art, and computing as well as dancing, music, and puppet shows.

This year, for the first time, Lorenzo the Magnificent will be performing magic on Saturday and Sunday. Meet-the-author sessions and book-signings take place daily.

147. At which of these times may only official school groups attend the fair?

(A) Thursday at 3 p.m.

(B) Friday at 11 a.m.

(C) Friday at 5 p.m.

(D) Saturday at 10 a.m.

148. Who may attend the fair May 21 to May 23?

(A) Only members of the European Book Foundation

(B) Only children and their parents

(C) Anyone who wants to

(D) Only publishers and bookstore owners

149. What is taking place at the book fair for the first time this year?

(A) Magic shows

(B) Computer workshops

(C) Book-signing sessions

(D) Puppet shows

Sherry Pendleton   2:32 P.M.

Hey Avi, congratulations. Just heard you were named team leader. Upper management must really be pleased with you.

Avi Chopra   2:33 P.M.

Thanks, Sherry. I just wish I had gotten a raise to go along with it.

Sherry Pendleton   2:35 P.M.

Well, typically, no one gets a raise until the end of the fiscal year. I'll bet you'll get one then.

Avi Chopra   2:35 P.M.

Well, we'll see.

Sherry Pendleton   2:36 P.M.

Anyway, it looks like you made the right decision, transferring to the Research and Development Department.

Avi Chopra   2:37 P.M.

I miss everyone in Engineering, but working in R&D is really exciting.

Sherry Pendleton   2:38 P.M.

Those new super-bright LED lightbulbs you guys are developing are really incredible. I had lunch with Mr. Philby from marketing, and he thinks they're going to be a really hot product.

Avi Chopra   2:38 P.M.

I sure hope so.

Sherry Pendleton   2:40 P.M.

Don't we all! We could use a big boost in sales.

---

150. Why does Ms. Pendleton congratulate Mr. Chopra?

(A) Because he got a job at another company

(B) Because he was recently promoted

(C) Because he made a good decision

(D) Because he was promised a raise in salary

151. What division did Mr. Chopra transfer from?

(A) Engineering

(B) Marketing

(C) Upper management

(D) Research and Development

152. At 2:40 P.M., what does Ms. Pendleton mean when she writes, "Don't we all"?

(A) Some people don't think the new product will sell well.

(B) She wishes that Mr. Chopra would start work on a new project.

(C) Everybody hopes the new LED lightbulbs will be successful.

(D) She doesn't agree with what Mr. Philby said.

GO ON TO THE NEXT PAGE

Pan-Pacific Airline's popular low-cost flights from Seattle-Tacoma to Tokyo and from Tokyo to Seoul are airborne once again. Four years ago, after Pan-Pacific acquired ailing Crown International Airlines, it was bound by an agreement made by Crown International not to fly from Sea-Tac to Tokyo. However, the path for the renewal of service was cleared by a liberalized aviation agreement signed earlier this year by the U.S. and Japanese governments.

153. What is the main purpose of this announcement?

(A) To discuss the merger of two airlines

(B) To describe Crown International Airlines' new image

(C) To report the restoration of a discontinued air route

(D) To announce direct service between Seattle and Seoul

154. According to the announcement, what allowed Pan-Pacific to fly from Seattle to Tokyo?

(A) An agreement between U.S. and Japanese government agencies

(B) A growing demand by the public

(C) The acquisition of routes from Crown International Airways

(D) An agreement between Japanese and U.S. airlines

You must rinse off all surfaces of your fountain, including the polished decorative stones (if provided with your unit), before using the fountain for the first time. Any dirt or residue which remains on the fountain may obstruct water flow, thereby causing unnecessary noise. Should you experience noise from the pump, please disassemble it, flush parts with water to remove particles, wipe dry, and reassemble. Please refer to our instruction manual should the noise remain, as this may be caused by a variety of other factors.

Due to the imperfect edges which are inherent in this fountain or any made from natural stone, water may splash outside the base of the unit. Therefore, we strongly recommend that you place your fountain on a waterproof surface or that you cover the surface with some waterproof barrier.

For further information, please call **1-800-SERENITY** or email us at **custserv@serenity.com**

155. Which of the following is the best heading for this notice?

(A) Hints for Using Your Serenity Fountain

(B) How to Repair Your Fountain's Water Pump

(C) Finding and Processing Decorative Stones

(D) Protecting Surfaces from Water Damage

156. What can be inferred about the decorative stones mentioned in the notice?

(A) They must be polished before use.

(B) They have already been rinsed.

(C) They may obstruct the flow of water.

(D) They do not come with all fountains.

157. What does the reading say about the imperfect edges of the fountain?

(A) They may scratch the surface on which they are placed.

(B) They may cause personal injury if not handled carefully.

(C) They are a flaw found in some fountains, but can be repaired.

(D) They may cause water to splash out of the fountain.

Trevor Baylis is best known for inventing the wind-up radio in 1992. It was designed for areas of Africa and other locales where there is no electricity and batteries are expensive. The radio is powered by the user winding a hand crank for several seconds. -[1]- For this invention, in 1996 he was awarded the BBC Design Award for Best Product and Best Design, as well as the World Vision Award for Development Initiative. He then perfected a wind-up laptop computer and a wind-up home lighting system. -[2]-

In 2001, Baylis completed a 100-mile walk across the barren Namib Desert in Southwest Africa to demonstrate his latest invention, a pair of "electric shoes," and to raise money for charity. -[3]- His "electric shoes" use piezoelectric contacts in the heels to charge a small battery that can be used to operate a cellular telephone. -[4]-

Since 2003, Baylis has operated a company called Trevor Baylis Brands. This company helps inventors develop and protect their ideas and inventions and then get them to market.

158. Which of these products was the first to be developed by Trevor Baylis?

(A) Electric shoes

(B) An indoor lighting system

(C) A radio

(D) A laptop computer

159. The article suggests that Baylis' products could also be marketed in which of these ways?

(A) As a high-technology substitute for existing products

(B) As a substitute for existing products in case of an electrical emergency

(C) As a low-cost substitute for existing products

(D) As a substitute for existing products when little or no maintenance is required

160. What do all of the products mentioned in the article have in common?

(A) They all must be wound up by hand.

(B) They do not require external electricity or batteries.

(C) They all won product awards for design.

(D) They were all marketed by Trevor Baylis Brands.

161. In which of the positions marked [1], [2], [3], and [4] does the following sentence best belong?

"This stores energy in a spring which then drives a small electrical generator to operate the radio receiver."

(A) [1]

(B) [2]

(C) [3]

(D) [4]

GO ON TO THE NEXT PAGE

SUBJECT: Additional time needed for audit
DATE: Thurs. 1 Aug. 20-- 15:45 EDT
FROM: Mark Chambers <mchambers@jcvassociates.com>
TO: Michelle Kinsdale <mich_kinsdale@sunburst.com>
CC: Paul Avila <paul_avila@sunburst.com>

Ms. Kinsdale:

It appears that it's going to take us a little longer than we anticipated to complete our audit of Sunburst Electronics.

From discussions with your marketing manager Paul Avila, I've learned that various members of the marketing team did not save all their travel receipts. We'll have to reconstruct these from the records of credit card companies, hotels, airlines, and so on. Of course, this will be more time-consuming than reviewing the original documents. I've discussed this problem with Mr. Avila and he will in the future hold all receipts for a period of three years.

As agreed in our contract, we will be billing you for this additional time at our regular rate of $120 an hour (in addition to the basic audit fee of $10,000).

On the positive side, all your employees have been remarkably cooperative and helpful. I can see that they have spent a lot of time getting ready for this audit.

Thanks!
Mark Chambers, CPA
Johnstone, Chambers, Voorhees & Associates

162. What basic message is Mr. Chambers sending Ms. Kinsdale?

(A) The audit will take longer and cost more than expected.

(B) He will be unable to finish the audit.

(C) He has lost some important documents.

(D) The audit fee has been reduced.

163. What problem does Mr. Chambers discuss in this email?

(A) He has been unable to get information from credit card companies.

(B) Some necessary documents are not available.

(C) The staff has been very uncooperative.

(D) Mr. Avila has refused to keep receipts in the future.

164. How much will Mr. Chambers' company charge Ms. Kinsdale's company for the additional work?

(A) A total of $120

(B) $120 for each additional hour

(C) A total of $10,000

(D) $10,000 a year for three years

Prices for patchouli oil have soared this year from about $10 a pound last January to over $75 a pound, and it is predicted that prices will reach $100 a pound by the end of the year. -[1]- This aromatic oil is distilled from the leaves of the patchouli plant and is one of the most important ingredients in nearly all commercially produced scents. Although sometimes used as a "stand-alone" scent, especially back in the 1960s, today it is primarily used to "fix" other scents in products: costly French perfumes, shampoos, hand soaps, scented candles, room deodorants, and many others.

Traders in essential oils are particularly concerned about the leap in patchouli prices because, until recently, they have been remarkably stable. -[2]- Traders say that prices have been driven up by a huge production shortfall on the Indonesian island of Sumatra, where the bulk of the world's patchouli plants are grown and the fragrant oil is distilled. -[3]- Sumatran farmers have been shunning patchouli production lately because of the static low prices. The prolonged drought in Indonesia has also contributed to lower production. Demand for patchouli, however, has continued to accelerate quickly, particularly in the United States, which account for 60 to 70 percent of annual patchouli consumption worldwide.

With prices at record levels, many farmers have returned to growing patchouli, but even in the tropics, it will be some time before the patchouli plants are ready to be harvested. -[4]- In the meantime, prices will probably continue to skyrocket.

165. How much will a pound of patchouli probably cost by the end of the year?

(A) $10

(B) $75

(C) $100

(D) $150

166. What part of the patchouli plant contains the aromatic oil?

(A) The flowers

(B) The roots

(C) The stems

(D) The leaves

167. Which of these products probably does NOT contain patchouli oil?

(A) Fragrant fruit juices

(B) Candles that smell like vanilla

(C) Expensive perfume from France

(D) Hand-milled scented soap

168. The word "shunning" in paragraph 2, line 9 is closest in meaning to

(A) increasing

(B) avoiding

(C) considering

(D) changing

169. In which of the positions marked [1], [2], [3], and [4] does the following sentence best belong?

"Once these plants are mature, prices will probably stabilize."

(A) [1]

(B) [2]

(C) [3]

(D) [4]

GO ON TO THE NEXT PAGE

Paul Matson   9:39

So, is everyone on this team as exhausted as I am?

Margot Zepeda   9:41

I sure am. I went into work an hour early yesterday and I was there until almost nine. I just got home.

Elizabeth Casey   9:42

And I'm going to have to work this weekend.

Cormin Kiritescu   9:42

We could do a much better job on this project if we had more people working on it. I don't understand why we don't.

Elizabeth Casey   9:44

You know the answer to that already, Cormin. It's because everyone else is working on the MacDougal contract.

Paul Matson   9:45

I get that the MacDougal contract is crucial, but what we're working on should be considered pretty important too, I think.

Margot Zepeda   9:45

Maybe we could have some temporary workers come in and give us a hand.

Cormin Kiritescu   9:46

You know, by the time the temps figured out how to do what we're doing, the deadline will have passed. Besides, I don't think the company could afford to hire temps right now.

Margot Zepeda   9:46

And anyway, there isn't any spare desk space or spare computers.

Elizabeth Casey   9:47

Eventually, though, I think we're going to need to hire some more full-time staff.

Paul Matson   9:47

If we could just have another week or so, we wouldn't have to break our necks trying to finish this by the end of the month.

Cormin Kiritescu   9:48

You're right. If Mr. Stern wants this done right, we need more time. Otherwise, we will have to cut some corners. There's no other way to finish it before the first of October.

Elizabeth Casey   9:50

All right, I have a meeting with Mr. Stern tomorrow to discuss our progress. If we're all in agreement, I'll bring it up then.

Paul Matson   9:51

The only positive thing about working on this project is—the overtime pay is nice.

Margot Zepeda   9:52

You're right, it is. But I just need some time away from work to spend with my family.

170. Which of the following is NOT mentioned as a problem with hiring temporary workers?

(A) There is not enough workspace for them.

(B) It would be too expensive for the company.

(C) It would take too long to train them.

(D) The project will end before they can be hired.

171. What will Ms. Casey ask Mr. Stern tomorrow?

(A) If he can extend the deadline for their project

(B) If he can hire more full-time workers

(C) If she can receive more overtime pay

(D) If she can avoid working on weekends

172. At 9:48, what does Mr. Kiritescu mean when he writes, "we will have to cut some corners"?

(A) They won't be able to complete their project in a thorough way.

(B) They won't have finished their task before the deadline has passed.

(C) They will have to work even longer hours to complete their project.

(D) They will have to assign some team members to work on the MacDougal contract.

Questions 173–175 are based on the following advertisement:

Think Globally

With World View Software!

Keep time with the rest of the world by converting your computer screen into a world clock. Clocks located at the top of the screen display the current time for every time zone in the world in an attractive graphical display. The display can be customized to display the local time for virtually any world city you choose. World View Software adjusts automatically for Daylight Saving Time. It can also be set up as a screen saver.

Typically costs $45.00 or more at retail stores and $40 when you order from the software maker, but now available for Nationwide Airline passengers at the discount rate of only $34.95 when you order directly from Sky Catalogue!

173. The advertisement indicates that which of these can be adjusted by users of World View Software?

(A) The colors of the graphical display

(B) The cities that are displayed

(C) The time zones that are shown

(D) The position of the clocks on the screen

174. According to the advertisement, where is World View Software available at the lowest cost?

(A) From retail stores

(B) On board most airline flights

(C) Directly from the software maker

(D) From the Sky Catalogue

175. Which of the following is NOT mentioned as a benefit of World View Software?

(A) It gives an overview of current local times around the world.

(B) It allows users to communicate with people from different time zones.

(C) Its display is nice to look at.

(D) It can function as a screen saver.

GO ON TO THE NEXT PAGE

The Art of Communicating Globally

by Richard Pryce and Sachiko Mori-Pryce   *St. George Press, Ltd.*

What's the best time to call someone in Australia if you are in New York? What greeting do you use to begin a business letter to someone in Turkey? How do you find the email address of a company in South Africa? What's the country code you'll need to call someone in Brazil? These and countless other questions are answered in this new guidebook. It covers the ins and outs of transnational contact by phone, fax, mail, and email. There are more than 500 pages of useful tips on how to address business people in 110 countries, how to polish your English for international correspondence, how to design stationery and forms for use in various nations, and how to say hello, thank you, and other important phrases in more than 70 languages. The book also provides information about translation software, postal codes, the meaning of various telephone signals in different countries, and many other topics. Like the popular guidebook *Negotiating Your Way Around the World* that the couple previously collaborated on, this volume should occupy a prominent place on the office bookshelves of all our readers.

Reviewed by Miles Winston

To: m.winston@newbusmag.com
From: Richard_Pryce@calcom.com
Date: 22 Jan 20-- 11:38 PM
Subject: Review

Dear Mr. Winston,

I would like to thank you for your kind review of *The Art of Communicating Globally*. It was the work of over three years, and Sachiko and I both appreciate your positive response to our book in "New Business Magazine."

One point I would like to make: the book *Negotiating Your Way Around the World* was not the result of a collaboration. That book was my wife's solo effort and was published before we were married. I wonder if you can publish a correction in your next edition.

Sincerely,

Richard Pryce

176. The magazine in which this review appeared is probably directed at which of these groups?

(A) Commercial artists

(B) International businesspersons

(C) Communication experts

(D) World travelers

177. The book that is reviewed probably does NOT answer which of these questions?

(A) What does it mean if I telephone an office in Malaysia and hear a series of chimes?

(B) What is the country code I need to send a fax to someone in Venezuela?

(C) How do I say "Hello" if I call someone in Finland?

(D) What should I wear to a business luncheon in Egypt?

178. The phrase "ins and outs" in line 4 of the review is closest in meaning to

(A) latest developments

(B) common difficulties

(C) important points

(D) helpful suggestions

179. How many pages does the book *The Art of Communicating Globally* probably have?

(A) 70

(B) 110

(C) 512

(D) 1,246

180. What mistake regarding *Negotiating Your Way Around the World* did Mr. Winston make in his review?

(A) He suggested that it was more popular than *The Art of Communicating Globally.*

(B) He stated that it was written by two authors rather than by a single author.

(C) He indicated that it took longer to write than *The Art of Communicating Globally.*

(D) He said that it was written by Richard Pryce, not by Sachiko Mori-Pryce.

Questions 181–185 are based on the following notice and email:

TRADE TIPS
From the ITC

1. **United Arab Emirates** is seeking direct sales to end users of insulated fiber optic cables, multimeters, pipes and fittings, paint, varnishes, lumber, and pumps.
2. **Tunisia** is seeking other investors for a frozen orange juice and dried milk plant.
3. **Hungary** is seeking a distributorship for digital imaging equipment.
4. **Egypt** is seeking an agency for second-grade paper.
5. **Brazil** is seeking a joint-venture opportunity with an environmental-technology firm.
6. **Australia** is seeking a distributorship for a picture-hanging system.
7. **India** is seeking an overseas partner to help develop and market a chemical scrubber for reducing air pollution and related environmental problems.

For further information and more tips, contact the information office at the International Trade Center Tip Program. Trade Tips is a service offered to our members, who may request as many tips as they desire. For nonmembers, there is a three-tip request limit. Email or call for membership information.

info.tradetips@ITC.org   202-555-1573

GO ON TO THE NEXT PAGE

Gomarco, Inc.

Sent: 3:02 p.m. 15 March 20--
From: P.G. Kuska <pgk@gomarco.com>
Subject: Trade tips
To: ITC Information Office <info.tradetips@ITC.org>

To whom it may concern:

I saw your recent notice in *International Business Daily* and I would very much like further information about the joint-venture opportunity in Brazil (Tip 5) and the partnership opportunity with the firm in India (Tip 7). If you have a tip on any other similar opportunity, could you please send that as well?

Also, please send ITC membership information. I believe the CEO of my firm would be interested in joining.

P.G. Kuska
Chief Information Officer
Gomarco, Inc.

---

181. What is Tunisia looking for?

(A) A distributorship

(B) A source of orange juice and milk

(C) Additional investment

(D) Further information

182. Which of these countries is seeking a joint-venture partner?

(A) Egypt

(B) Australia

(C) Hungary

(D) Brazil

183. How many tips can a nonmember request?

(A) None

(B) One

(C) Three

(D) An unlimited number

184. What can be inferred about P.G. Kuska from this email?

(A) He has received international trade tips from ITC many times in the past.

(B) He does not know the name of the information officer at the ITC.

(C) He has recently received permission from the CEO to become an ITC member.

(D) He is no longer interested in partnering with international companies.

185. What type of business does P.G. Kuska most likely work for?

(A) An environmental-technology company

(B) A food-processing company

(C) A banking and investment firm

(D) A chain of international hotels

Questions 186–190 refer to the following form, note, and email:

Sandia Technology Systems

Worksheet: Telephone Reference Check

Name of applicant: Carolina Sanchez

Previous/Current Employer: BFA Graphics

Dates of employment: May 1, 2015 **to** Present

Position: Data entry clerk **Salary:** $42,000

Reason for leaving: See "Additional comments"

Does applicant get along well with others? Yes _X_ No ____ Not sure ____

Does applicant have leadership qualities? Yes ____ No ____ Not sure _X_

Is employee reliable? Yes _X_ No ____ Not sure ____

Would you rehire? Yes _X_ No ____

Additional comments: Mgr of Accts Recvble Dept stated that he hated to lose Ms. Sanchez but that, because BFA is a relatively small co, there was not much room for her to advance in the near future. He also told me that Ms. Sanchez was very conscientious and that he was certain that she would make an excellent data coordinator for us.

Information received from: Dennis Longhurst, Mgr. Accts Recvble Dept at BFA

Information taken by: Michio Nakayoshi, Pers'l Officer

Michio,

From her interview, the information that you gathered on the phone, and the reference letters we've received, I'm inclined to offer this position to Ms. Sanchez.

One thing, though—I suppose Mr. Longhurst said that he didn't know anything about Ms. Sanchez's leadership qualities because she hasn't had any experience as a supervisor. Still, she's going to be overseeing a staff of eight data entry clerks if she comes to work for us. I wonder if you could get back to him and ask if he thinks she would do well in a managerial position.

Depending on what he says, go ahead and contact Ms. Sanchez. I'd say offer her $10,000 more than her current annual salary at BFA.

Kay Barrett
Director of Personnel

GO ON TO THE NEXT PAGE

To: Michio Nakayoshi <m_nakayoshi@sandia.com>
From: Carolina Sanchez <carolinasanchez@bfa.com>
Date: June 12, 20--
Subject: Data Coordinator position

Dear Mr. Nakayoshi,

I am delighted to be offered the position of data coordinator and happy to accept. This is exactly the kind of position I was hoping to land. And I consider the salary offer quite generous.

Mr. Longhurst, my boss at BFA, told me that you asked him if I had any experience as a supervisor. Although I did not mention it on my résumé, I did work at the university bookstore when I was an undergraduate, and one summer, I was promoted to manager with a staff of 16.

I look forward to starting to work at Sandia in two weeks. See you then!

Carolina Sanchez

---

186. What is the purpose of the form?

(A) To record information about a job applicant obtained from an employment reference

(B) To determine if an employee should be given a promotion

(C) To record notes taken during a phone interview with a job applicant

(D) To explain why a job applicant is unsuitable for a position

187. Who filled out the form?

(A) Carolina Sanchez

(B) Dennis Longhurst

(C) Kay Barrett

(D) Michio Nakayoshi

188. What position is the applicant seeking?

(A) Manager, Accounts Receivable

(B) Data Coordinator

(C) Personnel officer

(D) Data entry clerk

189. What salary does Kay Barrett recommend offering to Carolina Sanchez?

(A) $28,000

(B) $36,000

(C) $42,000

(D) $52,000

190. What incorrect assumption about Ms. Sanchez does Ms. Barrett make?

(A) That she would not be happy with the salary offered

(B) That she did not have any previous management experience

(C) That Mr. Longhurst would not give her a positive job reference

(D) That Mr. Nakayoshi would not want to offer her the position

Interoffice Memo

TO: All Employees
FROM: John Kendall, Managing Director

I am happy to announce that, as the next step in our ongoing water and energy conservation program, we have chosen Ms. Anna Fiori, currently serving as assistant financial officer, as our new energy management coordinator.

Ms. Fiori will be exploring areas in which we can save energy and boost our efficiency.
These areas include:

- The operation of our manufacturing processes
- Our lighting, heating/air conditioning, plumbing, and landscaping practices
- Our purchasing practices

Please email or call Ms. Fiori to communicate any ideas you may have for saving energy or improving efficiency here at Ventura Enterprises. Also, contact her if you believe that any changes create problems for you, your colleagues, or your department. She'll be announcing accomplishments and successes in our weekly newsletter.

Ventura

To: Anna Fiori <anna_fiori@ventura.com>
From: Rolf Erge <rolf_erge@ventura.com>
Subject: Suggestion
Sent: Apr. 12, 20--

Dear Ms. Fiori,

First off, congratulations on being named energy management coordinator.

I am contacting you because in my position as maintenance manager I see a lot of energy being wasted. Every night, I go into empty offices where all the lights are on. I've put up signs that say "Please turn off lights when leaving this room" but they are often ignored. What we need, I believe, are timing devices that will automatically shut off the lights at the end of the workday.

I have other suggestions for lowering energy costs, too. Let me know if you would like to talk! And good luck with your new job.

Rolf Erge
Manager, Maintenance Dept.

GO ON TO THE NEXT PAGE

Ms. Fiori,

I want to applaud the fact that the management has decided to "go green" and install a motion sensor to control the lights in my office. However, now, when I sit at my desk busily working at my computer—which is what I do pretty much all day—my lights go out after about 10 minutes. Apparently I sit too still while I type! To get the lights to come back on—and keep in mind, there are no windows in my office so I am sitting in the dark—I stand up and madly wave my arms over my head. This goes on all day and it is driving me crazy.

I've been thinking about buying a pendulum clock and putting it in front of the motion detector so that the motion of the swinging pendulum would prevent the lights from going off, but I realize that would utterly defeat the purpose of the motion detector, and I would have to buy an otherwise unnecessary clock.

So I am wondering if you have any better suggestions. Is there some way of turning up the sensitivity on the sensor so that it can "see" my busily moving fingers?

Thanks in advance,

Katie Snow

---

191. What is John Kendall's purpose in writing the memo?

(A) To notify workers about a new program

(B) To announce the start of a newsletter

(C) To discuss the opening of a new plant

(D) To announce that a position has been filled

192. According to the memo, how will employees be informed of changes by Ms. Fiori?

(A) In a newsletter

(B) By email

(C) By telephone

(D) In a memo

193. Why did Mr. Erge write the email to Ms. Fiori?

(A) Because changes that she made have caused problems for his department

(B) Because Mr. Kendall asked employees to send ideas to her about saving energy

(C) Because he is going to be working in her department

(D) Because Mr. Kendall asked employees to congratulate Ms. Fiori

194. How is the lighting system in Ms. Snow's office different from the one proposed by Mr. Erge?

(A) It is not as high-tech.

(B) It is less expensive.

(C) It is not as sensitive.

(D) It involves motion sensors.

195. How does Ms. Snow currently deal with the problem in her office?

(A) She gets out of her chair and moves her arms.

(B) She walks to the light switch and turns it on.

(C) She adjusts the level of sensitivity on the motion detector.

(D) She places a pendulum clock in front of the sensor.

LAKESHORE DESIGNS, INC.

Insure and personalize your business tools with engraved identification plates.
Made of Solid Brass!

✓ For briefcases and carry-on luggage

✓ Laptop computers

✓ Cameras and camera bags

✓ Golf bags

✓ Anything you want to identify and protect!

Style A: 1 or 2 lines, Up to 20 characters per line, $6.95 each, 2 for $12.95

Style B: 1-3 lines, Up to 24 characters per line, $9.95 each, 2 for $19.95

Style C: 1-4 lines, Up to 30 characters per line, $10.95 each, 2 for $19.95

Style D: 1-4 lines, Up to 30 characters per line, $12.95 each, 2 for $21.95

All styles except style A available in silver or gold colors. Style A is only available in silver.

Style D attaches with a leather strap. All other styles are self-adhesive. Simply peel off the adhesive paper from the back of the plate and press on. These plates permanently stick to plastic, metal, leather, and most other surfaces.

To:	Customer Service <customerservice@lakeshore.com>
From:	Martha B. Walker <walker.m.b.@calwood.net>
Subject:	Problem with ID plates
Date:	Nov. 3, 20--

Several weeks ago, I ordered four identification tags from Lakeshore Designs. I found them attractive and professional looking. I attached one to my tablet computer and one to my camera case. Within a few weeks, both of them had dropped off, and I was not able to find them. (The tags I attached to my briefcase and golf bag with straps were fine.) I was disappointed, of course, and I hope that you will replace the two lost tags with ones that will not detach so easily.

Martha Walker

GO ON TO THE NEXT PAGE

Martha B. Walker
288 Blossom Street
Chelsea, MA 02150

Nov. 7, 20--

Dear Ms. Walker,

Please accept our apologies for any inconvenience caused by the problem you experienced with our engraved identification plates. A number of customers have alerted us to this problem. It seems that one shipment of the double-sided adhesive strips used to affix the metal plates to surfaces was defective.

Please find enclosed replacements for the two tags that became unattached. We are also enclosing two more Style D tags with our compliments.

Again, we apologize and thank you for your business. We hope that you will continue to visit our website and to shop for quality products for discerning travelers and businesspersons.

Sincerely,

George Soto
Director, Customer Service Dept.
Lakeshore Designs, Inc.

196. What are the plates made of?

(A) Plastic

(B) Gold and silver

(C) Leather

(D) Brass

197. What is NOT true about Style A plates?

(A) They are the smallest in size.

(B) They are the least expensive.

(C) They can have a maximum of 40 characters.

(D) They are available in two colors.

198. Which type of plates did Ms. Walker attach to her briefcase and golf bag?

(A) Style A

(B) Style B

(C) Style C

(D) Style D

199. What problem did Ms. Walker have with two of the plates?

(A) They didn't stay attached.

(B) The cords broke.

(C) They were not the right style.

(D) Her name was misspelled.

200. In the letter, the word "affix" in paragraph 1, line 3, is closest in meaning to

(A) mark

(B) repair

(C) fasten

(D) decorate

THIS IS THE END OF THE READING COMPREHENSION SECTION. IF YOU FINISH BEFORE TIME IS UP, YOU MUST WORK ONLY ON PROBLEMS IN THIS SECTION.